The Media and the Far Right in Western Europe

This book examines the fascinating interplay of party and media behavior to explain one of the most important phenomena in Western Europe: the rise of Far Right parties. To account for the divergent electoral fortunes of these parties, this book examines how political parties and the mass media have dealt with growing public concerns over national identity. Mainstream politicians chose to "play the nationalist card," creating opportunities for the entry of Far Right parties into the political system. In some cases, the media gave outsized exposure to such parties, allowing them to capitalize on these opportunities; in other cases, they ignored them, blocking their entry into the political system. Using elite interviews, content analysis, and primary documents to trace identity politics since the 1980s, this book presents an original interpretation of identity politics and media behavior in Austria, Germany, Greece, and France since the 1980s.

Antonis A. Ellinas is an assistant professor of political science at the College of the Holy Cross. He received his Ph.D. from Princeton University and his B.A. from Hamilton College. His articles have appeared in various journals, including *Comparative Politics* and the *Journal of European Public Policy*. He has been a postdoctoral Fellow at the Reuters Institute and at Nuffield College of Oxford University and a Fulbright Scholar.

The Media and the Far Right in Western Europe

Playing the Nationalist Card

ANTONIS A. ELLINAS
College of the Holy Cross

CAMBRIDGE
UNIVERSITY PRESS

CAMBRIDGE UNIVERSITY PRESS
Cambridge, New York, Melbourne, Madrid, Cape Town, Singapore,
São Paulo, Delhi, Dubai, Tokyo

Cambridge University Press
32 Avenue of the Americas, New York, NY 10013-2473, USA

www.cambridge.org
Information on this title: www.cambridge.org/9780521116954

© Antonis Ellinas 2010

First published 2010

Printed in the United States of America

A catalog record for this publication is available from the British Library.

Library of Congress Cataloging in Publication data
Ellinas, Antonis A., 1975–
  The media and the far right in western Europe : playing the nationalist
  card / Antonis Ellinas.
    p. cm.
  Includes bibliographical references and index.
  ISBN 978-0-521-11695-4 (hardback)
  1. Political parties – Europe, Western. 2. Right-wing extremists –
  Europe, Western. 3. Mass media – Political aspects – Europe,
  Western. 4. Nationalism – Europe, Western. 5. Europe, Western – Politics
  and government – 1989– I. Title.
  JN50.E55 2010
  324.2′13094–dc22   2009044264

ISBN 978-0-521-11695-4 Hardback

Contents

List of Figures

List of Tables

Acknowledgments

This book began as a doctoral dissertation at Princeton University, and I am most grateful to Nancy Bermeo, Jonas Pontusson, and Ezra Suleiman for their constant support, critical insights, and wise advice throughout this period.

I was fortunate to get an opportunity to rework the manuscript at the Reuters Institute of Oxford University, and I am thankful to the Reuters Foundation for a generous fellowship that permitted this as well as to the Department of Political Science and its chair, Neil MacFarlane, for their unwavering encouragement. Nuffield College also provided a fellowship as well as an ideal working environment on the many rainy days when the Institute seemed too far to walk to. The European Studies Centre at St. Antony's College and SEESOX granted a useful forum for the presentation of my ideas, and Othon Anastasakis and Kalypso Nicolaides were wonderful hosts. Giovanni Capoccia provided good advice at critical phases of the project, and the Oxford Center for the Study of Inequality and Democracy was an exceptional source of insights.

On my return to the United States, at the College of the Holy Cross, I found an excellent working environment that facilitated the completion of this book.

For comments on parts or the entire book I am grateful to David Art, Mark Beissinger, Sheri Berman, Denise Demetriou, Erik Kuhonta, Jennifer Lieb, Kristine Mitchell, and the anonymous reviewers of Cambridge University Press. I would also like to acknowledge the excellent research assistance of Bénédicte Williams and Kris-Stella Trump. My editor at Cambridge University Press, Eric Crahan, deserves special thanks for his interest in the project as well as for the superb cooperation.

The Graduate School, the Hellenic Studies Program, the Program in European Politics and Society, and the French Studies Program at Princeton University have been particularly supportive throughout the various phases of the project.

I am also grateful for the assistance I got at the Austrian and French National Libraries, the Berlin State Library, the Constantine Karamanlis Democracy Institute, the Archive of the German Parliament, the Benakios Library, Nuffield College's Library, and, of course, Princeton's own Firestone Library.

I am deeply indebted to my mentors and good friends at Hamilton College, Alan Cafruny and Cheng Li, who sparked my interest in political science and have pushed me to think critically about important political questions.

My deepest gratitude goes to my parents, Andreas and Irene, for investing all the rewards from their hard work in the education of their three children.

Daphne Charalambidou has lived the dreams, hopes, and anxieties of this project from the very first day and has patiently awaited its completion. The book is dedicated to her.

Acronyms and Abbreviations

BZÖ	Alliance for the Future of Austria
CD	Center Democrats
CDU	Christian Democratic Union
CNCL	National Commission for Communication and Freedom
CP	Center Party
CSA	High Council for Broadcasting
CSU	Christian Social Union
DVU	German People's Union
FAZ	*Frankfurter Allgemeine Zeitung* (German newspaper)
FDP	Free Democratic Party
FN	National Front
FPÖ	Freedom Party of Austria
FYROM	Former Yugoslav Republic of Macedonia
LAOS	Popular Orthodox Rally
LN	The Northern League
LPF	Pim Fortuyn List
MNR	Republican National Movement
MP	Member of Parliament
MPF	Movement for France
MSI	Italian Social Movement
ND	New Democracy
NKZ	*Neue Kronen Zeitung* (Austrian newspaper)
NPD	National Democratic Party of Germany
ÖVP	Austrian People's Party

PASOK	Pan-Hellenic Socialist Movement
PCF	French Communist Party
PFN	Party of New Forces
PS	Political Spring
PVV	Party of Freedom
REP	Republikaner
RPR	Rally for the Republic
SPD	Social Democratic Party of Germany
SPÖ	Social Democratic Party of Austria
UDF	Union for French Democracy
UMP	Union for a Popular Movement
VdU	Federation of Independents
VVD	Party for Freedom and Democracy
WJC	World Jewish Congress

I

Introduction

On March 8, 2007, Nicolas Sarkozy created a political uproar during
the French presidential campaign when in a televised interview he
proposed creating a "ministry for immigration and national identity."
His political rivals immediately denounced his plans as an attack
against the French republican tradition and accused him of flirting
with the xenophobic ideas of Jean-Marie Le Pen's National Front.
Shortly afterward, though, the Socialist candidate, Ségolène Royal,
asked her supporters to "reconquer the symbols of the nation" instead
of "abandoning the national anthem to the extreme right." She said
that if elected she would "ensure that the French know the words to
La Marseillaise, and that every family owns a national flag" to "fly
from their window on national holidays."[1] So intense was the row
over French identity that it sidelined the more traditional materialist
concerns that tend to define Left-Right competition. As the *New York
Times* put it at the time, "the battle over French identity has over-
taken discussion of more practical issues like reducing unemployment
and making France more competitive."[2]

Although partisan appeals to national identity are not always as
explicit as in the French elections, they are a much broader phenomenon in Western Europe. In September 2007, for example, British

[1] Agence France-Presse, "French flag sparks tug-of-war in election race," *Agence
France-Presse*, March 25, 2007.
[2] Elaine Sciolino, "Identity, staple of the Right, moves to the center of French campaign," *New York Times*, March 30, 2007, p. 1.

Prime Minister Gordon Brown stirred controversy when he stated at the Labour Party's annual convention that he wanted to create "British jobs for British workers." The Conservative opposition accused Brown of stealing the phrase from a pamphlet of the extreme Right British National Party and of disregarding European Union (EU) law. A month later, international media spotlights turned to the Swiss legislative elections, where the Swiss People's Party relied on a controversial campaign against immigration to win a record 29% of the Swiss vote. A People's Party campaign poster showed white sheep kicking a black sheep out of Switzerland, alluding to the party's proposal to deport aliens who commit criminal offences. Even in Germany, where historical alarms go off whenever politicians make appeals to German identity, the Christian Democrats resorted in December 2007 to anti-immigrant rhetoric. Ahead of state elections in Hesse, the state premier, Ronald Koch, turned an incident of youth violence into a discussion about foreigners in Germany, explicitly associating certain ethnic groups with crime. "We have spent too long showing a strange sociological understanding for groups that consciously commit violence as ethnic minorities," he stated in an interview in the popular tabloid *Bild*.[3]

Partisan appeals to national identity are not a recent phenomenon. Since the 1980s, mainstream parties have incorporated national identity themes into their programs, creating a new axis of political competition. As this book shows, issues such as immigration, citizenship, asylum, and historical memory have become a constant source of partisan rivalry. This rivalry is often missed by conventional accounts of party politics, which tend to focus on traditional materialist themes. Although these themes continue to dominate partisan competition, in the past few decades, they have been supplemented by a set of non-materialist issues that cut across traditional party cleavages. Public apprehension over globalization has helped push these issues into the political mainstream by giving parties incentives to "ethnicize" politics in search of new electoral niches. The political turn toward national identity has taken different forms in different countries and in different times but has caused similar political rifts between those who defend or oppose certain conceptions of the national collective.

[3] Nikolaus Blome, "Wer in Deutschland lebt, hat die Faust unten zu lassen!" *Bild*, December 28, 2007.

It has also set in motion similar political processes and brought about comparable political effects. This book sets out to explicate these processes and to analyze their effects. It will show that the way political parties have competed over national identity explains why some West European countries have experienced a surge in electoral support for the Far Right, while other countries have not.

Party positioning in the competitive space is an important determinant of political outcomes, but its analytical utility is limited by the varying capacity parties have to communicate their messages to voters. Often missed by standard accounts of party competition, this variation is particularly strong between established and newer parties and, hence, most relevant to the discussion of Far Right parties, which sometimes lack the organizational and financial resources necessary to make their positions known. During their earlier phase of development, smaller parties need the media to publicize their views to national publics. The media can help small parties communicate their messages to much broader audiences than their organizational or financial resources would otherwise allow. Moreover, they can confer legitimacy and authority to political newcomers, and they can dispel voter doubts about their electoral viability. In this sense, the media control the gateway to the electoral market.

Politicians are acutely aware of this gate-keeping role of the media and are often critical of those helping give the Far Right publicity. In April 2007, for example, the leader of the Swedish Social Democrats, Mona Sahlin, was criticized for participating in a televised debate with the leader of the Far Right Sweden Democrats. She was accused of helping the party get much more exposure than its poor electoral standing would have justified or its finances would have allowed. Media treatment of Far Right parties has also come under fire in Greece. In June 2007, the leader of the Greek Communist Party, Aleca Papariga, accused the Socialists of "directing" certain media to grant the Far Right Greek Popular Orthodox Rally (LAOS) prime-time exposure to hurt the Conservatives. She complained that the leadership of LAOS frequently participated in major television shows and that its exposure far exceeded its limited electoral strength.[4] Her arguments echoed

[4] «Ενίσχυση ΛΑΟΣ από ΠΑΣΟΚ καταγγέλλει η κ. Παπαρήγα», *Καθημερινή*, 6 Ιουνίου 2007 ("Papariga reports strengthening of LAOS from PASOK," *Kathimerini*, June 6, 2007); Γιώργος Χρ. Παπαχρήστος, «Καραμπόλα για τον ΛΑΟΣ» *Τα Νέα*,

those of many French observers, who criticized Socialist president François Mitterrand for facilitating the rise of Le Pen in the mid-1980s by instructing public broadcasters to grant him exposure. This book seeks to subject these arguments into systematic comparative analysis. It will show that we cannot fully explain the divergent electoral fortunes of Far Right parties in Western Europe without examining the degree of communication resources they have at their disposal.

The focus on party and media behavior marks a departure from the voluminous literature that seeks to explain the divergent electoral trajectories of the West European Far Right parties. It similarly asks why Far Right parties have been successful in some but not other political settings, yet its answers differ. This book emphasizes political – instead of sociological, institutional, and economic – variables, and it focuses on explaining variation in Far Right performance across time rather than across countries. Using this temporal approach and a wide array of evidence, it traces party competition and media behavior in the past few decades. This book argues that the way mainstream parties have dealt with national identity issues has structured the political opportunities available to the Far Right and that the treatment of Far Right parties by the mass media has affected their capacity to make electoral advances.

Why the Far Right

Two decades after Klaus von Beyme complained that "there is virtually no comparative literature on the topic" (1988: 14), Far Right parties have earned more scholarly attention than any other party family in Western Europe. The empirical record justifies this burgeoning scholarly interest: in the past sixty years, no other party family has managed to make such significant electoral advances across so many countries in such a short time. As Figure 1.1 shows, since the mid-1980s, Far Right support has quadrupled in Western Europe. In sixteen West European countries, parties that are thought to belong to the Far Right polled

6 Ιουνίου 2007 (George. Chr. Papachristos, "Row over LAOS," *Ta Nea*, June 6, 2007); Γιώργος Χρ. Παπαχρήστος, «Πάγκαλος μαινόμενος κατά ΚΚΕ» *Ta Νέα*, 7 Ιουνίου 2007 (George Chr. Papachristos, "Pangalos angry with KKE," *Ta Nea*, June 7, 2007).

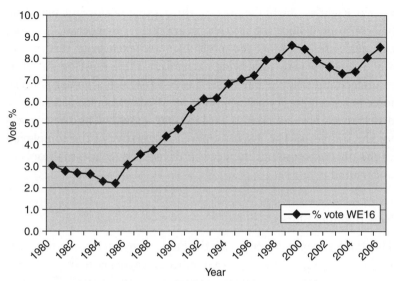

FIGURE I.I. Far Right support in Western Europe, 1980–2006
Mean vote for all parties included in scholarly literature as being on the Far Right, which ran in national legislative elections in sixteen West European countries (Norway, Switzerland, and EU15 except Luxembourg) between 1980 and 2006.
Sources: Mackie and Rose 1997; Caramani 2000; www.electionworld.org.

8.5% of the national vote in 2006 compared to 2.2% in 1985. They have consolidated a sizable presence in Austrian, Belgian, Danish, French, Italian, Norwegian, and Swiss politics. Yet, although this phenomenon is transnational, it is far from pan-European. In countries such as Finland, Germany, Greece, Ireland, the Netherlands, Portugal, Spain, Sweden, and the United Kingdom, the Far Right has failed to become a permanent force in national politics.

Apart from the geographical spread of the phenomenon, there are also good normative reasons to justify the exponential growth of the scholarly literature on the Far Right. Far Right advances have evoked memories of interwar democratic disintegration, and they have reshaped the contours of legitimate political discourse, injecting it with xenophobia, racism, and anti-Semitism. Even where Far Right parties have been least successful, as in Germany, they have had an important influence on policy outcomes, especially on issues such as immigration and crime. Many observers consider the rise of the Far Right as one of the greatest threats that democratic pluralism has confronted since the interwar years. Before democratic societies can successfully combat the intolerance and exclusivity that is usually associated with right-wing extremism, there must be an effort to understand why the Far Right has become such a potent political force in contemporary politics. That hundreds of books, articles, and dissertations have found it so hard to come up with definitive answers for the sources of Far Right support is suggestive of the complexity of the phenomenon and the need to devise new conceptual tools to understand it.

New Building Blocks

This book engages directly with the burgeoning literature on the Far Right, extending its findings in a number of ways. The first is by focusing on how parties compete over national identity issues. This study joins ranks with those works emphasizing the sociocultural effects of globalization and postindustrialism, linking socioeconomic development with changes in value priorities. There is already a significant body of literature making this link (e.g., Inglehart 1997; Inglehart and Welzel 2005). But in its emphasis on postmaterialist values, this literature tends to downplay the flip side of postmaterialism – what Piero Ignazi has called the "silent counter-revolution" (1992). Sometimes viewed as neoconservative backlash against postmaterialism, this revolution is thought to bring about heightened concerns about sociocultural values and issues, such as "nationalism, law and order, ethnocentricity and bourgeois morality" (Minkenberg 1992: 58). Such concerns create demands for self-affirmation, self-defense, and self-assurance (Ignazi 2003) that encourage individuals to seek refuge in collective forms of identification.

The most common of such forms is national identity. By eroding the link between the citizens and states, globalization creates an identity crisis that reinforces the need for national identification and creates demands for cultural protectionism. This book shows that mainstream parties sought to profit from these demands by playing the nationalist card – by radicalizing political competition over national identity issues. The radicalization of such issues sets in place a new axis of political contestation – the "national identity axis" – delineating partisan differences over perceptions of the national collective. Immigration has been at the epicenter of partisan arguments over national identity. But it is not the only issue contested on this axis. In the past twenty years, citizenship laws and asylum regulations have also led to highly charged debates in Western European parliaments. Recent decades have additionally witnessed the politicization of historical memory and the eruption of bitter partisan disputes over the way European societies remember their pasts (Art 2006). One contribution of this book is that it brings together primary and secondary evidence to carefully trace partisan competition over these issues and to assess its effects on electoral outcomes. It shows that party positioning on national identity issues has structured the political opportunities available for Far Right breakthroughs.

The second contribution of this book is the examination of how the media affect the electoral fortunes of Far Right parties. Scholarly analyses often acknowledge the role of the media in the rise of this phenomenon (e.g., Kitschelt with McGann 1995: 130; Norris 2005: 270; Mudde 2007: 248–253), but so far comparative analyses of media effects remain rare (e.g., Mazzoleni et al. 2003). For the most part, the literature assumes a perfect electoral market, in which parties can easily communicate their messages to voters. Although this assumption is valid for major parties, which have easy access to state and institutional resources (Katz and Mair 1995), it does not hold for most Far Right parties. Because of their smaller size, such parties tend to lack the organizational capacity to recruit and to mobilize potential voters and the funds to publicize their messages to national publics. The media, then, can make up for their organizational deficiencies and financial shortages by helping them become known. Moreover, media exposure can bestow prestige and legitimacy to controversial appeals and give the impression that political newcomers have a mass following. Far from being neutral bystanders, media outlets determine the capacity of new actors to take their message to a wide audience with minimum organizational effort (Tarrow 1998: 126–129). Simply put, the media is a political resource that can lift marginal parties from obscurity and push them into the political mainstream.

One of the main findings of this book is that the Far Right is more likely to thrive in those political contexts in which the media is willing to grant it exposure. Using evidence from the analysis of media content as well as from interviews with journalists, this book finds substantial variation in the way the media has treated the Far Right across time and across countries. In some settings, the media helped the Far Right to capitalize on the political opportunities available in the electoral market and to achieve electoral breakthroughs, whereas in others it blocked its entry into the mainstream political discourse. By systematically examining the association between political parties and the mass media, this book is suggestive of the role the latter can play in bringing about electoral change.

The third contribution of this book is the explication of a temporal approach to party development. Instead of focusing on variation in Far Right voting across countries, this book traces Far Right trajectories across time. It breaks party development into distinct phases and shows that some factors best explain the earlier trajectories of Far Right parties whereas others explain the later ones. The basic idea is that once parties pass a "threshold of relevance," their fortunes are shaped by different factors than before. Using this idea, this book examines the trajectory of Far Right parties before and after their initial electoral breakthrough and reassesses existing accounts of Far Right performance. It shows that mainstream party competition is more important during earlier phases of party development than in later phases. Mainstream parties have the biggest shares of the electoral market, and the way they position themselves in the competitive space structures the opportunities available for political newcomers. Tracing this positioning across time, this book identifies a particular pattern of competition that changes the structure of opportunities available to new contestants. The temporal analysis of party competition documents the programmatic oscillation (Ignazi 2003) of mainstream parties on national identity issues. The argument that runs through this book is that mainstream parties played but then retracted the nationalist card, creating opportunities for Far Right breakthroughs.

Moreover, the stage-based view of party development reassesses the emphasis often placed on party-specific characteristics. This book acknowledges the importance of party organization, leadership, and appeals but points out that prior to electoral breakthroughs these characteristics are of limited explanatory utility. Specific party attributes are more important after Far Right parties achieve electoral breakthroughs, for sustaining and extending their initial electoral gains. Badly organized, poorly led, and narrowly focused parties are likely to become flash phenomena. Such parties are likely to be co-opted by major parties and to quickly disappear from the electoral map. On the contrary, parties that manage to establish solid organizational structures, avoid leadership struggles, and extend their programmatic appeals are likely to resist subsequent efforts by their mainstream competitors to co-opt them. Using this temporal approach, this book suggests why some Far Right parties survive their first breakthrough whereas others do not. And why mainstream parties are sometimes able to regain the political space lost to the Far Right whereas in other times they are not.

"Ethnocrats" on the March

First, a few definitions and some context are necessary. What do Far Right parties have in common? And how do they differ from their predecessors? This section offers a definition of the Far Right, and the next one sketches its postwar electoral trajectory, identifying three distinct "growth waves."

The inclusion of parties such as the French National Front, the Austrian Freedom Party, or the Belgian Vlaams Blok in the same party family presumes they share basic characteristics that set them apart from other families. But no two scholars have so far been able to agree on what these characteristics are. In fact, the identification of a common set of features has proven so troubling that it became the subject of scholarly inquiry itself (Mudde 1996). This book adopts a minimal definition (Gerring 2001: 78) applicable to all Far Right parties across Western Europe. Whereas some have described the Far Right as antisystemic (Ignazi 2003), antidemocratic (Carter 2005), antiestablishment (Givens 2005), and populist (Betz 1994; Mudde 2007), there is an emergent realization that the most distinctive characteristic of the Far Right is nationalism (Eatwell 2000: 412; Hainsworth 2000; Mudde 2000; Givens 2005). In part, this growing scholarly consensus reflects a gradual ideological convergence of the parties themselves toward the ethnopluralist principles of the new right (Nouvelle Droite) and their programmatic shift to questions of national and cultural identity (Betz 2002). The concept of the "nation" is at the heart of this ideological turn and "certainly functions as a 'coathanger' for most other ideological features" (Mudde 2007: 16). According to two prominent students of the Far Right, its worldview is based on "a myth of homogeneous nation, a romantic and populist ultra-nationalism which is detected against the concept of liberal and pluralistic democracy and its underlying principle of individualism and universalism" (Minkenberg and Schain 2003: 162–163; cited in Ignazi 2006: 227). The scholarly consensus on the ideological essence of the Far Right is consistent with interviews with Far Right politicians in Austria, Germany, and Greece. Although they differed on other issues, they all shared an ethnocentric conception of politics. Adjusted to the particularities of each country, this conception approximates one of the most common definitions of nationalism – that it is the political principle calling for the congruence of the political with the national unit (Gellner 1983: 9).

Indeed, no other party family equates in such an explicit manner the state with the nation, citizenship with ethnicity, and the *demos* with the *ethnos*. This emphasis on a nationalist conception of politics – or "ethnocracy" – is what sets the Far Right apart from other parties. The introduction of the Hellenic Front's manifesto – a small Greek extremist party that boasted ties with the Le Pen's National Front – is not atypical of Far Rightist ideas: "The ideology of the Hellenic Front is Greek nationalism. Greek nationalism is inseparably linked with freedom of the Greeks and with the struggle for the national integration of Hellenism."[5] Echoing these ideas, the party's former leader and current LAOS MP, Makis Vorides, claims that "there are objective criteria for who belongs to the Greek nation. We speak the same language; we have lived through the same experiences and wars; we believe in the same God."[6] Despite their strong attachment to nationalism, all Far Right parties claim to be loyal defenders of democratic principles. But in their democracy, there is barely any place for non-nationals. In the manifesto of the Sweden Democrats, a small

[5] Hellenic Front, http://www.metopo.gr/idea.htm (last accessed: April 30, 2004; site no longer available); see also Ελληνικό Μέτωπο (1994) *Πολιτικό Πρόγραμμα: Αποφάσεις του Ιδρυτικού Συνεδρίου, Αθήνα 9–10 Απριλίου 1994*, Αθήνα: Ελληνικό Μέτωπο [Hellenic Front (1994) *Political Program: Decisions of Founding Congress, Athens 9–10 April 1994*, Athens: Hellenic Front].
[6] Interview #11, February 2004, Athens.

Far Rightist group that was allegedly funded by Le Pen, the tension between ethnocracy and democracy is apparent: "We are nationalist democrats and dissociate ourselves from all forms of totalitarianism and racism."[7] Nationalist rhetoric is not always as explicit in party platforms, but the political principle is similar across the Far Right spectrum. For example, Pia Kjærsgaard, the leader of the Danish People's Party, avoids overt references to nationalism, stating that "the essence of the party program is a warm and strong love of our country."[8] But her party's program allows no delusions as to what the "love of country" translates into: "Denmark is not an immigrant-country and has never been so. Therefore, we will not accept a transformation to a multiethnic society. Denmark belongs to the Danes and its citizens must be able to live in a secure community founded on the rule of law, developing *only* along the lines of Danish culture."[9]

The insistence on cultural homogeneity and cultural protectionism explains why nearly all Far Right parties oppose immigration. Calls for "Austria first!" or "France for the French" and demands for the expulsion of illegal immigrants are at the heart of this ethnocratic view of politics. It is through this view – adjusted to fit the historical particularities of each country – that Far Right parties filter their programmatic appeals. Hence, their forceful insistence on law and order is usually accompanied by suggestions for border police to block illegal immigration and for tougher asylum laws to end the flow of asylum seekers. Likewise, their complaints about crime tactfully associate criminality with immigration and foreigners. Similarly, their social policies are painted with strong nationalist hues. Income redistribution and welfare protection are limited to "those who belong to the ethnically defined community and to those who have contributed to it" (Kitschelt with McGann 1995: 22). The "little man" whom they seek to protect can be anyone but a foreigner.

This nationalist worldview also constitutes the basis for some of the most radical claims of the contemporary Far Right. The Vlaams Blok, which was dissolved by a court order in 2004 (and renamed

---

[7] Sweden Democrats: http://www.sverigedemokraterna.net/int_text.php?action=full news&id=225 (last accessed October 2007).

[8] *Ibid.*

[9] Dansk Folksparti, http://www.danskfolkeparti.dk/sw/frontend/show.asp?parent= 3293&menu_parent=&layout=0; emphasis added (last accessed October 2007).

Vlaams Belang), wants to unify all Dutch territory in one country and calls Belgium a historical mistake (Swyngedouw 1998). Similarly, Jörg Haider, whose electoral breakthrough in 1999 compelled the EU to impose sanctions on Austria, considers the country a "historical miscarriage." The German Republikaner refers to the five new German states as "Central Germany" and asks for the completion of German unification with the Eastern territories (Minkenberg 1997: 82). The German National Democratic Party (NPD) puts forth a biological explanation of national differences in its program, and LAOS calls for resistance to the foreign powers that want to impose foreign traditions on the Greek race.[10] The glue that ties these parties together is their shared understanding that the political should be congruent with the national. Interestingly, nationalism is also the definitional attribute that contemporary Far Rightists share with their interwar counterparts. As Juan Linz observes, "if there is one characteristic of fascism on which all analysts agree it is the central place of nationalism in its ideology, particularly the type of nationalism that goes as far as placing loyalty to the nation ahead of loyalty to the state" (1980: 161).

Sketching the Electoral Contours of the Far Right

Even if one looks beyond fascism, Far Right breakthroughs are not a contemporary phenomenon. Although scholarly interest in the Far Right focuses on its more recent trajectory, there were two more growth waves in Far Right support. The first wave occurred across a handful of postwar elections. It was most evident in Austria, where disenfranchised Nazis, unemployed civil servants, embittered war veterans, and dispossessed refugees took electoral shelter in the newly founded progenitor of the Freedom Party, the Federation of Independents, giving it almost 11.7% of the 1949 vote (Riedlsperger 1978). In Germany, gloomy forecasts of Far Right advances did not materialize, as only a tiny fraction of the millions of expellees, repatriates, and de-Nazified officials (Stöss 1988: 34) lent their support to the three Far Right

---

[10] LAOS (2001). *LAOS: For a Greece that belongs to the Greeks*, Athens: LAOS (in Greek).

parties that ran in the first two elections.[11] The French Far Right, led by Marshal Pétain's defense lawyer, managed to elect four deputies in the 1951 elections who subsequently joined other political groups (Ignazi 2003: 88). The political heritage of the prewar, fascist regime might also explain the extraordinary performance of the Far Right in the first postwar Greek elections. Although the fragmented extreme Right received only 3.4% of the vote in 1946, the electoral combination of former fascist officials and anti-Communist guerrilla fighters got 11% of the 1950 vote (Nicolacopoulos 2001: 43, 69–70, 107, and 112–113), the best result the Greek Far Right ever achieved in the past sixty years. Overall, the collapse of the interwar regimes left behind a significant group of people that remained attached to the old regime, refusing to accept the new status quo. But their resentment toward the new order faded away along with the circumstances that had created it in the first place. The growing democratic consensus and the extraordinary economic growth deflated much of the initial support for the Far Right. Subsequent spurts in Far Right support occurred under much different circumstances, hardly comparable to the conditions of human suffering and abrupt change under which the postwar Far Right thrived.

Although the first wave of Far Right growth occurred somewhat contemporaneously across countries that had undergone rapid regime change, the second growth wave spread across three decades of rapid economic development and relative political stability. Second-wave Far Rightists were a much more diverse group than their predecessors, but their breakthroughs proved just as short lived. The Poujadist Movement that received almost 12% of the French vote in 1956 is the most representative example of this second wave. Although it was originally founded as an antitax initiative for the defense of shopkeepers and artisans (as its name suggested), in the midst of the Algerian crisis the movement became host to a number of right-wing

---

[11] The three parties that made up the first wave of right wing extremism – the German Rightist Party, the German Empire Party, and the German Community – received less than 2% of the vote in the first national elections. Some scholars also categorize the German Party (DP) and the German Fellowship/Bloc of Expellees and Victims of Injustice (DG/BHE) as Far Right. Both received higher percentages in the early postwar elections before they were absorbed by the CDU and the FDP (Stöss 1991: 106–136, Kitschelt with McGann 1995: 207–208).

extremists, including Le Pen. The Poujadists foreshadowed the appearance of similar groupings in the Netherlands (1960s), Denmark, and Norway (1970s), where new, neoliberal, populist movements scored significant results in national elections at the expense of established parties. During this second phase, the German and the Italian political systems also experienced significant strains but of a different nature. Instead of antitax movements, both countries witnessed the surge in support of nationalist extremists associated with interwar authoritarianism. In Germany, the NPD received an alarming 4.3% in the 1969 elections, barely missing the 5% threshold for national legislative representation, and in Italy, the neofascist Italian Social Movement (Movimento Sociale Italiano, MSI) got 8.7% in 1972, its best result since 1946. Yet support for both parties quickly waned, along with scholarly interest in the subject. In fact, except for the 1972 MSI spurt, the 1970s were the Far Right's most "quiet" decade.

The current wave of Far Right growth differs from both previous ones. Recent Far Right advances have occurred almost simultaneously across Western Europe, and many of them have proven to be much more enduring than earlier breakthroughs (Betz 1994: 23). Since the mid-1980s, the Far Right has consolidated its presence across a number of West European countries.

Having defined the Far Right and sketched its postwar trajectory, we are now ready to return to the original puzzle: what explains the divergent electoral fortunes of the contemporary Far Right?

Far Right Parties Across Time

Scholarly efforts to account for the electoral fortunes of the radical right abound, and their findings vary depending on the relative weight given to voter and party behavior. Some works emphasize the effects of sociological (e.g., Ignazi 1992; Betz 1994; Kitschelt with McGann 1995), economic (e.g., Jackman and Volpert 1996; Knigge 1998; Lubbers et al. 2002), and institutional (e.g., Carter 2002; Golder 2003; Givens 2005; Norris 2005) variables on voter preferences; others focus on how the strategic positioning of parties in the competitive space affects their performance (e.g., Kitschelt with McGann 1995; Abedi 2002; Lubbers et al. 2002; Ignazi 2003; Carter 2005; Meguid 2005; Norris 2005; van der Brug et al. 2005); and a few concentrate on the internal characteristics affecting the behavior of radical right parties, especially their organization and leadership (e.g., Taggart 1996; Betz 1998a: 9; Immerfall 1998: 254; Eatwell 2002, 2005; Carter 2005; Mudde 2007; Art 2008).

While varying on the relative emphasis they place on these factors, scholarly exegeses of Far Right trajectories have been motivated by a single question: "Why have Far Right parties thrived in some countries but not in others?" This has pushed the search for answers along a common path: the examination of Far Right performance in national parliamentary elections across Western Europe. But this focus on spatial variation has diverted attention from the temporal dimension of the Far Right puzzle. One of the main suggestions of this book is that to fully understand the recent advances of the Far Right in Western Europe we must pay closer attention to the performance of these parties across time, not just across space. This requires the development of conceptual tools to analyze the electoral trajectory of the Far Right; developing these tools is the main topic of discussion in the remainder of this chapter. Chapter 2 uses these tools to develop a novel theoretical framework for understanding Far Right breakthroughs.

Attentiveness to the temporal dimension of Far Right development necessitates the breakdown of the electoral trajectory of Far Right parties into different phases (Ellinas 2007). As will be shown here, this deceptively simple analytical step allows the reexamination of conventional explanations for Far Right performance. It is plausible that the weight of each explanation varies depending on the stage of Far Right development. Some factors are likely to be more important during earlier stages in party life spans, while others might better explain subsequent phases. The task, then, is to identify the different phases and to draw clear lines of demarcation between them. Previous work shows that this is not an easy task (Harmel and Svåsand 1993: 71), in part because of the unavailability of clear criteria for distinguishing between the various phases. This book proposes a distinction between two phases, an early and a later phase, and the use of Giovanni Sartori's "threshold of relevance" (Sartori 1976: 121–129; see also Pedersen 1982) to differentiate between them. The basic idea is that once parties become electorally relevant, their electoral fortunes are determined by different factors than before.

The emphasis on parties' electoral relevance directs attention to one of the most intriguing moments in party life spans, that of their initial electoral breakthrough. This is the moment when a party's national electoral strength increases significantly to a point where it changes the parameters of political competition. This increase is most noticeable in national elections, when a small party's strength increases by a few percentiles or when a party passes the national electoral threshold and gains substantial legislative representation. But Far Right parties have also made headlines through breakthroughs in European or in local elections. Regardless of how an initial breakthrough is achieved, it marks a substantial increase in party strength that crowns minor players with the perception of national political relevance. This breakthrough is arguably the most important point in the trajectory of Far Right parties. Subsequent spurts in support are also significant, but they largely depend on the capacity of the party to use the initial breakthrough to strengthen its organization, improve its finances, and broaden its appeal. Initial breakthroughs lift small parties from relative obscurity and turn them from backstage understudies into important political actors.

This stage-based view of party development has important implications for the existing approaches to the study of the Far Right. The most serious implications concern the analysis of party competition: the breakdown of party life spans permits the assessment of the relative importance of mainstream and marginal parties across time. Current work assigns equal weight to both, measuring mainstream and Far Right positions in the competitive space. Based on the foregoing analysis, however, it is only reasonable to do so, only after Far Right parties pass the threshold of relevance. Before the Far Right becomes big enough to matter, it is more appropriate to focus primarily on the strategic choices of mainstream parties (e.g., on their programmatic convergence). In other words, the appeals of Far Right parties might be more important after their initial breakthrough (Schain et al. 2002: 6), while those of mainstream parties might be more significant beforehand.

The differentiation among various phases of party development has consequences not only for the relative importance ascribed to political agents but also for the analysis of their tactical choices. Once Far Right parties pass the threshold of relevance, they change the competitive environment and, consequently, the range of options available to mainstream parties. Before the Far Right becomes electorally relevant, mainstream parties might afford to ignore or co-opt their claims. But once confronted with a sizable opponent, the option of ignoring or dismissing (Budge and Farlie 1983; Meguid 2005) Far Right claims might no longer be available to mainstream parties. The improved political standing of the Far Right might compel its mainstream competitors to address these claims. The growth of Far Right parties also affects their own strategies. To gain electoral prominence, small parties initially target niche electorates and focus on signature issues that differentiate them from their mainstream competitors (Norris 2005: chapter 9). During their earlier stage of development, the smaller parties rely on the mobilization of narrower constituencies situated away from the median voter. But as parties grow, they can be expected to tactically moderate their appeals in order to attract more heterogeneous electorates. The analysis of partisan politics across time allows the consideration of changes in party positioning in the competitive space.

Party competition aside, the breakdown of party development into different phases can also facilitate the re-examination of organizational effects. Arguments about the impact of intraparty structures on Far Right performance usually do not distinguish between various stages in party life spans. But it is reasonable to expect the impact of organization to vary from the first phase to the second. Good organization can help a party sustain or extend its gains after its first breakthrough, but it might be irrelevant before. The empirical record is full of examples of disorganized parties that proved successful: Pim Fortuyn's List in the Netherlands, Pauline Hanson's One Nation in Australia, New Democracy in Sweden, Political Spring in Greece, and the Progress Party in Denmark. All are examples of newly founded parties that lacked a solid organizational basis when they achieved their initial electoral breakthroughs. But lacking stable organizational structures, some of these parties witnessed sharp drops in their electoral support, while others collapsed. In this sense, disorganized parties might be good candidates for flash phenomena – they are likely to disappear from the electoral map as quickly as they appear.

The emphasis on different phases of party development can also elucidate the impact of the media on Far Right performance. Have the critical cover stories of the Austrian weekly magazines *Profil* and *News* damaged or boosted the electoral appeal of Haider? Did Le Pen end up benefiting from bad publicity in the French media? If so, why did the treatment he received from the press in the late 1990s (Birenbaum and Villa 2003: 45–70) not undermine the National Front's electoral fortunes? The breakdown of party life spans into phases might help provide answers to these questions. It is plausible that the media have a stronger impact on the electoral performance of Far Right parties during the earlier phase of their development than afterward. Media exposure can push minor parties into the mainstream debate, give them visibility, and legitimate their claims. Yet, once minor parties become part of the mainstream discourse, media effects might subside in importance. Efforts to analyze the role of the media in Far Right performance might be more fruitful if they concentrate on the period prior to the parties' first breakthrough (see Chapter 2).

A stage-based view of party development might also help explain the difficulty mainstream parties have confronted in formulating effective policy responses to the Far Right. In line with the temporal logic explicated here, it is reasonable to expect that once Far Right parties pass the threshold of relevance, they are harder to combat. Electoral breakthroughs endow new parties with additional resources. Those parties that use these newly gained resources efficiently are likely to improve their organization, widen their membership base, and broaden their appeal. This makes it harder for mainstream parties to reclaim the constituencies lost to the Far Right. The enhanced strength of Far Right parties after their breakthroughs can perhaps explain why the adoption of tougher immigration policies by their mainstream competitors often fails to suppress electoral support for these parties and why strategies of *cordon sanitaire* have not achieved the desired results (Downs 2002; van der Brug and Spanje 2004). As Far Right parties grow, their electoral fortunes are less dependent on the tactical maneuvring of their mainstream competitors. They become increasingly more reliant on their own organization and appeals.

Overall, the breakdown of party development into distinct phases allows the re-examination of the conventional wisdom about the determinants of Far Right performance. This bears significant consequences for the analysis of party competition. First, it draws attention to the most intriguing moment in Far Right trajectories, their first breakthrough. Second, it suggests that the relative weight assigned to Far Right appeals and organization must vary across time, depending on their respective political clout. These factors are likely to be more important after the Far Right passes the threshold of relevance and less important before. Finally, it means that in the earlier phases of party development, before Far Right parties become big enough to matter, the emphasis must be on the actors that shape the structure of political opportunities available for the Far Right and on the factors allowing these parties to capitalize on these opportunities.

Plan of This Book

Chapter 2 uses this stage-based approach to develop a novel theoretical framework to account for Far Right trajectories. The analytical focus is on two explanatory variables: how mainstream parties compete over national identity issues and how the media treat the Far Right. The basic argument can be condensed into a few sentences: In the past few decades, globalization brought about a sociocultural change in Western Europe, increasing the salience of national identity issues. The change in value orientations created demands for cultural protectionism and encouraged mainstream parties to play the nationalist card – to radicalize political competition along national identity lines. The programmatic shift of mainstream parties alienated certain segments of their heterogeneous constituencies or key international allies, compelling them to moderate their initial positions. This created political opportunities for the rise of Far Right parties. Where the media were willing to give excessive exposure to the political newcomers, the programmatic retreat of mainstream parties allowed Far Rightists to enter the mainstream debate, gain public visibility, and legitimize their claims. Wherever major parties retracted the nationalist card and mainstream media gave them publicity, Far Right parties achieved electoral breakthroughs.

While the analytical emphasis of the theory is on the earlier phase of party development, the propositions explicated here also have ramifications for the subsequent development of the Far Right. Using this framework, this book explores why in some cases the Far Right was able to sustain and extend its initial electoral gains, while in others it quickly collapsed. In all the cases examined here, the advances of the Far Right triggered attempts by the mainstream right to co-opt their agenda by adopting tougher positions on national identity issues. Such attempts were only effective in some cases. The study attributes the varying effectiveness of mainstream party co-optation strategies to factors that are largely endogenous to the Far Right, such as the degree of its organization and the breadth of its appeals.

This book tests the utility of this analytical framework by applying it in the "most similar" cases of Austria (Chapter 3) and Germany (Chapter 4) and the "most different" case of Greece (Chapter 5). It then probes its generalizability by examining the case of France (Chapter 6) before concluding with a discussion of the findings and an explication of possible venues for future research (Chapter 7). This book relies on evidence from interviews with mainstream politicians and top journalists, on the examination of archived legislative and party records, and on the analysis of newspaper and television content from the past two decades. Unlike most studies on the Far Right, this book also uses evidence from interviews and meetings with Far Right leaders and from the observation of Far Right rallies and party functions.

2

Explaining Far Right Trajectories

This chapter develops a theoretical framework to account for Far Right performance. In line with Chapter 1, the emphasis is on the earlier phase of party development, although as suggested before, the theoretical propositions explicated here also have implications for the subsequent development of the Far Right. The focus is on two major actors: mainstream parties and the mass media. The basic argument presented here is that the fortunes of the Far Right largely depend on mainstream party and mass media behavior: on how mainstream parties compete over national identity issues and on how the media treat the Far Right.[1] Mainstream party competition structures the political opportunities available for the entry of Far Right parties into the electoral market. Access to communication resources allows them to overcome their organizational or financial shortcomings and capitalize on these opportunities. The rest of this chapter develops these basic theoretical propositions in more detail.

National Identity and Public Demand

The concentration on national identity uses and extends the theoretical insights of a significant body of literature on sociocultural change. Earlier contributions to this literature documented a shift in value

---

[1] National identity is defined here as the collective perception of "who we are." This perception rests on a combination of objective and subjective criteria, such as a historic territory, common myths and historical memories, a common culture, common

orientations of Western societies toward postmaterialism. This value change was thought to affect the most affluent members of society and was associated with the rise of Green parties in Western Europe (Inglehart 1971, 1977, 1990). More recent contributions have built on these earlier findings to suggest that a parallel process has been taking place on the opposite side of the political spectrum. Their central claim is that postindustrialism, globalization, and supranationalism set off a backlash against postmaterialist values and generated demands for self-affirmation, self-defense, and self-assurance, especially among the losers of the modernization process (Minkenberg and Inglehart 1989; Ignazi 1992; 2003: 201–204; Minkenberg 1992; 2003; Betz 1994).

This study is in line with this claim, associating political preferences with attitudinal changes brought about by the transformation of the socioeconomic environment. It differs from earlier work, though, in stressing the impact of socioeconomic changes on a particular set of dispositions: those connecting citizens with the national collective. By eroding the link between nationality and citizenship, globalization and supranationalism have brought about an identity crisis in European publics. The process has been aptly described by Jean-Marie Colombani, the editor of *Le Monde*: "Just when we need a strong sense of nationhood to help integrate and absorb a new generation of immigrants, with different races and religions, the French are asked to transfer their allegiance to some vague European idea. This contradiction is feeding an identity crisis and undermining trust in our political leadership" (Beiner 1995: 20). The identity crisis has reinforced public demands for collective identification. Such demands reflect individual needs to belong to the national in-group but also the need to define one's self through reference to the national collective.

Earlier work downplayed national identification in analyses of sociocultural change, in part because of the absence of reliable cross-time survey data. But a cursory glance at some of the existing evidence, presented in Table 2.1, is suggestive of a growing public attachment to the national in-group. The data from the various waves of the World Values Survey show a marked increase in national pride across the vast majority of West European countries since the early

legal rights and duties for all members, and a common economy (Smith 1991: 14; 1999).

TABLE 2.1. *Pride in Nationality (%)*

Very/Quite Proud	1981	1990	1996	1999	Diff.
Austria		92.5	91.3		−1.2
Belgium	79.6	81.2		75.1	−4.5
Denmark	76.5	86.7	92.6		16.1
Finland*		82.8	89.3	93.6	10.8
France	82.1	86.8		91.3	9.2
W. Germany*	67.1	68.8	57.1	64.6	−2.5
Greece				88.2	n/a
Ireland	94.3	98		97.9	3.6
Italy	82.2	88.9		98.3	16.1
Netherlands	65.5	76.6		80.3	14.8
Portugal		91		97.2	6.2
Spain*	87.4	87	92.2	89.3	1.9
Sweden*	70.4	84	89	87	16.6
Switzerland*		81.1	75.1		−6
UK	88.8	89.3		90.4	1.6

Responses to the question: "How proud are you to be [Nationality]?" Question G006 in World Values Surveys (www.worldvaluessurvey.org).
* 1996, 2000 (Finland), 1997 (Germany), 1995 (Spain), 1982 (Sweden), 1989 (Switzerland).
Note: The difference is calculated by subtracting the earliest available measure from the latest one.

1980s.[2] By themselves, these data do not provide any firm linkages to the Far Right, but they are indicative of sociocultural trends that are conducive to the rise of nationalist, xenophobic, and anti-immigrant parties. To establish a stronger connection between sociocultural and voting patterns, one needs to examine whether Far Right voters are more likely to share stronger views on national identity issues than the rest of the population. Indeed, a considerable amount of individual-level data shows Far Right voters have more negative views of immigrants, refugees, and multiculturalism than everyone else (Norris 2005: 181–185; see also Kitschelt with McGann 1995: 74).

My own analysis of the latest wave of the World Values Survey reinforces these earlier findings (Table 2.2). Far Right voters are more

[2] Interestingly, in two out of the four countries that witnessed a drop in national pride, Austria and Belgium, the concept of the "nation" is contested, especially by the Far Right. In a third, West Germany, it is controversial. Only the Swiss case is somewhat puzzling, although the lack of earlier data does not allow firm observations about the direction of change.

TABLE 2.2. *Profile of Far Right Voters, 1999*

	Austria FPÖ (N = 211)	Belgium VB, NF (N = 100)	Denmark DF, FP (N = 38)	France FN, MNR (N = 54)	Germany REP (N = 24)	Italy AN, LN, TF (N = 218)
I. National Identity						
Strict Immigration (3–4)	25.4	28.5	10.7	26.8	33.3	24.7
National pride (high)	–0.7	–1	11.5	5.6	43.8	3.7
Job priority for own nationals	15.5	36.4	41	42.3	25	17.7
II. Employment Status						
Unemployed	2.2	1.2	–1.5	–2.3	5.5	2.6
III. Political Interest						
Very interested in Politics	2.3	–1.2	9.1	6.2	–1.1	0.8
Frequently discuss political matters with friends	2.5	–1.7	11.5	5.4	8.1	1.5
IV. Civil Society						
Belong to labor unions	0.2	8.6	–0.6	–0.4	–3.4	–5.9
Do not belong to any associations	2.6	–0.9	3	8.2	–2.2	–2.1
V. Political System						
Having a strong leader (High)	2.8	3.9	–2.6	6.7	39.9	6.6
Confidence in armed forces (High)	0.4	2.5	3.3	21.9	6.2	4.6
VI. Gender						
Male	11.4	8.1	12.7	17.4	42.7	15.9

Responses to respective questions in World Values Survey, 1999; Author's calculations.

Note: The numbers refer to difference in percentiles between Far Right voters and the rest of the population.

likely to favor strict immigration laws, to want jobs reserved for their co-nationals, and to have a stronger sense of national pride than the rest of the populace. The data also confirm the existence of a gender gap among Far Right voters (Givens 2004) but are weaker when it comes to employment status and political participation. The unemployed are only slightly over-represented in the Far Right pool for voters and only in some of the countries. Furthermore, contrary to some expectations, Far Right voters are more likely to be interested in politics than not. The results are far from conclusive because the sample in some countries is relatively small. But the evidence is sufficient to justify the need to examine how public attachment to the national collective affects partisan politics.

National Identity and Party Supply

Changes in the sociocultural environment increase demands for cultural protectionism, but, unless political parties are conceived as mere reflectors of social sentiments, they do not automatically translate into Far Right support (Kitschelt with McGann 1995: 13–14). The match between individual attitudes and voting behavior points to the significance of national identity, but it should not exaggerate the explanatory weight of attitudinal changes. As some of the most careful analyses of public opinion trends have demonstrated, aggregate anti-immigrant attitudes are poor predictors of Far Right support. If Far Right performance could be read off attitudinal charts, we would expect the Far Right to thrive in those countries with the most xenophobic attitudes, such as Greece, Portugal, the United Kingdom, and Germany. But in none of these countries has the Far Right been successful (e.g., Norris 2005: 175–181). To understand the political ramifications of growing demands for cultural protectionism it is hence necessary to go beyond attitudinal studies of value change and focus on how political agents try to mobilize and profit from social sentiments. As the voluminous literature on the Far Right is progressively recognizing, this requires an analysis of the strategic interaction of political parties (Kitschelt with McGann 1995; Abedi 2002; Lubbers et al. 2002; Carter 2005; Norris 2005; van der Brug et al. 2005).

The examination of party responses to the challenges posed by the changing sociocultural environment necessitates a consideration of the specific appeals parties make. Analyses that focus on party shifts across a Downsian Left-Right scale aggregate party positions across a wide variety of issues but tend to miss differences in party appeals over specific policy dimensions (but see Meguid 2005). This might not have been as problematic for the analysis of the Far Right if appeals to national identity could be plotted along the traditional axis of political contestation. Yet, as the moderate Left came to belatedly realize in the 1990s, the sociocultural shift in Western Europe cuts across the traditional – mostly materialist – distinctions between Left and Right. To fully understand the electoral rise of the Far Right, it is important to appreciate the political implications of the sociocultural shift that has been taking place in Western Europe. One of most important consequences of this shift is the creation of a new axis of political contestation that supplements partisan competition over materialist issues. While the new axis partly overlaps with the older one, it is also different in that the issues at stake do not merely relate to economic preferences but also to cultural ones. At one pole on this axis, one finds preferences for cultural homogeneity and for various forms of cultural protectionism, whereas on the other, there is an inclination for cultural pluralism and for a more critical reflection of the dominant culture (see also Kriesi et al. 2008).

One of the main arguments of this book is that the way political parties compete along this axis goes a long way to account for the trajectories of Far Right parties. In line with the stage-based view of party development explicated earlier, the emphasis is on mainstream parties. The moderate Left and the mainstream Right are the biggest competitors in the electoral market, and it is reasonable to primarily focus on how *they* respond to the electoral opportunities and challenges posed by rising public demands for cultural protectionism. Analyses that emphasize the strategic positioning of Far Right parties along this axis take party entry for granted, discounting the ability of mainstream parties to block the gateway to the electoral market. But if mainstream parties can sufficiently address growing fears over the loss of national identity, they can prevent the defection of mainstream voters to the extreme Right or, even, broaden their electoral base. To address public demand for cultural protectionism, major parties will seek to incorporate national identity themes into their programmatic appeals, thereby pushing national identity into the public sphere. Themes related to national identity are ideal for politicization because of their great emotional potential and because they do not always create concrete policy commitments. Like the issue of race, these issues are "easy" in that they can be understood at the "gut" level, requiring "almost no supporting context of factual knowledge, no impressive reasoning ability, no attention to the nuances of political life" (Carmines and Stimson 1989: 11). To politicize these issues, politicians rely on national symbols, popular myths, and historical memories that are convenient referents to connect the elite with the citizenry.

This book shows that mainstream European parties politicized these issues in the early 1980s to capitalize on the electoral opportunities presented by increasing public demands for cultural protectionism. As the *New York Times* described this process at the time, "throughout Western Europe, the 7.5 million foreign migrant workers and their 5.5 million dependents have become fair game for politicians of the right and left willing to gain favor with their electorate."[3] In France, this "fair game" resulted in the radicalization of the immigration issue in the early 1980s, initially by the French Communists. A few months before the 1981 presidential elections, and as Le Pen was falling short of the 500 signatures necessary to run, the Communist mayor of Vitry led a bulldozer against an immigrant shelter, pushing mounds of earth in front of the entrances. In Germany, mainstream parties also tinkered with national identity issues during that time. In the late 1970s, Christian Democrats initiated a controversial parliamentary debate that led to the tightening of the asylum laws in 1980. When the Christian Democrats came to power in 1982, Helmut Kohl made immigration policy one of the four pillars of his new agenda, initiating what came to be known as "the conservative turn" (*die Wende*) in German politics (Minkenberg 2003). This turn preceded the founding of the anti-immigrant Republikaner in 1983, which splintered from the Bavarian Christian Democrats, as well as the official founding of the DVU as a party in 1987. Similarly, in Austria, mainstream parties politicized national identity during the Reder and Waldheim affairs. Both

---

[3] Jonathan Kandell, "Immigrant Workers in Europe Are Easy Targets for the Politicians as Jobs Tighten," *New York Times*, February 14, 1978, p. 18.

issues put historical memory on the political agenda by highlighting Austrian complicity in the Holocaust. Again, the debates over Reder and Waldheim preceded the electoral breakthroughs of the Austrian Far Right. What this cursory glance at the empirical record indicates is that mainstream politicians purposefully entered national identity issues into the political mainstream. Contrary to the conventional wisdom, this book suggests that in many cases it was major parties, not the Far Right, that played the nationalist card by radicalizing political competition along national identity lines.

The eagerness of mainstream parties to gain from growing public demands for cultural protectionism presents Far Rightists with opportunities to enter the political mainstream. The politicization of national identity sets in motion a process of intense political competition along this new political axis, which often materializes as a clash between defenders of different conceptions of the national collective. The intensity of the ensuing political debates increases public awareness to national identity issues, raises the political stakes, and leads to partisan polarization. The most marked consequence of the political clash over identity is the extension of the political space but also the shift in the boundaries of acceptable political behavior and discourse. The French Communists' bulldozer attack against the immigrant shelter; Jacques Chirac's reference to immigrant "noise and smell" or Nicolas Sarkozy's to "scum"; Margaret Thatcher's 1978 well-known remark about being "swamped by people of a different culture"; the controversial visit of Helmut Kohl and Ronald Reagan to a Bitburg cemetery in 1985; and the anti-Semitic remarks by leading ÖVP officials in Austria during the Waldheim affair are all examples of how mainstream party competition over national identity can stretch the limits of what is politically acceptable. This shift in the contours of legitimate political discussion allows Far Rightists to enter the mainstream debate, gain media attention, and publicize their views. Intense political competition over national identity helps push Far Rightists from the margins toward the center of the political discourse, legitimating their claims and justifying their insistence on an ethnocentric view of politics.

The increased salience of national identity issues and the enhanced visibility of the Far Right can become an electoral liability for mainstream parties if they cannot keep the nationalist card on the table.

This book shows that this is often the case: A number of reasons compel major parties – especially when they are in government – to retract the nationalist card, moderating their initial positions on national identity issues. The most common set of reasons relates to electoral pressures. Because national identity cuts across traditional party cleavages, its radicalization can upset the delicate balance between the heterogeneous constituencies of modern catchall parties. The threat might be more obvious for the moderate Right, which has to balance traditional concerns over loss of national identity with business demands for cheaper labor. But the politicization of national identity also constitutes a balancing act for the moderate Left, which has to cope with the contrasting preferences of progressive multiculturalists and more conservative unionists and workers. Major parties can also be compelled to retract the nationalist card by international pressures. In their urge to benefit from the politicization of national identity, mainstream politicians tend to discount the international ramifications of their actions. But as the Austrian or Greek conservatives found out, their swift movement into this new political space can backfire if it raises international eyebrows. The specter of international isolation can make major parties moderate their initial positions at the cost of losing domestic support.

Far Right parties can compete along the "national identity axis" more successfully than their mainstream competitors because they do not confront similar pressures to moderate their appeals. In their earlier phase of development, Far Right parties do not participate in government coalitions and, hence, they have no need to be concerned by international reactions to their ethnocentric appeals. Moreover, their size mitigates the electoral pressures confronted by major parties because their electorates are, initially, less heterogeneous. Absent international and electoral pressures, Far Right parties can take extreme positions on this axis in order to enhance their credibility on national identity issues. Calls for the repatriation of foreigners or for the redrawing of national borders push Far Rightists away from the "median voter" but enable them to establish themselves as credible defenders of national identity. Their credibility might be further reinforced, albeit inadvertently, by links with interwar fascism as well as by frequent denunciations by the mainstream parties, the mass media, and civil society activists.

As long as mainstream parties keep the nationalist card on the table, the reinforced credibility of the Far Right might be inconsequential. But when mainstream parties become compelled to retract the nationalist card, issue credibility gives Far Rightists the opportunity to improve their electoral fortunes. One of the basic propositions of this study, then, is that the capacity of mainstream parties to remain firm on national identity issues determines the structure of political opportunities available for the Far Right. When mainstream parties moderate their initial positions, Far Rightists gain opportunities to enter the party system.

Party Supply and the Mass Media

The consideration of partisan competition over national identity goes a long way to account for the electoral fortunes of the Far Right, but the proposed framework assumes a perfect electoral market in which political messages directly reach party voters without intermediation. This assumption is only partly valid, as it ignores the role the media can play in communicating messages to voters. Although analyses of the Far Right tend to downplay this role, a vast literature that largely focuses on American politics suggests that it is important. This literature focuses on individual-level effects of political communication and shows that far from having "minimal effects" (Klapper 1960; see also Patterson and McClure 1976), the media can set the political agenda (e.g., Iyengar and Kinder 1987), frame issues (e.g., Iyengar 1991; Gamson 1992; Mendelberg 2001), prime audiences (e.g., Iyengar and Kinder 1987; Krosnick and Kinder 1990), and, under some circumstances, persuade (e.g., McGuire 1968; Zaller 1992). This book joins this body of scholarly work in viewing the mass media as an important political actor. But at the same time, it departs from it in adopting a macro perspective that seeks to go beyond its "preoccupation with individuals" (Kinder 1998: 189). Instead of examining how the media affects political attitudes, it explores its systemic impact. The idea here is that the media can alter the parameters of partisan competition by granting or denying access to political newcomers. While mainstream party competition structures the opportunities available to new contestants, access to the media grants them the resources necessary to capitalize on these opportunities.

This book suggests that we can better understand the role of the media by treating it as a political resource for disseminating information to national publics. Standard analyses of party competition assume that this resource is evenly distributed across parties and then proceed to assess the spatial or issue proximity among them. But media access – and the capacity to reach voters that comes with it – varies considerably among parties, especially between established and new parties. Incumbency and size guarantee political insiders access to the media, while their cosy relationship with the state grants them institutional leverage to create barriers for outsiders; for example, by creating access rules based on prior electoral performance (Katz and Mair 1995: 15–16). The privileged position of "cartel parties" in the political system gives them the necessary means to reach voters and to carefully guard their positions against political newcomers. This results in an asymmetry in the distribution of media resources that exacerbates the overall resource gap between mainstream and smaller parties (see also Ivarsflaten 2005). For, apart from media access, the latter tend to also lack organizational and financial resources. Even the most persistent of marginalized parties are likely to have narrower membership bases and weaker organizational structures than their mainstream competitors. And they are likely to only have limited access to state subventions to finance their operations. Their scant resources hinder their capacity to spread their messages to voters. Before they can effectively compete against mainstream parties, smaller parties need to overcome serious visibility obstacles, raised in part by their more established competitors.

The media can change the parameters of political competition by furnishing smaller or new parties with the resources necessary to disseminate their messages to national publics. While mostly ignored in analyses of partisan politics, the transformative effect of media exposure on party system change does not go unnoticed by scholars of political communication. Analyses of the British media, for example, associate the enhanced electoral fortunes of the Liberals in the 1960s and 1970s to the advent of political television, which granted the party more airtime, allowing it to get more publicity that was otherwise granted to it by the daily press (e.g., Semetko 2000: 359; 1989). Similarly, studies of the Italian media are suggestive of the transformative impact of the Berlusconi-controlled media on the party system.

The control and use of enormous communication resources by the Italian media magnate is thought to have contributed to the electoral success of the newly founded Forza Italia and of the previously small and stigmatized Alleanza Nazionale and to have facilitated the emergence of the two parties as legitimate representatives of the Italian Right (e.g., Statham 1996; Gunther and Mughan 2000: 418). The media helps newcomers overcome their visibility obstacles and hence narrow the resource gap between political insiders and outsiders, facilitating the dissemination of information to much wider audiences than the resources of smaller or newer parties would have otherwise permitted.

More importantly, the media can give new players clout, legitimacy, and recognition. Frequent presence in the media gives the impression of a mass following and creates an image of political importance. Donald Kinder did not have the Far Right in mind, but his remarks help to illustrate this point: "the mere fact of recognition, of being singled out for attention, is evidently enough to bestow prestige and authority" (1998: 177). As Gianpietro Mazzoleni puts it, "Media coverage of movements, leaders, activists, and of specific events entails their reification, rendering those entities meaningful to other political subjects who can address and interact with them" (2003: 10). The impact of the media is similar to the "validation effect" noted by students of social movements: "the media spotlight validates the fact that the movement is an important player" (Gamson and Wolfsfeld 1993: 116). Apart from validation, media exposure can also give momentum to political newcomers, and it can signal their political viability (Bartels 1988). Such signals reduce voter uncertainty about the political prospects of new players and, possibly, the likelihood that the newcomers will be strategically deserted for those parties that are certain to win seats or office. Overall, the media can lower the barrier for the entry of new players into the electoral market by giving them access to national audiences, by granting them political legitimacy, and by signaling their political viability.

Media exposure is a critical political resource for all political newcomers, but it is particularly important for the Far Right. Because its political opponents often associate the Far Right with the legacy of authoritarianism, media exposure can be crucial for validating its political presence. Lacking such exposure, Far Right parties might be doomed to political irrelevance and relegated to the margins of the political discourse. But once the media start publicizing their views, Far Rightists gain respectability. A quote in a newspaper report or a spot on a television panel signals to media audiences the political significance of the Far Right, turning it from a marginal to a mainstream political player. Persistent presence in media spotlights helps lift the stigma that Far Right parties might carry and grants them authority as legitimate actors in the political game. While the exact impact of media exposure on the electoral performance of Far Right parties is hard to measure across time and across countries without survey or experimental data, there are a number of examples pointing to the role the media can play in facilitating the entry of smaller parties into the political system. One of the most-cited ones is Le Pen's 1984 appearance on a popular French television program, which reportedly boosted his popularity by 3.5 percentage points overnight. Le Pen claimed this to be the most important time in his career and in his party's history. His remarks about the impact of the appearance are instructive about the importance of the media for marginalized parties:

Just like that, I must have changed. Just like that, I became an acceptable politician. Just like that, I must have changed my "look," just as they are saying today. And yet, I had changed neither my look, nor my message, nor my language, nor my behaviour. What had changed was that a television network, Antenna 2, granted me an "Hour of Truth." Sixty minutes, after a battle that has been going on for 28 years. An hour is nothing, but it was enough for me to get rid of the monstrous and carnival-like mask that all my opponents have so generously applied to me. (Jean-Marie Le Pen, 1984, quoted in DeClair 1999: 76)

To understand why mainstream media have been willing to give free publicity to such controversial figures as Le Pen, it is important to appreciate the seismic changes taking place in the media industry in the past few decades. The dismantling of public broadcasting monopolies and the advent of new technologies have led to the proliferation of media outlets competing for advertising revenue. Competitive pressures have pushed traditional media to search for bigger audiences, often at the expense of the quality of their information content. In their quest for wider reach, the media are thought to have placed more emphasis on sensational and superficial – instead of serious and substantive – news reporting and to focus more on personalities than on policies. The turn to "infotainment" is particularly evident in television: "Seeking to entertain as well as inform citizens, television increasingly depicts politics as a game or personality contest, or reduces coverage of public policy issues, shifting attention to prominent personalities, human interest stories, and nonpolitical subjects in general. And when news articles deal with the substance of public policies at all, they convey little information to citizens" (Gunther and Mughan 2000: 430). While the "dumbing down" of news might be an intrinsic feature of commercial television, the press – the tabloid press, especially – is also thought to display different degrees of "media populism" (Mazzoleni et al. 2003: 8), adjusting its content to the tastes and preferences of its shrinking readership. Along with this "dumbing down" of news come a propensity for negativity in the coverage of the political process and a predilection for the use of conflictual frames and antipolitics themes that contribute to "videomalaise" – to media-induced public cynicism and political mistrust that is believed to undermine the quality of participatory democracy (e.g., Robinson 1976; Patterson 1993; Putnam 1995; but see Bennett et al. 1999; Newton 1999; Norris 2000).

The political repertoire of the Far Right satisfies the thirst of the media for sensational, simplified, personalized, and controversial stories. Exaggerated references to violent crime and urban tension, which are typical ingredients of Far Right appeals, match the growing tendency of the media to dramatize news. The "simplism" that also characterizes Far Right appeals (Lipset and Raab 1978) is in line with a media appetite for monocausal explanations and for the delivery of easy solutions to complex phenomena. The "us versus them" lens through which the Far Right usually understands the political world also conforms to a media logic that demands the simplification of news stories and the adoption of conflictual frames. Moreover, while populist outbursts against the government and notorious claims about history might not meet standards of basic political responsibility, they meet a persistent media demand for controversy. Personal attacks against political opponents and belittling remarks about the Holocaust are outrageous enough to keep audiences tuned. So are the unconventional rhetoric, unusual techniques, and eccentric tactics of Far Right leaders, who eagerly try to entertain audiences and to please ratings-conscious media hosts. The willingness of the media to grant Far Rightists exposure also relates to the ideological content of the Far Right. Unlike other appeals, which are directed to specific segments of the population, nationalist rhetoric can attract much wider audiences cutting across traditional societal cleavages. Nationalist appeals draw on common cultural symbols and collective understandings and hence allow their exponents to tap into widely held and deeply seated feelings of national solidarity and identification (Tarrow 1998: 6). The Far Right instrumentalizes these feelings by spreading and personifying fears about the loss of identity, security, and employment. Overall, then, media outlets give the Far Right opportunities to capitalize on popular apprehensions because its political repertoire helps them meet the commercial imperatives imposed by the dramatic transformation of the media landscape.

The willingness of the media to give Far Right parties publicity is often controversial because of the electoral effect this exposure could have for a small party. As the introduction of this book highlights, political opponents often accuse the media for giving the Far Right outsized publicity, explicitly linking media exposure with electoral success. While the literature on the Far Right acknowledges such a link, for the most part it has shied away from the systematic analysis of media effects. One of the most influential works on the Far Right, for example, argues that unless the media are willing to disseminate their messages, Far Rightists will not be able to capitalize on the opportunities that are made available in the electoral arena (Kitschelt with McGann 1995: 130). More recent work has similarly suggested that media coverage is likely to be an important part of Far Right success, especially if these parties "receive disproportionate attention relative to their size" (Norris 2005: 270). But apart from sporadic references, systematic comparative analyses of how the media deals with the Far Right remain rare.

One of the main goals of this book is to address this earlier neglect. This book treats communication as an intervening variable, mediating between partisan competition and electoral outcomes. Far from being unimportant, media agents can either block or facilitate the rise of the Far Right. Using evidence from interviews with journalists and from the analysis of newspaper and television content, this book demonstrates that media exposure can go a long way in accounting for when and how Far Right parties can capitalize on the political opportunities available in the electoral market. The treatment of the media as an intervening variable would have been superfluous if they simply reflected voter preferences and merely gave Far Right parties as much exposure as their electoral standing justified. Yet, as this book shows, there is considerable variation in the willingness of the media to provide exposure to the Far Right. On some occasions, they grant the Far Right outsized exposure, while in others, they completely ignore it. By tracing this exposure across time and across countries, this book helps highlight the fascinating interplay of the various factors that affect how the media treat the Far Right.

The most obvious set of factors is commercial. As suggested previously, commercial pressures tempt the mainstream media to grant oversized access to previously unknown Far Rightists whose nationalist and populist rhetoric are controversial and simple enough to attract large audiences. This book shows how commercial factors facilitated the revival of the Austrian Far Right in the mid-1980s, which benefited from enormous media publicity from both the tabloid and the elite press. While commercial considerations are important facilitators of media behavior, media outlets cannot merely be thought of as economic agents who solely care about maximizing profits. Analyzing how the media have treated national populists in Greece and in France, this book shows how political considerations are also important. In Greece, the conservative government accused the media of publicizing – and even funding – a new nationalist party in the early 1990s to bring about its collapse. And in France, the Socialist government was accused of granting Le Pen access to prime-time spots on public television to hurt the mainstream Right. Yet another set of distinct factors relates to journalistic norms about publicizing Far Right opinions. In Germany, the study finds a strong journalistic consensus against giving too much exposure to Far Right parties. The remarks of a veteran journalist are indicative of this consensus and of the normative motivations guiding editorial choices: "In *Die Zeit* we don't give any publicity to extreme right views. This is our policy. Even bad publicity is good for them, and we are not willing to expend any space to host the views of extreme right politicians. Our policy is to keep quiet."[4] Instead of presenting the entire spectrum of political

---

[4] Interview #16, May 2004, Berlin.

opinion, the German media tend to consciously ignore Far Right parties. The example of Brandenburg broadcasters, who allegedly project the shoes instead of the faces of the DVU parliamentary speakers, is somewhat radical, but it is telling of the hesitation the media have in granting publicity to the Far Right.[5] This approach contrasts with that in other countries, where journalists and editors choose to publicize extremist opinions, claiming norms of impartiality, objectivity, and pluralism. By highlighting the various factors affecting the treatment of the Far Right by the media, this book points to the multiple and complex ways the media affect the political system.

Research Design

The consideration of partisan competition over national identity and the analysis of media behavior yield specific expectations about the conditions facilitating the entry of Far Right parties into the party system. This is when mainstream parties radicalize national identity issues, but are then compelled to moderate their positions, and when the Far Right gets higher media exposure than its electoral standing justifies. While the analytical emphasis is on earlier party trajectories, the framework developed here also creates expectations for the trajectory of Far Right parties after their initial entry into the party system. It attributes their electoral persistence or collapse to the parties' own organizational characteristics and to their positioning in the competitive space. The study examines these basic expectations against evidence from the "most similar" cases of Germany and Austria and the "most different" case of Greece (Przeworski and Teune 1970; Meckstroth 1975). It then probes the generalizability of the findings to the case of France.

Historical legacy and sheer size make Germany one of the most important cases in analyses of the Far Right in Western Europe. It is also

---

[5] This is what the press officer of the Brandenburg DVU, Thilo Kabus, claimed in an interview with the author in June 2004. While this example seems far fetched, newspaper coverage of a fire that almost burned down the headquarters of NPD, in Köpenig, verifies some of the claims about non-neutral reporting. Out of the few newspapers that covered the issue, some merely referred to a burned NPD car rather than a building. The author visited the charred building only a few days after the incident in May 2004.

one of the most puzzling cases because despite scholarly expectations, high unemployment and postindustrial change have not alleviated the electoral misfortunes of the three German Far Right parties in the past few decades. Austria shares more similarities with Germany than any other country in Western Europe. The commonalities among the two countries go beyond their Nazi past: They have similar cultures, postindustrial economies, and federal structures, while their legal and electoral institutions pose similar albeit not identical obstacles to new entrants. Prior to the electoral breakthrough of the Freedom Party in 1986, Germany and Austria also had comparable party systems, dominated by the Christian and Social Democrats. Moreover, Austria has similar immigration levels with those of Germany and one of the lowest unemployment levels in Europe. Given the emphasis of this book on the role of the media, it is also notable that the two countries have comparable media systems (Hallin and Mancini 2004). Also, the structure of the newspaper industry is similar, with one major tabloid – *Bild* in Germany and *Neue Kronen Zeitung* in Austria – dominating the market.

The Greek case is quite different. The Greeks endured the Nazi occupation, fought a bloody civil war, and suffered from a seven-year dictatorship before returning to democracy in 1974. Unlike most postwar democracies, Greece has not enjoyed a long period of peace and prosperity that scholars associate with postindustrial development. Earlier work associated the seeming failure of the Far Right in Greece with this developmental "lag." With the benefit of hindsight, this study re-examines this claim. It demonstrates that despite marked socioeconomic, cultural, and historical differences across the Greek and the other two cases, a similar process permitted notable electoral breakthroughs of the Political Spring in 1993 and LAOS in 2007. To further examine the generalizability of the findings, this book analyzes the trajectory of one of the best known Far Right parties: the French National Front. The French case provides an opportunity to further examine the relative effect of party-specific attributes by going beyond the particularities of the Freedom Party, the most successful party examined in the earlier country cases. Unlike the Austrian Far Right, the National Front was a fringe political force before its series of electoral breakthroughs in the mid-1980s; it put forth more extremist appeals and had the same leader since 1972, thereby limiting the plausibility of explanations focusing on leadership charisma.

The emphasis placed in this book on party competition over national identity and on media exposure poses a methodological challenge, as both variables are hard to quantify and measure. Over the years, Europeanists have come up with standardized measurements of party shifts on the Left-Right scale (e.g., Budge et al. 2001; Klingemann et al. 2006), but gauges of partisan rivalry over national identity remain underdeveloped (but see Kriesi et al. 2008). This might be because, unlike partisan disputes over economic policy, national identity does not constitute a constant feature of electoral politics. It is only during certain periods that issues related to national identity gain political limelight. This confines the analysis to those periods and issues and creates the task of identifying them. To do so, the study relies on evidence from elite interviews, press reports, and secondary sources. Table 2.3 presents a list of the eight periods identified and highlights the issues that were contested during each period. Throughout each of these periods, national identity issues became heavily politicized by mainstream parties and the media covered them for an extended period of time. All the issues included in this study made numerous headline stories for at least two months, while some, such as the Historians' Debate or the Waldheim Affair, became important reference points for casual observers and political

TABLE 2.3 *Periods of Intense Partisan Competition over National Identity*

Country	Issue(s)	Period
Austria	Austrian complicity in Nazi crimes (Reder and Waldheim affairs)	1985–1988
	Immigration/"Austria First"	1989–1993
Germany	Asylum Policy	1979–1980
	Die Wende	1982–1989
	Asylum Policy	1991–1993
	Citizenship/Immigration law	1998–2002
Greece	"Greekness" of Macedonia	1991–1995
	Orthodoxy and National Identification Cards	2000–2002

pundits alike. Moreover, some of these issues, such as the "Austria First" campaign, the Macedonia affair, and the Greek controversy over identification cards, have provided the impetus for the biggest citizen mobilizations in those countries' histories.

To trace patterns of political competition in each period, this book uses a combination of primary and secondary sources. It relies on interviews conducted with mainstream party politicians and leading Far Rightists; the analysis of newspaper reports and party programs; and the review of archival documents and parliamentary records. It uses evidence from these sources to trace the position of mainstream parties to national legislative outcomes. To assess the role of the media, the study utilizes information from interviews with top journalists in each of the three primary country cases and from the systematic analysis of newspaper and television content.

3

Party and Media Politics in Austria: The Rise of the FPÖ

In the universe of cases the literature often associates with the West European Far Right, Austria is one of the most fascinating and puzzling ones. Up until the mid-1980s, the Alpine country had one of the most stable party systems in Europe. "Exceptionally predictable" (Sully 1981: ix) and with "a reputation of a very high degree of stability" (Plasser 1989: 41; see also Müller 1993), the Austrian system had nearly fallen out of favor among political scientists who were increasingly more interested in explaining electoral change (e.g., Inglehart 1971; Flanagan and Dalton 1984; Przeworski and Sprague 1986; Lawson and Merkl 1988; Pedersen 1990; Kitschelt 1994; Pontusson 1995) than rigidity (e.g., Rose and Urwin 1970; Lipset and Rokkan 1990). It took the spectacular growth of the Far Right Freedom Party (FPÖ) to push Austrian politics back into the international scholarly limelight.

The FPÖ, which had stagnated at about 5.5% of the overall vote for almost twenty years and "had already been on its deathbed" (Müller et al. 2004: 174), witnessed a five-fold growth in support during a thirteen-year period. Through a series of electoral breakthroughs, it managed to break the forty-year duopoly of the Socialist Party of Austria (SPÖ) and the Christian democratic or conservative Austrian People's Party (ÖVP).[1] This put Austria back on the political science

---

[1] The SPÖ changed its name in 1991 to the Social Democratic Party of Austria. Here, the current and previous name of the SPÖ is used interchangeably.

map, but it problematized the conventional scholarly explanations for Far Right performance. For unlike many of its European counterparts, the FPÖ did not thrive in a high-unemployment environment. In fact, Austria still enjoys one of the lowest joblessness rates in Europe. Nor did the FPÖ's electoral advances follow politically motivated changes in electoral laws, as was arguably the case with the National Front's 1986 spurt in France (Mayer 1998). It is this obvious weakness of economic and institutional explanations that makes Austria one of the most fascinating and puzzling cases for the study of the Far Right.

Given the apparent drawbacks of economic and institutional accounts, academic efforts to analyze the FPÖ's performance have instead focused on the impact of long-term socioeconomic change. The shift from the industrial to the postindustrial economy is said to have shaken the structural foundations of Austrian society, eroding traditional party loyalties and creating new political issues. Tough budgetary constraints and painful economic slowdown highlighted government inefficiencies and gave rise to voter alienation and protest against the established parties. The disgruntled postindustrial electorate got tired of Austrian "partocracy," government corruption, and political inefficacy and became estranged from the cozy relationship between the Socialists and the conservatives. According to this logic, the FPÖ succeeded by tapping into this pool of disgruntled and alienated voters (Luther 1987; Pelinka and Plasser 1989; Plasser and Ulram 1989; Kitschelt with McGann 1995; Ignazi 2003).

Socioeconomic explanations are necessary starting points of analyses of Far Right performance but they cannot sufficiently account for the pace and the direction of electoral change. The rise of the FPÖ is a case in point: The abruptness and unexpectedness of its breakthroughs cannot be attributed to processes that take decades to evolve. Moreover, such processes cannot predict the direction of electoral realignment; that is, why voter alienation benefits Far Rightists instead of other small parties. Finally, the emphasis on socioeconomic processes risks sidestepping two important aspects of the Austrian case: those relating to partisan competition over national identity and to media exposure.

This chapter intends to show that the two factors can go a long way to account for the trajectory of the Austrian Far Right in the 1980s and 1990s. Using the analytical framework developed in earlier chapters, this chapter breaks down the trajectory of the FPÖ into an earlier and a subsequent phase, separated by the party's first breakthrough in 1986. To account for this breakthrough, this chapter examines the controversy over Austria's Nazi past. Sparked by the Reder and Waldheim affairs in the mid-1980s, the partisan row over historical memory allowed the nationalist wing of the FPÖ to enter the mainstream debate, gain media visibility, and legitimize its claims. When the Austrian conservatives became compelled by international pressures to moderate their position, the FPÖ achieved a major electoral breakthrough. This chapter also examines the subsequent trajectory of the party. It shows how the 1986 breakthrough became the impetus for organizational developments that granted its leadership considerable discretion to maneuver in the competitive space. Capitalizing on this flexibility, the party managed to continuously broaden its appeal to accommodate the preferences of its increasingly more heterogeneous electorate. Along with the party's easy access to the mainstream media, its organizational growth and its programmatic shift away from pan-Germanic nationalism allowed the FPÖ to consolidate and extend its early electoral gains.

To appreciate the magnitude of the electoral earthquake caused by the rise of the Austrian Far Right, it is important to understand its postwar trajectory. The first section of this chapter sketches the electoral contours of the postwar Far Right, tracing its roots to the FPÖ's progenitor: the Federation of Independents (Verband der Unabhängigen, VdU). The second section shows how the radicalization of national identity issues in the mid-1980s changed the structure of opportunity available to the FPÖ and how media exposure allowed the party to capitalize on this opportunity. The third section discusses the trajectory of the FPÖ after its 1986 breakthrough, pointing to its organizational and programmatic evolution and to the inherent difficulties this posed to the government parties. The last section concludes with a summary of the findings and with a brief discussion of the reasons for the party's collapse in the 2002 elections and of the subsequent revival of the Austrian Far Right.

From the VdU to the FPÖ

Until recently, the Austrian Far Right was synonymous with the ambiguity surrounding the concept of Austrian nationhood. This ambiguity

relates to the country's relationship with Germany (Katzenstein 1976).
It was epitomized in 1918, when all Austrian political parties voted for
"union" with Germany, a decision that was later annulled by the allied
powers, paving the way for the 1920 constitution (Luther and Müller
1992: 4–5). The defeat in World War II and the horrendous crimes of
Nazi Germany helped dissolve much of the ambiguity about Austrian
nationhood but left behind a considerable segment of the populace that
continued to embrace pan-Germanism and to reject attempts to create a
distinct Austrian identity. Fervent pan-Germanists took political shelter
in the VdU, along with former Nazi party members, unemployed civil
servants, embittered war veterans, and dispossessed refugees. Founded
by two prominent media figures and with the help of the SPÖ,[2] the VdU
put forth a platform that revived the third political camp (*Lager*), com-
bining a mix of economic liberalism and German nationalism.[3] The
party also pledged to protect the political rights and to restore the social
status of ex-Nazis. The revival of the nationalist camp paid off electorally, as the party received 11.7% and 10.9% of the vote in the 1949 and
1953 elections, respectively, upsetting the duopoly of the Socialists and
the conservatives.

Ideologically, the founders of the Federation were more on the liberal than the national side of the political spectrum, but by the early
1950s, ex-Nazis took the upper hand within the party. Reflecting this

[2] In his comprehensive study of the VdU, Riedlsperger (1978) argues that the SPÖ
tacitly supported the formation of a fourth party on the right of the political spectrum, thinking that this would damage their main rivals, the ÖVP. He presents the
Socialist interior minister, Helmer, as the "godfather" of the new party. He further
suggests that SPÖ's decision to "protect" the new party from possible Allied objections was based on the assumption that the "VdU would win a sufficient number of
seats in the coming parliamentary elections to reduce the ÖVP to a rough parity with
the SPÖ" (49). "Whenever local ÖVP authorities threatened to confiscate Die Neue
Front for alleged neo-Nazi publicity, all editor Reimann had to do was to telephone
Minister of Interior Helmer to prevent the action" (62–63). Riedlsperger suggests
that it was only after it became evident that the VdU's initial breakthroughs hurt the
SPÖ as much as the ÖVP that the Socialist leadership openly distanced itself from
the VdU and started to link the VdU and Nazism. Riedlsperger's analysis confirms
the emphasis given here on mainstream party actors. It also shows the importance
of media actors in the initial breakthroughs of newer parties: Both founders of the
party were significant media figures who used the *Salzburger Nachrichten* as a platform to establish a "third force" in Austrian politics.

[3] Apart from the Nationalists, the other two other Austrian political camps are the
Socialists and the Catholics. (See Shepherd 1957; Bluhm 1973; Katzenstein 1976;
Sully 1981; Thaler 2001.)

power shift, the VdU's 1954 Ausseerer Program stated that "Austria is a German state" and espoused "the strengthening of the German *Volk* (national community) in the Austrian area." It also asked for the restoration of "the rights of those who, because of their national views were persecuted and deprived of these rights." Even during the period of allied occupation, the Federation made no secret of its nationalist roots: Its slogan in the Vienna local elections was "Nationalists, vote VdU!" (Riedlsperger 1978: 142, 145). The VdU's attachment to pan-Germanism was not enough to undermine the growing consensus for Austrianism, but it set the basis for the re-establishment of a significant nationalist force in the Austrian party system. Contrary to the "patriotism" or "Austrian nationalism" of the ÖVP, VdU's nationalism had strong anti-systemic elements, as it was inherently antithetical to the existence of a truly independent Austrian national or political community.

The VdU's Far Rightist core did not have much trouble transplanting its pan-Germanic principles into the program of the Federation's successor party: the Freedom Party. Under pressure from its nationalist wing and after the 1955 State Treaty smashed the dreams of pan-Germanism by securing Austrian neutrality, the VdU merged with a number of other nationalist groups in 1955 to form an umbrella group that Herbert Kraus, co-founder of the VdU, called a "successor organization of the NSDAP" (Riedlsperger 1978: 158). In its 1955 program, the party renewed its commitment to pan-Germanism: It avowed the "social community of the *Volk*" and demanded "an education conscious of the *Volk*." Friedrich Peter, the former SS officer who took over the leadership of the party from 1958 to the late 1970s, "dismissed the idea of Austria being a 'nation' and advocated a positive appraisal of the efforts made by soldiers who had defended the fatherland in the Second World War" (Sully 1981: 103). Pan-Germanic nationalism was also the root for some of the most absurd FPÖ demands. For example, in its 1968 program, the party demanded the application of modern genetics to ensure that the *Volk* remained of healthy stock. The four FPÖ programs drafted between 1955 and 1968 relied on an organic vision of a single German *Volk*, on staunch anti-Communism, and on a peculiar form of antisystem protest that combined economic liberalism with pan-Germanic nationalism (Luther 1988: 233).

Throughout the 1970s, the party became less hostile to the reality of Austrian statehood but remained attached to pan-Germanic ideals. Bruno Kreisky's pragmatic approach to Austria's wartime past and the inclusion of four former NSDAP members in his Cabinet encouraged tacit FPÖ support for his minority government in exchange for a change in the electoral law that worked in FPÖ's favor (Stadler 1981: 9). The Socialist chancellor's cooperation with the FPÖ marked a sharp contrast with the approach of his predecessors, who showed little hesitation in associating the VdU and the FPÖ with Nazism. An example of the new SPÖ strategy toward the FPÖ was Kreisky's defense of Peter, when he was accused of complicity in the extermination of Jews and Gypsies during the war. Yet, while Kreisky's pragmatism pulled Peter and his party closer to the acceptance of Austrian statehood, it did little to dilute its commitment to pan-Germanism. In its 1973 program, the party described the *Volk* as a "natural community of those sharing a common language, history and culture" and proposed the return of guest workers to their home countries (Sully 1981: 113). The FPÖ's continued attachment to pan-Germanism was not only shown in its program but was also shared by its sympathizers. Surveys in the 1970s showed that as in the past, the concept of Austrian nationhood had least resonance with FPÖ supporters. For example, in a 1979 survey, 23% of FPÖ voters rejected entirely the idea that Austria is a nation, compared to 7% and 3% of ÖVP and SPÖ voters, respectively (Bruckmüller 2003: 62). Moreover, anti-Semitic attitudes, dating back to the Schönerer tradition of the nationalist camp, were more prevalent among FPÖ voters than among SPÖ or ÖVP voters (Pelinka 1998: 191).

The strong hold of pan-Germanism on party supporters obstructed subsequent efforts to push the party on a liberal course. Although the liberal roots of the FPÖ can be traced as far back as the late nineteenth century, they remained a marginal force within the nationalist camp because of the dominance of pan-Germanic nationalist traditions. Hence, there were no explicit references to liberalism in the five party programs drafted before 1985, but there was a peculiar effort to blend individual with collective freedom. Things started changing, though, in the 1970s, as young liberals, such as Friedhelm Frischenschlager and Norbert Steger, formed the Attersee Circle "to generate new ideas with which the FPÖ's liberal and intellectual profile could be enhanced" (Luther 1988: 233). These efforts led to the acceptance of the party in the Liberal International in 1979 and to Steger's ascendance to FPÖ's leadership in 1980.

But Steger's efforts to enhance the FPÖ's liberal profile alienated the party's nationalist wing, leading to a dismal result in the 1983 elections: The party's strength, which had stagnated at around 5.5% after 1966, dropped to its lowest point (Table 3.1). The subsequent alliance with the SPÖ caused further rifts within the party, undermining its capacity to present itself as an antisystem protest party, fighting patronage and corruption. By 1986, these rifts prepared the ground for the rise of Jörg Haider to the leadership of the FPÖ. Capitalizing

TABLE 3.1. *Results in Austrian Parliamentary Elections, 1945–2008*

	SPÖ	ÖVP	FPÖ*	Others
1945	44.6	49.8		5.6
1949	38.7	44	11.7	5.6
1953	42.1	41.3	10.9	5.7
1956	43	46	6.5	4.5
1959	44.8	44.2	7.7	3.3
1962	44	45.4	7	3.6
1966	42.6	48.4	5.4	3.6
1970	48	44.7	5.5	5.5
1971	50	43.1	5.5	1.4
1975	50.4	42.9	5.4	1.3
1979	51	41.9	6.1	1
1983	47.6	43.2	5	4.2
1986	43.1	41.3	9.7	5.9
1990	42.8	32.1	16.6	8.5
1994	34.9	27.7	22.5	14.9
1995	38.1	28.3	22	11.6
1999	33.2	26.9	26.9	13
2002	36.5	42.3	10	11.2
2006	34.3	35.3	11	19.3
2008	29.3	26	17.5	27.2

* Until 1953, VdU.
Note: In 2006, another Far Right party, the BZÖ, received 4.1% of the national vote and entered the parliament; in 2008, it received 10.7%.
Source: Bundesministerium für Inneres.

on the nationalist fervor caused by the controversy over Austria's
Nazi past, Haider replaced Steger ahead of the 1986 parliamentary
elections.[4] The next section examines how the intense partisan competition over Austrian history changed the structure of opportunities
available to the Far Right.

Reder, Waldheim, and the 1986 Breakthrough of the FPÖ

Two bitter controversies helped make the 1986 elections a landmark in
Austria's postwar history: the Reder and Waldheim affairs. The controversies sparked a heated political debate about Austrian national
identity by challenging the conventional historical account of the
country's association with Nazism (Art 2006). As the remainder of
this section will show, the radicalization of Austrian national identity
enhanced Haider's media visibility and political capital, helping him
to topple the liberal FPÖ leadership and become the natural leader of
the Austrian war generation. This proved an important electoral asset
when international pressures compelled major parties to de-radicalize
the issue.

The Reder and Waldheim affairs might not have been so critical
for Austria's electoral politics had the official memory of the Nazi
period caught up with historical reality. For four decades, a combination of political pragmatism and electoral opportunism prevented
Austria from confronting its Nazi past. But the political rationale
that kept Austria silent about the past started changing in the early
1980s, when the social democrats found themselves in a tenuous
coalition with the then more liberal FPÖ. The conservatives remained
in opposition and sought every opportunity to expose the ideological rift between the governing parties and exacerbate the tensions
the coalition created within the social democratic party. One such
opportunity came in January 1985, when the FPÖ defense minister,
Frischenschlager, gave an official welcome to a freed Nazi war criminal, Walter Reder, who had returned to Austria after spending thirty
years in an Italian prison. The conservatives quickly politicized the

---

[4] For a detailed account of Haider's rise within the FPÖ in the early to mid-1980s see
Höbelt 2003: 37–47.

issue, demanding the minister's resignation and later calling for a motion of no confidence against the government. The politicization of Frischenschlager's seemingly naive handshake with seventy-year-old Reder was largely tactical: Through the affair, the conservative ÖVP sought to increase tensions within the Socialist SPÖ, reviving scepticism about its coalition with the FPÖ. Furthermore, the ÖVP looked to block FPÖ's liberal opening (which threatened to make inroads into ÖVP's constituencies) by strengthening the nationalist wing of the FPÖ. The most important consequences of the Reder affair were to confront Austria with its wartime past and trigger the radicalization of the political discourse over Austrian historical memory (see also Pick 2000: 155–158).

Periods of intense political competition over national identity are characterized by the widespread coverage of the issues at stake. The heated political debate over the Reder incident lasted for enough time to bring considerable public attention to Austria's Nazi past. An analysis of newspaper content in the two most influential Austrian publications a month after the affair broke out is telling: Barely a day went by without a newspaper story on it.[5] The way the media covered the affair reflected the deep political chasm that ensued. The influential liberal weekly magazine *Profil* portrayed Reder as a war criminal, gave extensive coverage to his war crimes, and questioned Frischenschlager's action. Moreover, it used the occasion to critically reflect on Austrian historical memory and on right-wing extremism. By contrast, the popular conservative tabloid *Neue Kronen Zeitung* celebrated the secure release of a war prisoner – not a war criminal. The *NKZ*'s first editorial on the issue set the tone for the way the newspaper approached the affair: It presented Reder as a soldier who

---

[5] Analysis of newspaper and magazine content in the month that followed the Reder incident demonstrates the extent of the coverage the affair received. In its limited Politik section, the conservative *Neue Kronen Zeitung* (NKZ) devoted at least a news article or opinion piece on the issue in all but one day during this period. The attention the press gave to the Reder incident is also reflected in the liberal weekly magazine *Profil*'s coverage, which featured the issue on its cover for four consecutive weeks. The *NKZ* is the most widely read newspaper in Austria, with a market share of about 42%. *Profil* was the top Austrian weekly magazine in the 1980s, although it slipped to second place in the 1990s, after the establishment of *News*. Its market share approximates 9%. See http://www.aussenministerium.at/up-media/13_t_z_englisch.pdf, pp. 214–217 (last access: February 14, 2007).

simply followed the orders of his German superiors and as a "victim" of Italy's failure to master its fascist past.[6]

The controversy over the Reder affair opened a window of opportunity for the Austrian Far Right to join the debate, voice its support for the Austrian war generation, and benefit from the extraordinary public attention the issue had received. When the affair broke out, Haider aligned his position with that of the *NKZ*, arguing that Reder was not a war criminal but a war prisoner who had done his duty. He hence distanced himself from the liberal FPÖ leadership and gave full support to the defense minister, who, like Haider, was a son of a Nazi army (*Wehrmacht*) soldier. When Frischenschlager reportedly apologized to the Israeli government for his handshake with Reder, Haider's insistence that no apology was needed cast him as natural leader of FPÖ's pan-Germanic wing. Haider even went a step further, saying: "If you are going to speak about war crimes you should admit such crimes were committed by all sides."[7]

In a country that tactfully denied its Nazi past for forty years, this "relativization" of the Nazi crimes granted Haider a national platform to publicize his views. The analysis of the content published by the *NKZ* in the first thirty days after the Reder incident demonstrates the impact of the affair on Haider's visibility in the Austrian press. Haider's position received significant publicity in the newspaper, especially after Frischenschlager's apology (Figure 3.1). In the earlier phase of the affair, Haider was only quoted in related articles; in the latter phase, however, he made newspaper headlines and was featured in political cartoons.[8] But it was not only the *NKZ* that opened its pages to Haider. So did *Profil*. Throughout the period of radicalization, the influential magazine repeatedly warned about the revival of right-wing extremism, but showed no hesitation in interviewing Haider and featuring his picture on its cover.[9]

[6] Viktor Reimann, "Endlich in Freiheit," *Neue Kronen Zeitung*, January 25, 1985, p. 4.
[7] This is quoted by James M. Markham, "A Handshake Awakens Austria's Wartime Pain," *New York Times*, March 6, 1985, p. 2.
[8] See, for example, Peter Gnam, "Jetzt Gegenschlag der FP-Spitze gegen Haider," *NKZ*, February 16, 1985, p. 2 (and the cartoon on p. 3); "Steger: Haider über der Grenze des Zumutbaren," *NKZ*, February 18, 1985, p. 2.
[9] Helmut Voska, "Reder hat seine Pflicht getan," *Profil*, February 18, 1985, pp. 18–21. Throughout the interview, the journalist keeps a critical distance from

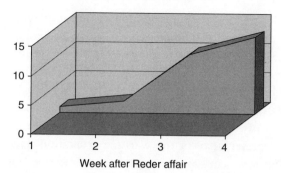

FIGURE 3.1. Number of references to Haider after Reder affair broke out
Note: References to "Haider" in the *Politik* section of the *NKZ* between January 25 and February 24, 1985.

Profil's "critical publicity" was to become typical of the treatment Haider and the FPÖ received in the following years from the liberal press. Publications such as *Profil*, *Standard*, *Kurier*, and *Salzburger Nachrichten* would rather give Haider negative publicity than ignore him altogether. According to one influential commentator, the stance of the liberal press toward Haider was partly influenced by commercial motivations:

During this period a lot of liberal journalists (in the *Kurier*, *Standard*, *Profil*, *Salzburger Nachrichten*, and the ORF) wrote frequently about the misdeeds of Haider. We wrote that he said this and that, that he wants to establish an authoritarian state, that he is a liar, etc. What did this achieve? We tried to tell the strong minority of liberals that were antithetical to Haider that they were rightly so. But we could not have hurt Haider. Not when the *NKZ* and *Presse* were against us. Some people said we made him stronger. When *Profil* or *News* hit the stands with covers picturing Haider, they would sell 30% more copies. The truth is he was a hot topic. ...[10]

Haider's stance on the Reder affair not only allowed him to enter the mainstream discourse and to gain media attention, but it also proved to be a valuable political asset a year later, when the controversy about Kurt Waldheim's wartime past erupted. Confronted with evidence that

Haider, continuously pressuring him to state his views on the Third Reich, war criminals, and concentration camps. Characteristic of this critical stance is the journalist's introductory question as to whether one still uses the typical Austrian greeting (Grüß Gott!) in Haider's home state of Carinthia or the Nazi salute (*Sieg Heil*).

[10] Interview #29, July 2004, Vienna.

Waldheim had concealed important details about his association with the Nazis, the ÖVP presidential candidate and the party leadership put forth a strikingly similar argument to the one Haider had made about Reder: that the ex–United Nations general secretary had only done his duty, like a whole generation of Austrians. The public debate that ensued shook Austrian memories of the Nazi past and shattered the long-standing myth of Austrian victimhood. Indeed, Waldheim was the archetypical representative of the wartime generation. His association with the Nazis was not an exception to the experience of many Austrians, whose traditional version of history was now challenged both at home and abroad (Uhl 1997: 80–86).

Publicized only a day after the ÖVP had announced his presidential candidacy, the Waldheim story became the focus of an otherwise uneventful campaign. The Socialists argued that the possible election of Waldheim to the presidency would harm Austria's image abroad, while the conservatives charged that the revelations were part of a defamation campaign orchestrated by the Socialists (Mitten 1992: 50–55, 204–205). The conservatives also accused the *New York Times* and the World Jewish Congress (WJC) for interfering in the Austrian elections – the former by publishing supporting evidence for Waldheim's past and the latter by calling Waldheim a liar and a Nazi and by threatening Austria with an economic boycott. The conservatives' defense of Waldheim shifted the parameters of legitimate political discourse, injecting it with high doses of xenophobia and ethnocentrism. This shift was evident in ÖVP's election slogan, which stated that "We Austrians elect whomever *we* want."[11] It was also echoed in numerous press commentaries and in ÖVP's attacks against the WJC, which had strong anti-Semitic overtones, including a comment by the ÖVP's general secretary, Michael Graff, who called the WJC leadership a "dishonorable lot" (Mitten 1992: 227–236).

The coverage of the Waldheim affair by the press contributed to this nationalist outburst. For the most part, newspaper coverage mirrored the charged environment, reproducing the heated political debate over Waldheim's past. But some newspapers, such as the *NKZ*, also had an independent effect on the radicalization of

---

[11] See, for example, the advertisement in the *NKZ* on March 29, 1986, p. 4.

the campaign. The most widely read Austrian publication not only dismissed *Profil*'s reports, but it also tried to present the issue as a defamation campaign against Waldheim and Austria. Reflecting the newspaper's sympathetic stance toward Waldheim, several cartoons showed Waldheim being sprayed with swastikas by political opponents.[12] Moreover, rather than examining the validity of the *Profil*'s allegations, the *NKZ* shifted readers' attention to the "story behind the story" (Mitten 1992), as it sought to expose the ones who instigated the "campaign" by supplying the WJC and the *New York Times* with archival documents on Waldheim.[13] When the WJC presented more evidence about Waldheim's wartime past, the newspaper largely ignored it, attributing WJC secretary Israel Singer's "emotions" and "anger" to his father's horrible experience under the Nazis in Vienna, where he was forced to clean the streets with a toothbrush.[14] Overall, the radicalization of the Waldheim affair broke the taboos against making anti-Semitic remarks in public (Wodak and Pelinka 2002: x, xii). Surveys carried out by the Department of Journalism at the University of Vienna suggest that the net effect of this nationalist radicalization was also an increase in Austrian pan-Germanic nationalism (Gehmacher et al. 1989: 107–109).

The radicalization of Austrian historical memory during the Waldheim affair and the pan-Germanic turn in parts of the Austrian electorate was the best Haider could hope for in his struggle against the liberal wing of the FPÖ. The Waldheim affair crystallized the rift between the liberal and the national factions of the party, which increasingly widened after the Reder affair and a series of government failures. Haider chose to tacitly support Waldheim in the elections, which put him at odds with the liberal FPÖ leadership that invested its decreasing political capital with the Socialist candidate: Kurt Steyrer

[12] See, for example, the cartoon in *NKZ*'s, March 3 and March 23, 1986 editions.
[13] In one of its many top stories on the issue, *NKZ* proudly proclaims to have found the person who ignited the "Waldheim-bomb." The newspaper links the issue with a "Leftist" historian with links to the SPÖ, Georg Tidl, who is said to have supplied the material to the *NYT* and to have gotten paid for it. See Peter Gnam, "Die 'Krone' deckt auf, wer in Wien den Waldheim – Bombe gezündet hat," *NKZ*, March 8, 1986, p. 5.
[14] Kurt Seinitz, "Weshalb der Jüdische Weltkongreß und dessen Chef Israel Singer jetzt so zornig sind: Singers Vater mußte 1938 in Wien mit Zahnbürste Straße, reinigen'!" *NKZ*, March 29, 1986, p. 4.

(Höbelt 2003: 43). Waldheim's victory and the subsequent response of the international community sustained the nationalist momentum in Austria for long after the election. This enhanced Haider's position within the party and prepared the ground for the toppling of the liberal FPÖ leadership. By September, when the FPÖ met in Innsbruck for its regular congress, the fallout from the Waldheim controversy strengthened the national faction at the expense of the liberals. Haider won the election for the party chairmanship, replacing Steger and revitalizing the national camp. Reflecting the changed equilibrium within the FPÖ, Haider supporters showed little restraint during the Congress: They reportedly made *"Sieg Heil"* calls and told Mrs. Steger that her husband ought to be gassed (Luther 1988: 245). So radical was the FPÖ's departure from its liberal course that the ousted party chairman threatened to withdraw from the party altogether if the new leadership did not clearly distance itself from these Nazi incidents. In a *Profil* interview, Steger suggested that Haider is an Austrian version of Le Pen.[15] This view echoed that of a number of European liberal parties that moved to expel Haider's FPÖ from the Liberal International because it was no longer a liberal party but rather an extreme-Right party.[16]

This view was also shared by SPÖ chancellor Franz Vranitzky, who abruptly ended the Socialists' three-year partnership with the FPÖ and called for new elections because the "liberal element in the FPÖ had been shoved into the background."[17] This was the beginning of Vranitzky's exclusion (*Ausgrenzung*) policy. Sensitive to the mounting international criticism against Austria after Waldheim's election, Vranitzky chose to isolate the Haider-FPÖ from the political process. In essence, this blocked the prospect of a future SPÖ coalition with the FPÖ, boosting Haider's efforts to present the party as the true opposition. The credibility of this image was reinforced by the growing realization that because both main parties would fail to win an absolute majority, the country was heading for a grand

---

[15] Christian S. Ortner and Josef Votzi, "Ex-FPÖ-Obmann Norbert Steger: 'Ich bin geistig emigriert'," *Profil* 39, September 22, 1986, pp. 26–27.
[16] Christoph Kotanko, "Der Aparthaider: Die Haider-Partei soll aus der Liberalen Internationale ausgeschlossen werden" *Profil* 39, September 22, 1986, pp. 18–20.
[17] James M. Markham, "The Austrian coalition collapses over party election of a rightist," *New York Times*, September 15, 1986, p. 4.

coalition for the first time since 1966. There were a number of factors that made the grand coalition seem likely. One of the most important was the de-radicalization of the Waldheim controversy. After the June presidential election and in the wake of Austria's growing international isolation, the conservatives toned down their bitter exchanges with the Socialists over Waldheim's past. Realizing the damage the Waldheim debate had done to Austria's image abroad, the two parties attempted to leave the issue out of the electoral campaign, focusing instead on economic issues (e.g., unemployment, taxation, pensions, and working hours).[18]

Despite bipartisan efforts to de-radicalize the Waldheim controversy, a combination of international events kept the issue alive. Israel's decision not to replace its ambassador to Vienna until the results of the election became known; Israeli charges of Nazi and anti-Semitic overtones in the campaign; and reports on "American attacks on Austria" kept the controversy over Austrian historical memory alive in the *NKZ*.[19] So did the newspaper's editorial columns, which charged Israel with interference in Austrian politics and blamed the "powerful WJC" for tarnishing the country's international image.[20] Despite the numerous political scandals that had erupted in the past few years and a widespread call for clean politics, the newspaper's coverage of such issues was limited compared to that of the Waldheim controversy.

The residue of the Waldheim affair in the electoral campaign, along with the two main parties' efforts to de-radicalize the issue, presented the FPÖ with a political opportunity for an electoral breakthrough. But it was Haider's growing visibility in the Austrian media that allowed him to capitalize on this opportunity. His

[18] Peter Gnam, "Torloses" TV-Match, Mock kämpfte mehr," *NKZ*, November 7, 1986, pp. 2–3. According to the article, these were the most important issues discussed during the Vranitzky-Mock television debate. These were also the issues that the two major parties focused on in their newspaper advertisements. The ÖVP stressed the unemployment issue, and the SPÖ argued that all ÖVP proposals will be financed through higher taxation.

[19] Several of the articles made cover stories in the newspaper, including an anonymous report published six days before the election on a *Washington Post* editorial piece that argued that the Austrians are not ready to confront their wartime history. *NKZ*, "Wieder Angriffe gegen Österreich in den USA!" *NKZ*, November 17, 1986, pp. 1–3.

[20] Almost 40% of the references to the Waldheim controversy were opinion articles.

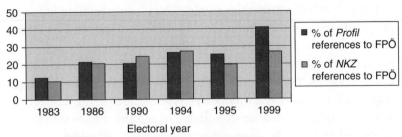

FIGURE 3.2. References to FPÖ as percentage of total references to all political parties in *Profil* and *NKZ*, 1983–1999

continued defense of the *Wehrmacht* generation, his toppling of the liberal FPÖ leadership in September, and his controversial style had granted Haider considerable media access and attention from sympathizers and critics alike. This exposure preceded FPÖ's 1986 breakthrough; it did not follow it, as some have suggested. The analysis of press coverage during the electoral campaign demonstrates Haider's high visibility in the Austrian media (Figure 3.2). Measured as a percentage of all references to Austrian political parties and their candidates in the two most influential Austrian publications, FPÖ's was more than a fifth of the total exposure granted to Austrian political parties.[21] Notably, the party's exposure was nearly four times higher than its predicted electoral result.[22] During the 1986 electoral campaign, the Freedom Party received 21.2% of all party-related references in *Profil* and 20.6% in the *NKZ*.[23] The exposure

[21] For the analysis of the *NKZ*, the author counted all party-related references in news and opinion articles published in the Politik section during the month before each national parliamentary election between 1983 and 1999. In those articles that included more than one reference to a particular party, only the first one was counted. For the analysis of *Profil*, the author counted all articles included in the index of the magazine that explicitly related to specific parties two months before each election.

[22] The author came across two public opinion polls during this period. The first one predicted that the FPÖ would get 5.5% of the vote. The other one, in the *NKZ*, predicted 6%.

[23] The content analysis of *NKZ* reports has yielded similar results to those cited in Plasser (1987: 100). He reports that FPÖ's exposure in the *NKZ* two months prior to the election was 24% of all party-related statements in the newspaper. FPÖ exposure in the other four newspapers included in the analysis ranged from 15.6% to 18.4%. The FPÖ also received 18.9% of all the exposure granted to parties by the television news program " Zeit im Bild."

TABLE 3.2. *Analysis of Profil's Coverage of the FPÖ, 1983–1999**

Election Year	Top Cover Story with picture	Top Cover Story, No Picture	Other Story on Cover	Picture in Index	Number of Articles	Number of Pictures in Articles
1983	0	0	1	0	5	2
1986	1	0	4	3	12	12
1990	0	0	0	0	6	3
1994	1	0	1	0	12	12
1995	1	2	2	2	20	15
1999	1	1	1	2	28	31

* Number of articles and pictures four months up to national elections.

the FPÖ received in the two publications in 1986 was approximately double its 1983 exposure. Reflecting Haider's capacity to gain media attention, almost two-thirds of *NKZ's* 1986 references to the FPÖ were about Haider himself. Moreover, Haider's name appeared in *NKZ* headlines more times than those of the Socialist and conservative leaders.

The *NKZ's* exposure of the FPÖ should not be surprising because the newspaper had a similar agenda to Haider's. But *Profil's* exposure of the FPÖ in the 1986 elections is more puzzling because the magazine was highly critical of Haider's pan-Germanic appeals. To reinforce the findings of the first analysis, the study includes a second measure, focusing on the publicity *Profil* gave to the FPÖ. This measure counts the number of articles or pictures published in the influential magazine four months prior to each election between 1983 and 1999. The results of the analysis are presented in Table 3.2. Between July and November 1986, *Profil* devoted one of its top cover stories to the FPÖ; published several secondary cover stories; and wrote 12 articles on the party, including many pictures. Like the previous analysis, this second measure shows that the FPÖ received a lot more publicity from *Profil* during the 1986 election than in 1983. But unlike the first assessment, the latter analysis suggests that the 1986 exposure was higher than the exposure the FPÖ received in 1990 and in 1994.

The FPÖ Trajectory after the 1986 Breakthrough

Mainstream parties and the mass media command the gateways to the electoral market, but once a party breaks through, its electoral destiny is less dependent on exogenous factors than before. As a party grows, it is better positioned to shape its own electoral fate. To do so, the party needs to sustain the electoral momentum. The remainder of this chapter analyzes the factors that allowed the FPÖ to build on its 1986 breakthrough to become the second-largest Austrian party by 1999. Consistent with the theoretical framework developed in the previous chapters, the emphasis here is on the party itself, especially on its strategic positioning in the competitive space. The next section shows how the party used its early breakthrough as the basis to improve its organizational capacity and to extend its initial appeals beyond pan-Germanism in order to profit from growing public apprehension over immigration.

Organizational Development. Electoral breakthroughs can become mere flashes of electoral support if parties fail to use them as opportunities to improve their organizational capacity and to broaden their ideological appeal. To sustain their electoral gains, parties need to set in place intraparty mechanisms to establish contact with the new constituencies, recruit new members, and mobilize voters. Ideally, these mechanisms allow parties to expand their membership base without hindering their capacity to respond effectively to new stimuli in the political environment. Unlike many of its counterparts in Western Europe, the FPÖ already had the organizational infrastructure to contest elections, participate in parliament and formulate legislative proposals. But by the time Haider rose to the FPÖ's leadership, the party's organizational capacity had reached its limits, as government participation started taking a toll on new member recruitment. In the early 1980s, party membership peaked at 37,517 and then dropped after the small coalition came into effect in 1983 (Figure 3.3). The 1986 breakthrough reversed this downward trend. In the next fifteen years, party membership grew by nearly 39%, from 36,925 in 1986 to 51,296 in 2000. This growth was smaller than the multifold growth of FPÖ's electorate during this period, but it sharply contrasted with the membership decline of the two major parties (Müller 1992; Luther 2000; Luther 2006).

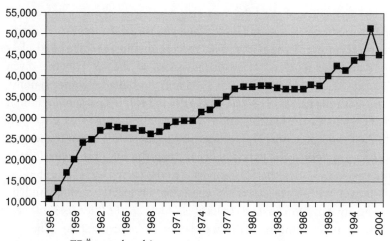

FIGURE 3.3. FPÖ membership, 1956–2004
Sources: Müller 1992 up to 1990; Luther 2006 after 1990. Reproduced with permission of authors.

Despite its organizational growth, the FPÖ apparatus remained small enough to grant the party leadership the flexibility necessary to maneuver in the competitive space. Even at its peak, FPÖ membership was merely a fraction of that of the SPÖ and the ÖVP, which boasted more than a half-million members each, or nearly a third of their respective electorates. This made the party more responsive to the changing political environment. Unlike its mainstream competitors, the FPÖ apparatus afforded the party leadership considerable discretion rather than constraining it through elaborate control mechanisms or bureaucratic decision-making procedures. As the next section will show in more detail, the slim organizational structure allowed the party to swiftly claim ownership of new issues and drop older ones. In the late 1980s, the party gained ownership of the immigration issue before mainstream parties could formulate effective policy responses to address widespread public concerns. In the early 1990s, it started distancing itself from old-fashioned pan-Germanism adopting a new sense of Austrian nationalism, and it quickly reversed its pro-EU stance to become the most vocal opponent of EU membership and, later, eastern enlargement. In the latter half of the 1990s, the FPÖ dropped its liberal antithesis to the growth of the welfare state and its long-standing anticlericalism.

The flexibility of the FPÖ was also because of changes in internal power relations that gave Haider leverage to determine the ideological positioning of the party. The success in the 1986 national elections and the repeated electoral advances of the FPÖ in the seven *Landtag* elections held between 1986 and 1990 made Haider synonymous with the party. This was especially so after his personal triumph in the 1989 Carinthian elections and his appointment as governor. Unlike his predecessor, Haider was able to make full use of the formal powers granted to the party leader to turn the FPÖ into what critics unflatteringly called the Führer party. In the early 1990s, he extended his power within the party by changing the party statutes and by setting up new intraparty structures, such as the "leader's office." These changes reinforced the trend toward centralization. The late 1990s witnessed increased intervention of the national leadership in provincial party activities, including those related to candidate selection. The recruitment of party outsiders to stand for key elected posts strengthened the national leadership, as the new recruits lacked organizational footholds within the party and were directly dependent on Haider (Luther 2000: 434). Up until 2000, he made all important strategic and personnel decisions in the party, often announcing them in public before discussing them internally (Müller et al. 2004: 161). Haider's leadership style created tensions with party functionaries, especially toward the late 1990s, when a number of regional organizations refused to give in to pressures from the national party leadership on candidate selection. But overall, his power position within the party was so strong that he managed to emerge from these internal battles unscathed.

Issue Extension: From Waldheim to Immigration. Along with the organizational development of the FPÖ came the gradual broadening of its appeal beyond the issues that facilitated its 1986 breakthrough. The first few years of the grand coalition gave the party new opportunities to benefit from the political controversy created by the Waldheim affair. The decision of the Reagan administration to bar the Austrian president from entering the United States; the findings of an independent commission about Waldheim's association with the Nazis; the publication of new evidence in the local and foreign press; and the growing isolation of Austria kept the issue alive for several years, causing significant tension in the governing coalition. The ÖVP's participation in government limited its capacity to defend Waldheim because it had to take into consideration the danger of Austrian ostracism abroad and the reactions of the Austrian business community, which saw the deterioration of relations with Washington as a threat to Austrian exports and tourism. The tenuous position of the ÖVP was exposed in November 1987 when two prominent ÖVP officials had to step down after making anti-Semitic remarks[24] and when the conservative leader had to grudgingly agree to an official visit to the United States, despite the blacklisting of Waldheim. The weakened position of the ÖVP allowed the FPÖ to secure a near monopoly over the defense of the war generation. Through rhetorical attacks on Austria's international critics, the FPÖ managed to take the position that the conservatives had previously occupied but abandoned under increasing international pressure.

When the Waldheim affair started receding in public attention, the FPÖ tactfully weakened his emphasis on old pan-Germanic themes and introduced new issues into its repertoire. Hence, in the 1987 Vienna elections and in the midst of the nationalist backlash that Austria's international isolation had caused, the FPÖ started focusing on immigration. In comments that raised memories of the past, Haider made a connection between the 140,000 unemployed Austrians and the 180,000 immigrant workers in Austria – a calculation he repeated many times afterward (Gärtner 2002: 18–19). Moreover, the FPÖ also linked immigration with rising crime rates. Playing on public anxiety about urban crime, a poster of the Vienna FPÖ in the 1990 election campaign read: "Vienna must not become Chicago" (Riedlsperger 1996: 360). FPÖ's growing hostility to foreigners was documented in the "Declaration of St. Lorenzen," a

---

[24] Defending Waldheim, ÖVP general gecretary M. Graff told a French newspaper that Mr. Waldheim was innocent "so long as it's not proved that he strangled six Jews with his own hands." Similarly, deputy mayor of Linz, Carl Hödl, had to step down after writing a letter to Edgar Bronfman, the president of the WJC, in which he compared the campaign against Waldheim with the "persecution of Jesus by his fellow Jews." Serge Schmemann, "The Angst over Waldheim Just Won't Go Away," *New York Times*, December 9, 1987, p. 4. For the resignation of Graff, see also Peter Michael Lingens, "Warum nur Graff: Alois Mock hat den Ton angegeben in dem sich sein Generalsekretär vergriffen hat," *Profil*, November 23, 1987, p. 13.

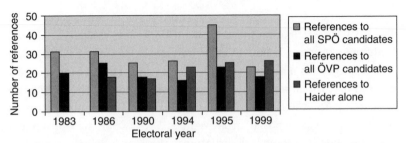

FIGURE 3.4. Number of references to main party candidates in Politik section of *NKZ*, 1983–1999
Note: One month before each national parliamentary election.

paper presented in October 1989 that set the ideological basis for the party's anti-foreigner policy. One of its drafters, Raimund Wimmer, later warned on Austrian television that "suddenly even the Negroes will be the majority here."

As Chapter 4 shows, in Germany, journalistic norms limited the reproduction of such views by the media. In Austria, though, the FPÖ enjoyed easy access to the media and received considerable publicity. Toward the late 1980s, the party continued to benefit from outsized media visibility, especially from the *NKZ*. The largest Austrian daily had a "soft spot" for Haider (Höbelt 2003: 15) and contributed in several ways to FPÖ's 1990 breakthrough. First, the *NKZ* gave Haider a lot of free exposure, which was often disproportionate to the FPÖ's electoral strength. During the 1990 electoral campaign, for example, Haider received almost as much attention as all ÖVP candidates combined (Figure 3.4).[25] In addition, the newspaper reinforced and legitimized the FPÖ's agenda by providing extensive coverage to the same issues that Haider raised, implicitly signaling to its readers that these issues are important. This coverage was not always based on actual events or happenings. In its account of the critical television debate between Vranitzky and Josef Riegler (ÖVP) in the last phase of the 1990 campaign, for instance, the newspaper chose

---

[25] Haider's exposure is even more remarkable if one takes into account that the SPÖ and the ÖVP were governing at the time, which gave their candidates (e.g., Vranitzky) more opportunities for exposure. The number of references for SPÖ and ÖVP candidates and for Haider totaled 410.

to report on what was *not* discussed: the series of scandals, the "foreigner problem," and Austrian neutrality – the same issues Haider campaigned on.[26]

More importantly, the newspaper helped create a hostile climate against immigration by framing it in negative terms. Along with other conservative newspapers, the *NKZ* "used a metaphorical language that represented migration as a natural catastrophe or as a highly alarming phenomenon." Various newspapers used phrases such as "migration of Eastern European nations," a "state of siege," or a "tidal wave of emigrants to Austria" to describe the phenomenon (Joskowicz 2002: 315). The reporting on Romanian immigrants is a case in point: From March 1990 onward, the *NKZ* started to depict them as a serious threat to the social order in Austria,[27] portraying them as criminals and welfare scroungers. While the precise impact of the newspaper's reporting on reader attitudes is hard to assess, there is some evidence suggesting a strong association between the two. A 1992 study, for example, shows that regular readers of the *NKZ* and the tabloid *Täglich Alles* were more likely to be fearful of foreigners than readers of daily prestige newspapers, such as *Die Presse* and *Der Standard* (Table 3.3). This notable relationship held even after the introduction of controls for sociodemographic background.

With the help of the mainstream media, which gave the party a platform to voice its antiforeigner rhetoric, the FPÖ stood to benefit from growing public concerns over immigration. A few months before the 1990 national election, two out of three Austrians thought that with foreigners in Austria, the rate of insecurity, disorder, and crime would rise. The ranking of political issues according to their importance reflected this change in public mood: The "foreigner problem" was not on the list of issues in 1989, but it ranked tenth in 1990 and second in 1992 (Gärtner 2002: 19–20). It was the top issue in Vienna in the 1990 national elections. In October 1992, a Gallup opinion poll showed that 76% of those polled were strictly against allowing more

---

[26] Dieter Kindermann, "Fernsehduell der Kanzlerkandidaten: Brisante Themen wurden ausgespart, Kein Wort über Skandale, Neutralität und Ausländerproblematik," *NKZ*, September 28, 1990, p. 2.

[27] A series of articles that appeared in spring 1990 in the *NKZ* were titled "Threats by Foreigners!" (Gärtner 2002: 19).

TABLE 3.3. *Political Orientations: Readers of Daily Prestige and Tabloid Newspapers*

Political Orientation (%)	Prestige *(Presse, Standard)*	Tabloid *(NKZ, TA)*
Authoritarian potential	20	51
Fear of foreigners core*	16	43
Party weariness core	18	37
Alienated core	10	23
German national core	5	9
German national potential	11	24
Low subjective policy efficacy core	23	16
Government critics core	11	10

* Core refers to those people holding strong convictions, as opposed to those who only tend in that direction.
Source: FESSEL-GfK, Life-Style (1992), cited in Plasser and Ulram 2003: 31–33.

foreigners into the country, while 66% would have preferred to close the borders to war refugees (Reisigl and Wodak 2001: 150).

Mainstream Party Responses to Immigration. The appearance of a new issue in the political environment presents mainstream parties with dilemmas on how to address it. Political scientific research suggests that one way of doing so is to ignore it (Budge and Farlie 1983). But this might only be an option when opponents lack the means to publicize their views or when the new issue fails to generate media attention. If the new competitors have the necessary resources to put the issue on the political agenda or if the new issue is important enough to generate media publicity, this might no longer be an option. Once the issue enters the mainstream debate, established parties need to take up positions on the new issue dimension.

To address the political challenge posed by the politicization of the immigration issue, the governing coalition attempted to co-opt the FPÖ position by introducing a number of legal measures to restrict immigration. In 1989, Vranitzky appointed to the interior ministry Franz Löschnak, a Socialist hard-liner who adopted a tough immigration stance against Eastern European immigrants, introducing visas for Bulgarians, Romanians, and Turks. The SPÖ general secretary,

Josef Cap, asked that visas also be introduced for Poles on account of their allegedly high crime rate – prompting Haider to ironically proclaim the fulfilment of his immigration policy (Gärtner 2002: 20). Shortly before the 1990 national legislative elections, the government did indeed introduce travel restrictions for Poles, responding to xenophobic appeals against "criminal tourism" but also reacting to strong public concerns over immigration (Reisigl and Wodak 2001: 149–150). Moreover, in August 1990, the government introduced a new law to regulate the distribution and aid to refugees and asylum-seekers (Mitten 1994: 37). During the 1990 electoral campaign, the ÖVP sought to counter the FPÖ's "Vienna must not become Chicago" with "Vienna for the Viennese."

The 7% spurt in FPÖ support in the 1990 elections, the FPÖ's shocking breakthrough in the 1991 Vienna elections, and the continued flow of refugees – this time from neighboring, war-torn Yugoslavia – reinvigorated government efforts to reclaim ownership of the immigration issue. During the next two years, the governing coalition introduced a series of legislative measures that turned Austria's immigration regime into one of the most restrictive in Europe. The 1991 Asylum Act established narrower criteria for granting political asylum, accelerated the evaluation procedure for applications, and introduced logistical and organizational changes to restrict the illegal entry of asylum applicants into the labor market. The 1992 Alien Act introduced administrative restrictions for obtaining entry visas, applying them even to those who were already in the country. Moreover, it extended the police power of immigration officials, allowing them to enter private residences or perform identity checks in search of illegal immigrants. The most controversial piece of legislation, though, was the Resident Act, passed in June 1992 and enacted a year later, which sought to codify the conditions for granting residence permits. The law threatened the deportation of legal aliens under conditions that civil society groups considered to be very restrictive, such as the accommodation of at least ten square meters per person per housing unit (Mitten 1994: 37–41).[28] The restrictiveness of these series

---

[28] About 103,000 foreigners and 73,000 Austrians did not meet this condition (Mitten 1994: 40–41).

TABLE 3.4. *Issue Competence of the FPÖ, 1990–1998**

Issue Area	Policy Competence Ranking					
	1990	1993	1995	1996	1997	1998
Fighting corruption	3	1	1	1	1	1
To get control of the "foreigners' question"	1	1	1	1	1	1
Prevent waste of public money	2	1	1	1	1	1
Fighting crime	n.a.	3	3	3	3	3

* In response to the question: "Could you please tell me for each of the following items, which of the parties – the SPÖ, ÖVP, FPÖ, Greens, or LF – will be all the more likely to work hard in…"
Source: Müller 2002: 169.

of legislative measures became obvious when new figures showed a sharp squeeze in the flow of immigrants, from 91,000 in 1991 to only 9,000 in 1995, the lowest in almost a decade (Höbelt 2003: 84).

Despite the restrictiveness and effectiveness of the newly intro-duced measures, the governing coalition failed to recapture the for-eigner issue from the FPÖ, which managed to retain the ownership of the immigration issue throughout the decade (Table 3.4). In fact, the repeated attempts to recapture the issue helped to sustain its salience among the electorate and seem to have benefited the FPÖ, which was widely perceived as the most competent party to handle it. In part, the failure to co-opt FPÖ's immigration agenda related to the belated responses of the established parties on the issue. By the time they decided to take drastic measures to address public concerns, the FPÖ had used its organizational and media resources to portray itself as a credible defender of national identity.

Moreover, the issue was too thorny to allow the governing parties to present credible solutions to immigration, as it cut across tradi-tional class-based divides. On the one hand, the ÖVP had to carefully balance the interests of its business constituents, who benefited from cheap foreign labor, with the conservative inclinations of its voters. On the other hand, the SPÖ had to uphold its traditionally more mul-ticultural principles while easing the concerns of wary trade unionists (Höbelt 2003: 80, 87, 113). Both parties were also cautious to avoid tarnishing Austria's image abroad, as the country slowly recovered from the damage caused by the Waldheim controversy and started confronting its Nazi past.[29] This cautious approach was reinforced by survey evidence that showed that anti-Semitism was on the rise again, this time because of the antiforeigner rhetoric.[30] Restrained by the conflicting preferences of their heterogeneous constituencies, the governing parties sent mixed signals: While criticizing Haider's anti-foreigner rhetoric, they made some efforts to address public concerns and minimize defections from disgruntled constituents. In effect, the coalition's approach to immigration helped legitimate Haider's claims, despite their accusations that FPÖ's programmatic appeals were xenophobic and racist.

The effectiveness of major parties' co-optation strategy was also limited by the FPÖ's adoption of increasingly more restrictive positions on immigration. Unrestrained by the burden of implementing its policy proposals and unhampered by the inflexible organizational structures of its competitors, the FPÖ used its easy access to the media to continuously move the goalposts on immigration beyond the point that the governing parties could afford to move. The most notable example of this strategy of outbidding was the initiation of a petition drive in early 1993 called "Austria First" to "secure the right to a fatherland for all Austrian citizens and, from this standpoint, ensure a restrained immigration policy in Austria" (Reisigl

[29] One of the defining moments of Austria's confrontation with the past was Chancellor Vranitzky's statement in the Austrian Parliament in July 1991 that the country "is partly responsible for the suffering, that not Austria as a state but citizens of the country had brought over other human beings and other nations" (Manoschek 2002: 9).

[30] The results of the survey are presented in "Was is da passiert?" *Profil*, November 4, 1991, pp. 28–29. Responses to the various questions asked by the IMAS Institute show a similar pattern: Anti-Semitism increases significantly in 1986–1987, during the Waldheim controversy, drops in the late 1980s, and then rises again in 1991. For instance, one out of ten Austrians agreed in 1991 with the statement "Actually one must be grateful to the Nazis for having driven the Jews out of Austria," while 26% said they "don't know." In 1988, 86% of the population responded "no," only 3% said "yes," and 11% said "don't know." In the early 1990s, there were also a number of anti-Semitic incidents reported in the press, including the desecration of Jewish graves in Eisenstadt. One of the pictures printed in *Profil* illustrates the connection between the anti-foreigner campaign and the rise of anti-Semitism. On one of the Jewish graves, the young neo-Nazis sprayed a swastika and wrote 'Foreigners out!' The picture was printed in Tanzer R. Tramontana, "No, und sonst?" *Profil*, November 9, 1992, p. 15.

and Wodak 2001: 152, chapter 4). The twelve-point petition included many of the measures already introduced by the government but went beyond them in calling for a constitutional ban and an immediate halt on immigration as well as a quota on foreigners in classrooms. Haider could have raised the issue through normal parliamentary routes but chose to launch a public initiative to help the FPÖ attract media attention and establish direct contact with SPÖ and ÖVP supporters, who seemed to be split on the issue.

The signature drive put even more urgently the immigration issue on the political agenda, polarizing Austrian society. Charging Haider with racism and xenophobia, civil society groups staged a massive demonstration at Vienna's Heroes' Square (*Heldenplatz*), a symbolic contrast with Hitler's address to a large crowd in 1938, after the Union (*Anschluß*). Liberal publications, such as *Standard* or *Profil*, gave a lot of publicity to the issue and urged their readers to attend the demonstration.[31] Among the participants were NGOs, church and business representatives, and the new federal president. By contrast, the *NKZ* generally supported the FPÖ petition, attacked its critics, and largely ignored the "Sea of Lights" demonstration at the Heroes' Square (Joskowicz 2002: 319–320). Although the number of people who signed the petition fell far short of initial expectations, the controversy over "Austria First" sustained public attention to the immigration issue for several years and helped the FPÖ stand out as the single-most important political force to oppose immigration. Despite the series of immigration measures passed by the government, the party boosted its credibility on the issue. Those who believed that the party "could work hard to get control of the foreigner issue" increased from 23% in 1990 to 32% in 1993 and to 44% in 1997 (Müller 2002: 169).

Beyond Immigration. As parties grow, they need to address the demands of increasingly more heterogeneous constituencies. To do so, they have to keep broadening their appeal. In the early 1990s, the FPÖ managed to use the immigration debate as a springboard for the incorporation of Austrian nationalism into its public appeals. Targeting non-German speakers, the immigration debate allowed the

[31] Interview #27, July 2004, Vienna.

FPÖ to replace the earlier emphasis on the German ethnic community with a subtler call for the preservation of German cultural identity. The departure from old-fashioned pan-Germanism was heralded in the 1992 Vienna Declaration, a paper delivered by Haider, in which he called for a "credible distance from National Socialism" and a "commitment to Austria" (Sully 1997: 62–63). The official farewell to straightforward pan-Germanism came in late 1993 in Haider's "Theses for the Political Renewal of Austria," which omitted terms such as "nation" or "national conscience," to the dismay of FPÖ hard-liners. To sustain their support, he would occasionally defend the war generation or make controversial statements about the Nazis, such as his damaging remarks about "proper" Nazi employment policies in 1991 or his reference to "penal camps" in 1995. But for the most part, the FPÖ would now try to distance itself from pan-Germanism, as there was virtually no political competitor for the pan-Germanic vote. The turn away from pan-Germanism was reflected in the new party program, drafted in 1997, which made vague references to the German cultural community, marking a clear departure from the 1985 program's reference to the German ethnic community. One of the first casualties of the country's gradual embrace of Austrian nationalism was the FPÖ's earlier support of European integration. Although the party traditionally supported the European integration project, in the early 1990s, it opposed Austria's entry into the EU, and it was the only party to reject the single currency. Consistent with its new rhetoric, the FPÖ protested the supranational authority of the EU and demanded the shift of EU competencies to the national level. Once the country joined the EU, in 1995, the party sought to mobilize public concerns for the loss of Austrian jobs because of the eastern enlargement.

Through general appeals to Austrian identity and sovereignty, the FPÖ provided a unifying theme for an increasingly more heterogeneous electorate and an ideological venue for the expression of what many observers viewed as anti-establishment protest. Nationalism provided an antidote to the insecurities caused by globalization and supranationalism as well as to the growing disillusionment with mainstream parties. To aggravate this disillusionment, Haider carefully mixed nationalist appeals with cleverly planned attacks against the ideological consistency of the major parties, especially the Social Democrats. The most memorable of these attacks was during an election television debate with chancellor Vranitzky in 1994, during which Haider took out a big white placard showing the provocatively high salaries of the top executives in the SPÖ-dominated Chamber of Labor. The *NKZ* backed Haider's allegations with a series of top stories on the issue, which showed that the officials enjoyed salaries and pensions that were beyond the wildest imaginations of the workers they were supposed to represent. By exposing the exorbitant privileges of the Socialist elite, Haider was able to undermine the ideological consistency of the Socialist party and to present himself as the honest representative of the "common people."[32] At the same time, the FPÖ's nationalist rhetoric provided an ideologically appealing venue for the disillusioned SPÖ voters, especially for workers. As Caspar Einem, one of Vranitzky's ministers in the mid-1990s and a prominent member of the SPÖ, put it:

> Haider understood that the SPÖ and the ÖVP are moral parties. He understood that the social democratic beliefs and program have a strong moralistic content and background. The social democrats built their postwar profile by securing the earnings of labor and by managing labor relations. Haider was able to show successfully that some exponents of the social democratic movement, especially unionists, said one thing and did another. There was a particular issue with their tremendous earnings, which exceeded by far those of workers. This came at a time when people were losing their jobs during the restructuring of the state industries. He made a very emotional appeal to social democratic workers, which proved to be successful. He said "Look at them! They are a big party and they are corrupt." This "Robin Hood" approach along with his unwillingness to accept any taboos in the propagation of nationalist and xenophobic ideas helped the FPÖ grow.[33]

The FPÖ was not the only party to attack social democratic inconsistencies. Both the Greens and the Liberals pointed to the exorbitant privileges of Socialist elites and to the scandalous mismanagement of public resources.[34] But it was the combination of anti-establishment

---

[32] One of the FPÖ's advertising slogans at the time stated: "Simply honest, simply Jörg."

[33] Interview #32, July 2004, Vienna.

[34] For example, Maria Vassilakou, the head of the Green party in Vienna, blamed social democrats because "they have stopped having philosophical concerns. They have been turned into pure administrators of politics. The social democratic party has become a huge organization for administering and distributing power and benefits." Interview #30, July 2004, Vienna.

rhetoric and nationalism that seems to have won the hearts of Socialist workers. In the 1994 elections, one out of ten SPÖ voters defected to the FPÖ.[35] Not surprisingly, a significant number of the defectors were blue-collar workers. The SPÖ's share of the blue-collar vote dropped from 52% in 1990 to 47% in 1994, while the FPÖ's grew from 21% to 29% (Ignazi 2003: 122). Overall, the FPÖ received 22.5% of the votes, compared to 16.6% in 1990.

The 1995 elections, called after the collapse of the grand coalition over budgetary disagreements, reaffirmed the strength of the FPÖ: it drew 22% of the vote and increased its number of votes. But the slight drop in FPÖ's percentage – which was largely because of the mobilization of SPÖ non-voters (Sully 1997: 117) – was enough to raise questions about the future of the party.[36] By May 1998, such questions seemed prophetic, as FPÖ's popularity dropped to 18%, partly because of a scandal involving an FPÖ MP that undermined the party's pronouncements against corruption. But the party managed to rebound by further extending its appeals and by retaining its ownership of the immigration issue. First, the party sought to make inroads into traditionally conservative constituencies by abandoning the anticlerical position of the national-liberal camp. In its 1997 program the FPÖ devoted an entire chapter to Christianity and saw itself "as an ideal partner of Christian churches." The party rejected anticlericalism as "outdated" and viewed Christianity as a moral bulwark against "the increasing fundamentalism of radical Islam which is penetrating Europe" (FPÖ 1997: 8–9). Second, the party tried to attract female voters, who were underrepresented in the FPÖ electorate. In 1999, it called for the introduction of a new welfare benefit, dubbed the Children's Cheque (*Kinderscheck*), a monthly allowance paid to mothers for each child. This was the most prominent demand in the party's campaign in Carinthia, Haider's home state, and part of its broader turn toward welfare-friendly positions. The stunning electoral victory in Carinthia encouraged the party to insist on this proposal in the national legislative elections to be held later in the year (Müller 2002: 167–168).

[35] Josef Votzi, "Alles fließt," *Profil*, October 11, 1994, p. 21.
[36] "Is this the limit of FPÖ's growth?" asked *Profil* in its post-election coverage on December 19, 1995.

In addition to its attempts to reach Christian conservatives and women, the FPÖ tried to sustain the ownership of the immigration issue through a series of legislative proposals. The proposals sought to lower the quota for legally employed foreign workers from 8% to 6% (1997); to introduce a clause that "Austria is not an immigration country" in the citizenship law (1997); and to tighten the asylum law (1998). That the Austrian parliament passed all three proposals was yet another indication of the growing capacity of the party to affect policy outcomes, even when in opposition (Minkenberg 2001: 13). The firm positions of the party on immigration benefited the party when the issue regained salience in May 1999 after the death of a Nigerian asylum seeker, Marcus Omofuma. The death occurred as the young Nigerian was deported from Austria; he had been bound and gagged by Austrian police. It caused an outrage to human rights groups and liberal intellectuals, reviving the debate about immigration. Aided by the *NKZ*, Haider again managed to stand out on the opposite side of the debate. Ahead of the national elections in the fall, the Vienna branch of the FPÖ resorted once more to the mobilization of xenophobic sentiments: Its posters called for an end to "overforeignization" and warned against the misuse of asylum rights. In September 1999, Haider went on Austrian radio and erroneously accused Omofuma of drug dealing.[37] He was largely repeating the sweeping generalizations about African drug dealers reported in the *NKZ*. Aided by outsized exposure in both *Profil* and the *NKZ* – the FPÖ received almost as much coverage from *Profil* as the ÖVP and the SPÖ combined (Figure 3.5) – the FPÖ received 27.9% of the vote, becoming the second-largest party in Austria after the Socialists. Reinforcing the earlier trend, the FPÖ became the largest workers party, attracting almost half of that constituency.[38] As in previous elections, there were important defections of both Socialist and conservative voters to the FPÖ: 9% of SPÖ voters and 11% of ÖVP voters defected to the Freedom Party.[39]

---

[37] A first order court ruled that Haider's charge was "untrue and blasphemous." APA, "Haider convicted for 'drugs dealer' charge against Nigerian," Austrian Press Agency, April 24, 2001.

[38] *Profil*, October 4, 1999, pp. 40–41.

[39] SORA-Institut, quoted in Thomas Hofer, "Blau frisst Rot" *Profil*, October 4, 1999, pp. 40–41.

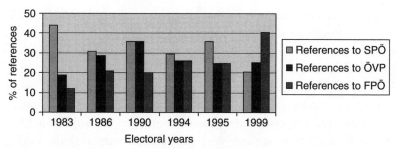

FIGURE 3.5. References to each main political party as percentage of total party-related references in *Profil,* 1983–1999
Note: N = 258. The percentages for the three parties do not add up to 100 because references to smaller political parties are not included in the chart.

Conclusion

The examination of Far Right voting in Austria has traced partisan competition and media exposure up to the 1999 elections, when the FPÖ became Austria's second-largest party, receiving 27.9% of the vote. In February 2000, the ÖVP formed a coalition with the FPÖ, causing an outrage among Austria's fourteen EU partners, who responded with unprecedented and ineffective diplomatic sanctions. Soon afterward, Haider resigned from the party leadership and became one of the coalition's biggest critics. Struck by bitter infighting, scandalous mismanagement, and allegations of patronage, electoral support for the party quickly collapsed. In the 2002 elections, the FPÖ received only 10% of the vote, with the majority of its supporters defecting to its coalition partner: the ÖVP. Party functionaries interviewed in 2004 attributed its electoral misfortunes to the inexperience of the party in holding public office and to a contentious decision to purchase 24 Eurofighters. FPÖ critics stressed the party's inability to match the expectations it had created while in opposition, especially with regard to patronage and corruption. Others emphasized Haider's mistakes, among which they include his two provocative visits to Saddam Hussein. And some noted the change in *NKZ*'s stance toward Haider: After the FPÖ joined the government, the newspaper withdrew its tacit support of Haider.[40]

---

[40] Interviews with FPÖ functionaries, with journalists, and with Green and SPÖ politicians, Vienna, July 2004.

The search for overarching explanations for the sudden collapse of the FPÖ points to the organizational difficulties and programmatic constraints confronted by the party in this new phase of development – that of government participation. During the previous phase, its slim organizational apparatus proved to be an electoral asset, granting its leadership enough flexibility to maneuver in the competitive space and respond swiftly to environmental stimuli. As long as the party could communicate with voters directly through the media, the relatively small membership base did not pose organizational challenges for the party. But once the party participated in government, the lean organizational structure hindered its capacity to perform the dual task of winning votes and executing policy. Not only did the FPÖ lack the organizational resources to perform such tasks, but it also lacked effective internal mechanisms to ease the resulting conflict between the governing team and the party grassroots. Absent such mechanisms, the party underwent a period of intense strife, changing five leaders in two months. In this sense, the competitive advantage granted to the party by the media seems to have undermined its capacity to develop the necessary structures that would allow it to perform its new tasks. The media provided a venue for direct communication with voters but at the expense of organizational development.

Apart from these organizational difficulties, government presence placed programmatic constraints on the FPÖ, limiting the political space available for voter mobilization. Its previous success relied on the programmatic flexibility granted by its opposition status and by its leadership strength. But once in government, the party lost the ability to move freely in the competitive space because it had to implement, not just advocate, its proposed policies and because the international community was very attentive and apprehensive of its presence in the coalition. Simply put, government participation and international condemnation helped to deradicalize the party by forcing it to moderate its appeals (Luther 2000). One example of this moderation was the party's agreement to a compensation scheme for forced labor during World War II and the restitution of property lost under "Aryanization" politics during the Nazi era.

Despite this brief analysis, it is still unclear which of these factors can best explain the trajectory of the Austrian Far Right after 1999. What is less unclear is that notwithstanding its 2002 collapse, the

Far Right is not about to disappear. The 2006 elections – in which Haider's newly formed Alliance for the Future of Austria (Bündnis Zukunft Österreich, BZÖ) got 4.1% and the "Haider-less" FPÖ increased its share of the vote to 11% – dissolved expectations for the relegation of the Far Right to the margins of Austrian politics, where it once was. The snap 2008 elections, in which the two parties received 28.24% of the vote, increasing their percentage by 6.5% and 6.54%, respectively, demonstrated the persistent difficulty of mainstream parties to compete with the Far Right on identity issues. While the death of Haider in a subsequent car accident might undermine the electoral momentum of the BZÖ, the non-incumbency status of the two Far Right parties might give them enough room to maneuver in the competitive space and, hence, to capitalize on the electoral opportunities presented by the global economic crisis.

4

Competing over German Identity: Conservatives and the Nonvisible Far Right

Historical legacy makes alarmism the natural companion of scholarly efforts to map the electoral trajectory of the German Far Right. But a quick glance at the postwar German electoral landscape suggests no reason for alarm: The German Far Right has never managed to gain national legislative representation. This contrasts with the striking advances of the Far Right in Austria, a country that shares Germany's Nazi past; enjoys similar levels of socioeconomic development; has an analogous political party and media system; and has a comparable culture.

With the Austrian experience in mind, then, the first task of this chapter is to account for the noticeable failure of the German Far Right. Given the advance of the Far Right elsewhere in Europe, it is tempting to attribute this failure to the traumas and memories of National Socialism and their impact on German political culture. But a closer examination of German politics reveals the intense partisan competition over German history and identity, which is concealed by arguments about German exceptionalism. Moreover, it exposes a small but noticeable variation in Far Right performance since the late 1970s, which some observers of German politics tend to miss. The second and more tedious task of this chapter is to account for this variation by analyzing, as before, how party and media behavior has affected the electoral fortunes of the Far Right.

Investigating the electoral fortunes of the German Far Right necessitates a departure from conventional explanations for Far Right

performance. Postindustrial development has harmed certain segments of German society, but contrary to historical prejudice and
scholarly expectations, the losers of modernization and the millions
of jobless Germans have not been swayed by Far Right appeals.
Furthermore, like all postindustrial democracies, Germany has also
witnessed electoral de-alignment (Flanagan and Dalton 1984), but
except on a few occasions, the re-alignment of the German electorate
has not moved in the direction of the Far Right. Those few occasions
cast doubt on another common explanation: the prohibitively high
barriers that constitutional drafters erected against political extremism. The sporadic breakthroughs of the Far Right, especially in state
elections, suggest that institutional constants, like the 5% threshold,
cannot sufficiently account for electoral variation.

Departing from sociological, economic, and institutional explanations, this chapter examines how identity politics and media access
have affected the electoral fortunes of the German Far Right. Using
evidence from interviews with politicians and journalists, from party
documents, from legislative records, and from hundreds of journalistic
reports and accounts, this chapter traces patterns of competition over
national identity to national legislative outcomes since 1980. Given the
stagnation of the Far Right in federal elections below the 5% threshold, this chapter also looks at secondary elections, in which Far Right
performance has been more varied. The basic point is that in the past
two decades the Christian Democrats have toyed with identity politics,
and, throughout most of this period, they were able to sustain their
conservative positions on identity issues, thereby blocking the rise of
the Far Right. The crowdedness of the competitive space presented the
Far Right with an unfavorable opportunity structure, which can go a
long way to account for its failure. Apart from this, the three German
Far Right parties confronted the unwillingness of the German media to
give them access to a national audience. Despite the enhanced saliency
of national identity issues during certain periods, the Far Right failed
to attract media attention even when it purposefully tried to. A widespread journalistic ethos and a strong media consensus against publicizing Far Right views raised this additional obstacle for the Far Right,
which can explain its overall failure.

The first section of this chapter sketches the historical trajectory
of the Far Right in postwar Germany. The second and largest section

seeks to account for Far Right performance by examining German identity politics since the late 1970s. This chapter discusses several episodes throughout this time when the Christian Democrats played the nationalist card: the 1980 debate on asylum policy; the 1983–1989 conservative *Wende*; the 1991–1993 asylum controversy; and the 1998–2002 discussion of the citizenship and immigration law. The chapter concludes with a discussion of the main findings.

The Electoral Trajectory of the German Far Right

Scholarly alarmism about the electoral fortunes of the German Far Right contrasts with its electoral failure. The German Far Right is among the least successful in Europe. But while the overall performance of the Far Right has been consistently low, a closer look at the electoral data shows some variation in Far Right performance (Table 4.1). In the past sixty years, the Far Right has gone through three distinct, albeit minor, "waves" of development, approximating Klaus von Beyme's observations (1988: 6–12; Ignazi 2003: 62–74). Each wave lasted roughly twenty years, characterized by the relative growth and subsequent decline of Far Right support. The first wave was the smallest of the three. Widespread concerns that the disruptive social conditions of the early postwar years would create public support for extremist parties did not materialize. Such concerns were fed by repeated survey evidence, which showed that a considerable percentage of Germans displayed antidemocratic attitudes.[1] However, despite the gloomy forecasts, the millions of expellees, repatriates, homeless, and de-Nazified officials (Stöss 1988: 34) did not lend their support to the German Far Right. The three parties that made up the first wave of right-wing extremism – the German Rightist Party, the German Empire Party, and the German Community – received

---

[1] For example, when asked in 1954 whether they would "vote in an election for or against a man like Hitler" 15% of the respondents replied that they would vote for. And when asked in 1955 whether "Hitler would have been one of the greatest German statesmen had it not been for the war" almost half the respondents (48%) responded "Yes" (Stöss 1991: 43–44).

TABLE 4.1. *Results in German Parliamentary Elections, 1949–2005*

	49	53	57	61	65	69	72	76	80	83	87	90	94	98	02	05
CDU/CSU	31	45.2	50.2	45.3	47.6	46.1	44.9	48.6	44.5	48.8	44.3	43.8	41.5	35.1	38.5	35.2
SPD	29.2	28.8	31.8	36.2	39.3	42.7	45.8	42.6	42.9	38.2	37	33.5	36.4	40.9	38.5	34.2
FDP	11.9	9.5	7.7	12.8	9.5	5.8	8.4	7.9	10.6	7	9.1	11	6.9	6.2	7.4	9.8
Greens									1.5	5.6	8.3	3.8	7.3	6.7	8.6	8.1
PDS*												2.4	4.4	5.1	4	8.7
NPD					2	4.3	0.6	0.3	0.2	0.2	0.6	0.3		0.3	0.4	1.6
REP												2.1	1.9	1.8	0.6	0.6
DVU														1.2		
Other	1.8	1.4	1.1	0.9	0.2			0.1								

Gray shade, Far-right parties.

* Ran with Party of the Left.

Note: Based on second ballot votes.

Source: Der Bundeswahlleiter 2005.

less than 2% of the vote in the first national elections.[2] Struck by fragmentation and factionalism, the Far Right entered the "doldrums years" in the 1950s, especially after the 1952 banning of the neo-Nazi Socialist Empire Party (Sozialistische Reichspartei, SRP), which had received 11% and 7.7% in the state elections in Lower Saxony and Bremen, respectively. Notwithstanding occasional advances in state elections, Far Right support deteriorated throughout the 1950s, dropping to a mere 0.9% by 1961.

The establishment of the National Democratic Party (National-demokratische Partei Deutschlands, NPD) in November 1964 reversed this downward trend and marked the beginning of the second "wave" of Right-wing extremism. The party was formed by ex-Nazi functionaries of the German Empire Party, and it sought to unite the various Rightist groups. The NPD got 2% in the 1965 elections and made a long series of notable advances in state elections, in which it won a total of 1.9 million votes and gained representation in seven state parliaments.

Political observers attributed these advances to the programmatic convergence of the mainstream parties brought about by the Grand Coalition and made dire predictions about the likelihood of NPD advances in the next federal elections. Indeed, NPD support jumped to 4.3% in the 1969 elections, the best result for a German Far Right party after World War II, but the party fell short of the representational threshold (Nagle 1970; Warnecke 1970; Backes and Jesse 1993: 78–100). To the relief of domestic and foreign observers,

---

[2] Some scholars also categorize the German Party (DP) and the German Fellowship/ Bloc of Expellees and Victims of Injustice (DG/BHE) as Far Right. Both parties participated in the first German elections with considerable success. In the first German election the DP received 4% of the vote and gained legislative representation. In the subsequent elections it won 3.2% and 3.4% of the vote respectively, but failed to surpass the newly introduced national threshold of 5%, and was hence deprived legislative representation (e.g., Backer 2000). The DG/BHE got 5.9% of the 1953 vote and 4.6% in the 1957 elections. It was able to win legislative seats due to a law that yields full proportional representation to those parties that win at least three mandates in single-member districts. The CDU is thought to have helped the party win legislative representation by asking its supporters to vote for the DG/BHE in safe conservative districts. Evident of the ambiguity in their categorization as Far Right, both parties participated in the Adenauer government and their constituents were later absorbed by the Christian Democrats and, in the case of the DP, by the Liberals (Stöss 1991: 106–136; Kitschelt with McGann 1995: 207–208).

this last mobilization of the "old warriors" (Kitschelt with McGann 1995: 209) was short-lived: By the 1970s, the German Far Right returned to the doldrums, where it stayed for nearly two decades.

The third "wave" began in the late 1980s, after the surprising successes of the newly founded Republikaner (REP) in the Berlin elections and in the 1989 European elections, where it won 7.1% of the national vote. During the late 1980s, the German People's Union (Deutsche Volksunion, DVU) also started participating in secondary elections, receiving 1.6% of the national vote in the European elections and making a notable advance in the Bremen elections (3.4%). In the 1990 elections, the two Far Right parties that participated in the elections, the REP and the NPD, received 2.4% of the vote. This was much lower than the pre-unification forecasts, but it was the best performance for the Far Right since 1969, reinforcing the earlier signs of electoral recovery. A series of advances in state elections between 1991 and 1993, along with increasing incidents of antiforeigner crimes, revived the fears of a Far Right resurgence. But the fears were again belied by the poor performance of the Far Right in the 1994 federal elections, where the REP received 1.9% of the vote. Ever since, Far Right support has remained at that level, occasionally boosted by the electoral participation of the DVU, which has mostly been active in state elections. The 2002 elections seemed to mark the decline of the Far Right, but a number of state-level successes in 2004 and 2006, including the participation of the NPD in two state legislatures for the first time since 1968, suggest that this third "wave" of Far-Right development will last longer than the previous ones. It is on this last "wave" that the rest of this chapter focuses – the period when identity politics started gaining currency in Germany.

National Identity Enters Politics: The 1980 Asylum Controversy

Much discredited after World War II, national identity remained for decades on the sidelines of political competition in Germany. But globalization and postindustrialism pushed it back into the political limelight, tempting conservatives to "ethnicize" the political discourse. Confronted with public apprehension about the presence of foreigners and popular unease with the Left's critical reflection of German history, in the late 1970s, the Christian Democrats broke long-established taboos about the politicization of national identity issues. Their first target was the country's liberal asylum policy. The politicization of this issue created a new political space, which was quickly captured by the Christian Democrats. By sustaining its firm position against asylum, the CDU/CSU opposition limited the opportunities for a Far Right breakthrough. The rest of this subsection traces the politicization of the asylum issue to the federal election of 1980.

The politicization of the asylum issue was a conscious political effort to profit from growing public concerns over the presence of foreigners in Germany. Such concerns were exacerbated by the economic downturn that followed the two oil crises but also by the steep rise in the number of asylum seekers after the restrictions that were imposed on the recruitment of guest workers (*Gastarbeiter*) in 1973. The restrictions inadvertently encouraged guest workers to stay in Germany and to bring their dependents. Throughout the 1970s, a growing number of people relied on the generous provisions of Article 16 of the Basic Law to circumvent the 1973 recruitment ban.[3] By 1980, the number of asylum applications, which had averaged 7,100 between 1953 and 1978, exceeded 100,000.

Despite the 1973 ban, the foreign population in Germany continued to grow (Figure 4.1), compelling Helmut Schmidt's SPD-led coalition to formulate for the first time a broader policy framework for foreigners. In 1977, a government commission upheld the long-held principle that Germany is not a country of immigration. Demonstrating the amorphous and inconsistent nature of German immigration policy, it proposed measures for the integration but also for the repatriation of foreigners. Not surprisingly, the proposals failed to curb the flow of immigrants: In 1981, they totaled 4.6 million compared to 4 million in 1973 (Esser and Korte 1985: 165–205; Brubaker 1992: 171–177; Green 2001; Geddes 2003: 79–101).

The social impact of these immigrant flows became apparent when pollsters started gauging public attitudes toward foreigners. For example, one poll established that almost half the population showed

---

[3] A deliberate measure of atonement for the persecution of minorities by the Nazis and of recognition for other countries' granting of asylum to Germans who were persecuted by the Nazis, the German constitution granted asylum to the politically persecuted, entitled them to welfare benefits and gave them the right to work for as long as their application was processed.

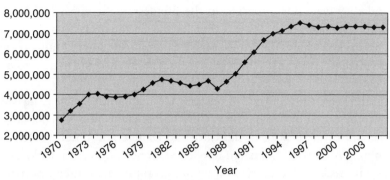

FIGURE 4.1. Foreign population in Germany, 1970–2005
Source: Statistisches Bundesamt Deutschland; includes all individuals residing in Germany who held a foreign citizenship.

overt signs of hostility toward foreigners (Stöss 1991: 50). In another poll, 43% of the respondents thought that children of Turkish immigrants born and raised in Germany should not receive German citizenship when they turn eighteen.[4] Similarly, an Emnid poll showed that 35% of respondents believed that it was better for foreign workers to live in their own areas rather than with Germans. Such surveys also showed that antiforeigner attitudes cut across traditional party lines. While xenophobic attitudes were more prevalent among Christian Democratic supporters, Social Democratic voters were almost as likely to share such views: 54% of Christian Democrats held hostile views toward foreigners, compared to 47% of Social Democrats (Stöss 1991: 49–50). Toward the late 1970s, antiforeigner sentiments started giving rise to public demands for cultural protectionism. Citizen groups began mobilizing against plans to move asylum seekers to their localities, exercising pressures on local officials to resist the agreed allotment of the incoming foreigners (Karapin 1999: 434).

Popular demands for cultural protectionism created incentives for the politicization of the asylum issue. In 1978, recognizing problems in the asylum process, the German parliament approved a set of legislative measures to address them. Reflecting a partisan consensus against the electoral exploitation of the issue, the measures were passed unanimously within three weeks of their introduction in the Bundestag,

---

[4] "Wo nimmst Du das Geld her?" *Der Spiegel* 20, 1980, p. 100.

and they were not discussed in the Bundesrat, the upper legislative body (Steiner 2000: 69–70). But as the national election of 1980 approached, this earlier consensus began to break down. Mainstream politicians, especially Christian Democrats, turned the issue into an electoral theme, structuring political competition along national identity lines for the first time in postwar German politics. The issue was initially raised by the Bavarian Christian Social Union (CSU) and by the conservative wing of the Christian Democratic Union (CDU) in 1979.[5] "A massive campaign developed, concentrating on Turks and asylum seekers and carried on by important media sources, particularly the influential elite paper *Frankfurter Allgemeine*" (Thränhardt 1995: 327).

By 1980, the asylum issue had become a central campaign theme in state elections, like the one in Baden-Württemberg. In February, a month before the election, the CDU candidate and incumbent prime minister of the southwestern state, Lothar Späth, announced his plan to ban the employment and to restrict the cash benefits of asylum seekers. He blamed the Schmidt government for the "inundation" of the state with "fake asylum applicants" and warned that unless the "obvious abuse" of the German asylum law is stopped, "civil-war like discussions" and "inadvertent hatred for foreigners" would occur.[6] Within weeks, the politicization of the asylum issue by local politicians turned it into a national theme. Shortly before the Baden-Württemberg election, the government announced visa requirements for all citizens of Afghanistan, Ethiopia, and Sri Lanka. It later extended these to Turkish citizens, which made up almost two-thirds of asylum applicants in 1980 and the biggest portion of Germany's foreign population. Moreover, the Schmidt government formed a commission consisting of the interior ministry and the most affected German states (*Länder*) not only to formulate policy responses but also to "depoliticize the issue and thereby to limit the conflict over it" (Perlmutter 2002: 273).

---

[5] The CSU is the Bavarian sister-party of the CDU. The two parties have separate party structures but cooperate at the federal level, have a common caucus in the lower house and do not compete against each other. The CDU runs for election in all states but Bavaria, where the CSU enjoys unusually high support. In state elections, the CSU has enjoyed a majority and has run the Bavarian government since 1946.

[6] "Asylrecht: So drastisch," *Der Spiegel* 8, 1980, pp. 24–25.

Yet, as the Schmidt coalition found out, once the "identity genie" was out of the bottle, it was hard to put it back in. Despite government efforts, the asylum issue remained on the political agenda and snuck into the national electoral campaign. This was partly because of the significant media attention it received: Both the Leftist and the conservative press covered the unfolding asylum controversy at great length.[7] The influential liberal weekly *Spiegel*, for example, devoted two of its cover stories to the asylum and the immigration issue, one only a few weeks before the national election.[8] The conservative *Frankfurter Allgemeine Zeitung* (FAZ) had numerous front-page stories on the issue throughout the summer, covering extensively the ensuing partisan conflict, at both the national and the state levels.[9] But it was the frequent opposition attacks against the SPD-led coalition that kept the issue alive. The successful opposition tactics did not escape the attention of the Interior Minister, Gerhardt Baum (FDP), who complained that "this issue has been dragged into the election. We experience for the first time in the Federal Republic that xenophobia becomes an election issue" (Steiner 2000: 72).

Indeed, the parliamentary debate over the asylum law started in March but lasted until the end of July, two months before the national election. It peaked in July, when the CDU/CSU opposition rejected

---

[7] The labels attached to the various publications mentioned in this chapter are based on a survey that asked journalists to place both parties and news organizations on the political spectrum from left to right. Journalists placed the *Frankfurter Allgemeine Zeitung* close to the CDU position on the political spectrum and the *Spiegel* close to the SPD position. *Die Zeit* and the *Süddeutsche Zeitung* were also placed on the left of the political spectrum, while the two publications of the powerful Springer Group, the *Bild* and the *Welt* were placed on the rightmost positions (cited in Hallin and Mancini 2004: 181–182). Like the *NKZ* in Austria, the *Bild* dominates the newspaper market. According to 2006 figures it sells 3.6 million copies per day compared to 0.44 million of the second most widely read newspaper, the *Süddeutsche Zeitung*, and 0.36 million of the third, the *FAZ*.

[8] The liberal magazine reported on the social problems created by the increase in asylum applications, especially the growing hatred for foreigners. See, for example, "Die Ausländer Asyl Deutschland" *Der Spiegel*, June 16, 1980, pp. 28–42; "Ausländer raus? Fremdenhaß in der Bundesrepublik" *Der Spiegel*, September 15, 1980, pp. 19–26.

[9] A few days before the election the newspaper published an editorial by Theodor Schmidt-Kaler, who wondered how many foreigners Germany can have. The editorial presented ethnocultural arguments about the impact of foreigners on German culture and expressed concerns about the declining birth rates of Germans; September 30, 1980, p. 11.

government proposals insisting that asylum seekers be put in camps and that border judges decide on their entry into the country. Structuring the political discourse along cultural lines, they repeatedly referred to floods of "sham-asylees" and "economic-refugees" and argued that Muslims and Hindus are harder to integrate than Christians. Social Democrats and Liberals accused the Christian Democrats of "sham humanitarianism" and "sham statesmanship" and charged them with stirring xenophobia to win the upcoming elections. Setting the stage for the mid-1980s debates on historical memory, the Christian Democrats called for the normalization of German asylum laws to match the restrictiveness of those in other European countries, while the Social Democrats connected the asylum regime with the country's moral obligations for Nazi crimes (Steiner 2000: 69–78).

By politicizing national identity issues, mainstream actors enhance public awareness on the topic and create expectations among voters about policy outcomes. Such expectations can become an electoral liability if parties cannot sustain their firm positions. To do so, they need to present themselves as firm defenders of national identity. The Christian Democrats were able to demonstrate their resolve on the asylum issue by voting against the government's legislative proposals in the lower house in early July 1980. The government majority passed the amendments to the asylum law through the Bundestag without the support of the opposition.[10]

The opposition's rejection supplied local Christian Democratic leaders with political ammunition to use against the government amendments. Reports on the arrival of new asylum seekers and problems with accommodation, especially in Frankfurt and Bavaria, gave Union politicians frequent opportunities to remind their constituents of governmental failures in addressing the rise of asylum applications.[11] During the subsequent debate in the upper house, the majority of Union-led state governments remained critical of the government's "half-hearted steps" but eventually approved them. Only the CSU

---

[10] "Bundestag beschließt Beschleunigung des Asylverfahrens" *Frankfurter Allgemeine Zeitung*, July 3, 1980, pp. 1–2.

[11] "Bonn: Unterbringung der Asylanten ist Sache der Bundesländer" *Frankfurter Allgemeine Zeitung*, July 8, 1980, p. 2; "Der Zustrom von Asylbewerbern wird zu einem großem Wahlkampfthema" *Frankfurter Allgemeine Zeitung*, July 14, 1980, p. 1.

voted against the regulations in the Bundesrat, demanding more drastic measures to curb the flow of asylum seekers.[12] The Bavarian position allowed the Union parties to distance themselves from the governing coalition and to remain critical of its policies throughout the electoral campaign. Their credibility on the asylum issue was reinforced by the candidacy of CSU leader and Bavarian prime minister, Franz Josef Strauss, for the chancellorship. Known, among other things, for his statement that "there must never be a democratic party to our Right," Strauss's fervent anticommunism and national conservatism put him on the fringes of the political spectrum.[13] Along with the Christian Democrats' firm position on the asylum issue, Strauss's candidacy created an unfavorable opportunity structure for the Far Right.

Presented with an adverse political environment, the Far Right's own efforts in 1980 to enhance its electoral standing proved inconsequential. Such efforts concentrated on programmatic renewal and organizational consolidation. The only Far Right party that existed at the time, the NPD, sought to tune in to the latent xenophobia by campaigning hard on the issue of immigration and by incorporating "New Nationalist" ideas into its platform. Tapping into antiforeigner attitudes, the NPD also enhanced its organizational reach: Its members founded the "Citizens Action Group to Stop Foreign Immigration" in January 1980. Based in North Rhine-Westphalia, the group collected signatures for a referendum and for a petition to the Bundestag. Similar groups later appeared in Hamburg and in Schleswig-Holstein.

After a decade spent in the political wilderness, the politicization of the asylum issue allowed the NPD to renew its program and improve its organization. But in the absence of a favorable political opportunity structure, the NPD's efforts to revitalize its electoral presence proved ineffective. The firm positions of the Union parties on the asylum issue prevented the rise of the Far Right. Moreover, the German

---

[12] "Die Mehrheit der Unionsländer stimmt dem Asyl-Gesetz der Koalition zu" *Frankfurter Allgemeine Zeitung*, July 19, 1980, p. 1–2.

[13] A Spiegel poll put Strauss at 8.12 on a 1–10 Left-Right scale, farther to the Right than the CDU/CSU's 7.59. The same poll put Schmidt at 4.26, also to the Right of SPD's 3.66 and the Greens' 3.46. "Wo nimmst Du das Geld her?" *Der Spiegel* 20, 1980, p. 98. For his remark on the need to be the rightmost party on the democratic spectrum, see Art 2006: 163.

press completely ignored the party during this period. An analysis similar to the one of the Austrian press highlighted the difficulty the party had in attracting media attention. The few references in both *Spiegel* and *FAZ* during the campaign disregarded the party's positions and indirectly connected it with terrorist attacks, such as the one in Munich a few days before the federal election. Lacking communication resources and political opportunities, the party merely received 0.2% of the 1980 vote, its worst result ever.

Die Wende

The political controversy over the asylum law broke the consensus against the politicization of national identity issues and opened the way for the "conservative turn" in German politics during the 1980s – what some have dubbed as *die Wende*.[14] But whereas the asylum debate lasted for only a few months, Helmut Kohl's 1982 election to chancellor put national identity issues on the political agenda for years, until his Pyrrhic 1987 victory compelled the Christian Democrats to change course. The subsequent de-radicalization of political competition opened a "window of opportunity" for the Far Right Republikaner. Electoral successes in the Berlin and European elections in 1989 granted the party some media exposure, and it seemed for the first time that the Far Right would enter the federal parliament. But the reunification of Germany allowed the Christian Democrats to reclaim the national conservative space before the Far Right had time to organize and to resolve leadership tensions.

While the controversy over the German asylum regime put national identity on the electoral map, it was the Christian Democratic *Wende* that turned it into a top political theme. Upon the assumption of power in October 1982, Kohl made no secret of his goal to bring about a moral and spiritual change by revitalizing German national identity. The intellectual stage for the political seizure of the identity

[14] The term "Wende" literally means change or turnover and it is sometimes used to describe the changeover brought about by the German reunification. It is also used to describe the turnover in government in 1982, from the Social Democrats and to the Christian Democrats. When using the term some emphasize the change in economic policies, while others (e.g., Kitschelt with McGann 1995: 213–214; Art 2006: 62) refer to the spiritual, moral and cultural change the Kohl administration sought to bring about.

theme was already set by conservatives like Armin Mohler, who argued in 1966 that "a nation is sure of itself if it lives in accordance with its history" (quoted by Müller 2000: 214), calling for a German version of Gaullism. Going a step further, Henning Eichberg later echoed the "ethnopluralist" ideas of Nouvelle Droite, popularizing the term "national identity" in 1978, basing it "on differentiation, the recognition of one's own ethnic and national particularities, and the particularities of others" (Betz 1988: 132). These earlier ideas formed the basis of conservative antithesis to immigration. The "Heidelberg Manifesto," a statement drafted by fifteen German university professors, argued that "the integration of large masses of non-German foreigners and the preservation of our nation cannot be achieved simultaneously; it will lead to the well-known catastrophes of multicultural societies." Published in early 1982, the statement concluded that the "return of the foreigners to their native lands will provide ecological as well as social relief."[15] Besides immigration, the conservative search for national identity also led to a reaction against the "negative nationalism" of the Left and to an effort to push German historical reflection beyond the twelve years of Nazi rule. In the early 1980s, Karl Lamers, a CDU member of the Bundestag, argued that to regain self-confidence, Germany would have to be allowed "once again to be proud of the really great evidence of their cultural contributions to the history of Europe and humanity" (quoted in Betz 1988: 143).

The new chancellor's efforts to revitalize German identity concentrated, then, on both immigration and history. In his inaugural speech, Kohl announced that curbing immigration was one of the main pillars of his policy, along with combating unemployment and controlling inflation. He pledged to reduce the already-declining foreign population by a million in the next five years (Castles 1985: 528; Faist 1994: 57; Minkenberg 2003). Kohl's spiritual change was also to come about through a return to German tradition and, more importantly, through the reassessment of German history. Kohl espoused

---

[15] Eileen Hennessy, "The Heidelberg Manifesto: A German reaction to Immigration" *Population and Development Review* 8:3 (September 1982), p. 637. The manifesto was drafted by Professors Bambeck, Fricke, Karl Götz, Haberbeck, Illies, Manns, Oberländer, Rasch, Riedl, Schade, Schmidt-Kahler, Schröcke, Schurmann, Siebert, Stadtmüller.

the idea that Germans must not only focus on Nazism but also on the positive sides of German history. In his first speech to the Bundestag in 1982, he announced his plan to build a museum of West German history in Bonn. In March, after winning the 1983 elections, he stressed that German history must become a "spiritual home" for the younger generation and sought to instill national pride through references to Germany's cultural inheritance (Art 2006: 62).

Immigration. Kohl made the first steps toward the materialization of the *Wende* as soon as he walked into the chancellery. He appointed Friedrich Zimmerman to the ministry of interior, with the mission of changing Germany's immigration policy. The conservative deputy chairman of the CSU quickly put together a commission to draft new regulations for foreigners. The commission reported its more than 80 recommendations in March 1983, a few days before the federal elections. They aimed at restricting immigration, encouraging repatriation, and facilitating the deportation of foreigners. For example, one of the recommended measures (approved by the federal parliament in November 1983) was offering foreigners cash to permanently return to their countries. Another proposal, a much more controversial one, was to reduce the maximum age for entry of dependent children from 16 to 6 and to limit or prohibit the entry of foreign spouses (Castles 1985: 528–530).

The government proposals were accompanied by the gradual radicalization of the political discourse over immigration. As the *Wende* progressed, statements like the "boat is full" or "Germany for the Germans" became an inseparable part of the German political repertoire. Much like dire warnings about Germany becoming a "thoroughly racially mixed society" or a "multicriminal multiconflict society," these references signaled a shift in the contours of legitimate political discourse. The alarmist rhetoric also reflected a significant change within the CDU, as the balance of power shifted away from more liberal members, such as the general secretary Heiner Geissler, toward more conservative ones, such as Heinrich Lummer, Rolf Olderog, and Alfred Degger (Young 1995: 64–65).

By the 1983 federal elections, the radicalization of the immigration issue by the "national conservative" faction of the Christian Democrats started to bear fruit: The majority of respondents in a survey commissioned by *Spiegel* believed that the current coalition was the most capable to address the country's immigration issues. Asked whether a CDU- or an SPD-led coalition was more competent in "reducing the number of foreigners in the Federal Republic," 54% chose the former and only 9% the latter. This was the highest percentage for the Kohl coalition across thirteen policy areas and the biggest difference between the government and the opposition.[16] While the radicalization of the issue enhanced the political capital of the CDU, it also helped to reinforce xenophobic attitudes among the electorate. A 1982 Emnid poll found that 55% of respondents thought that the best way to fight unemployment was to deport foreign workers (Stöss 1991: 50).

Christian Democrat efforts to tighten the immigration regime met significant resistance from other parties and from civil society groups. The most important source of opposition came from the SPD. The Social Democrats insisted on the need to socially integrate foreign workers rather than repatriate them. The right to citizenship (*Optionsrecht*) constituted the cornerstone of their approach. In the early 1980s, the SPD tabled proposals for granting this right to German-born and German-educated children of migrant workers, but their legislative motions were quickly rejected by the Christian Democrats. More liberal proposals, tabled by the Greens in 1984, had a similar fate. The Greens, who entered the federal parliament in 1983, agreed with the Social Democrats in viewing the issue from a human rights perspective and in stressing the moral obligation of the German government toward foreigners. But the Greens went a step further, rejecting ethnic criteria for citizenship, defending multiculturalism, and advocating equal rights for immigrants in all areas. Moreover, they explicitly linked the immigration issue with Germany's Nazi past, arguing that, contrary to Hitler's "German blood" policies, Germans had a political responsibility to grant immigrants political rights without requiring them to assume German identity or culture (Castles 1985; Murray 1994).

By 1985, when another controversy over asylum broke out, national conservatives and Leftist multiculturalists had already taken firm positions on this new national identity axis. The new debate over

[16] "Zweifeln zu viele SPD-Wähler an der SPD?" *Der Spiegel* 7, 1983, p. 36.

asylum, stirred by a relatively small rise in asylum applications, lasted for almost two years. The heated discussions in the German parliament showed the deep chasm between the opposing sides and the increasing radicalization of the political discourse. Lummer (CDU) claimed, for example, that "the drug scene is largely tied to the phenomenon of asylum-seekers. And when one thinks of Ghana, one also knows that prostitution is tied in as well." Similarly, Olderog (CDU) complained that the press increasingly "reports brawls, disturbances, knife fights, prostitution and theft in connection to this problem. All this is unfortunately leading to antiforeigner sentiment." In the midst of the Bitburg affair and the Historians' Debate (*Historikerstreit*), Christian Democratic efforts to curb asylum applications were instantly perceived as a conservative attempt to do away with Germany's past. During a parliament debate of the issue, an SPD parliamentarian accused the Christian Democrats of "deliberately neglecting to remind people of our moral and ethical obligations." Hans-Christian Ströbele, another SPD member, charged: "The political responsibility for our past is onerous for Kohl, Zimmerman, Lummer, Späth, Olderog and the rest of them; they would like to bury it, seal it and forget it" (Steiner 2000: 78–84). Despite the strong objections of the opposition, the majority government passed a new, more restrictive law in late 1986 that demonstrated its commitment to defending German identity.

Historical Memory and Bitburg. The debate over Germany's immigration and asylum policies prepared the ground for the controversy that accompanied the Bitburg incident. The announcement of Ronald Reagan's visit to a military cemetery in Bitburg in late 1984 led to a charged debate in both Germany and the United States after it became known that among the fallen were Waffen-SS. The visit was meant to symbolize the historical healing and the contemporary strength of the transatlantic partnership. But domestic and international critics saw it as a tasteless effort to bury the Nazi past and to shift the burden of collective responsibility away from the perpetrators of Nazi crimes. After the announcement of Reagan's itinerary, American and German legislators, Jewish organizations, and war veterans pressured both Reagan and Kohl to cancel the visit to Bitburg. Their strong reactions, which included a letter sent to Kohl by 257 House Representatives, confronted the Christian Democrats with the prospect of accepting a setback in their efforts to revitalize German national identity only a few weeks before the election in Germany's most populous state, North Rhein-Westphalia. If Kohl dropped Bitburg, he would have also alienated the national conservative faction of the CDU, which became increasingly more influential after the *Wende*. In an open letter to the 53 American senators who had urged Reagan not to go to Bitburg, a prominent member of the national conservatives, Alfred Dregger (CDU), warned that a cancellation of the visit would be an insult to his brother who died during the war. The emotional stakes were too high for Kohl to back down. Realizing this, he stated: "If we don't go to Bitburg, if we don't do what we jointly planned, we would deeply offend the feeling of our people. The Germans consist of more than minds. They also have hearts and souls."[17] In the end, both Reagan and Kohl went along with the trip, refusing to yield to the pressures (Maier 1988: 9–16; Art 2006: 69–72). Unrelenting to critics, a few months later Kohl met the Paraguayan leader Alfredo Stössner, creating a new wave of protest because in the past, the general had allegedly provided asylum to ex-Nazis and had denied Israeli extradition requests.

The Bitburg affair cleared the way for an open debate of Germany's past, removing the remaining inhibitions against public historical discourse. This discourse "revolved around the nature of the Federal Republic's historical and therefore national identity, its self-understanding" (Baldwin 1990: 27). It was part of the broader dispute over questions of national identity, but unlike earlier debates, it centered on the role of the Nazi past in Germany's democratic present. Moreover, unlike the Bitburg incident, the debate about Germany's past went beyond the realm of partisan politics into the domain of intellectual discourse. On one side of the debate stood those who sought to compare Nazism with other atrocities, hence disputing its uniqueness or, as their critics charged, "relativizing" it. The most controversial refutation of the Holocaust's singularity came from Ernst Nolte, a prominent historian of fascism. In an often-quoted article in the *FAZ*, in June 1986, he compared Nazi with Stalinist terror,

---

[17] James Markham, "As Bitburg visit nears, Kohl, under fire, says it will go on" *New York Times*, April 30, 1985, p. 10.

suggesting that Nazi crimes were a response to horror caused by those of the Soviets. Joachim Fest, *FAZ*'s editor, defended Nolte's views, comparing the Nazis' racial crimes with the Bolsheviks' class murders.[18] Both were thought to be partly responding to President Richard von Weizsäcker's 1985 speech at the fortieth anniversary of the Nazi surrender. In a well-known address to the German parliament, the German president argued that contemporary Germany should keep alive the memory of the Nazi past, emphasizing the uniqueness of the Holocaust, and stressing German complicity in Nazi crimes.[19] In the polarized political environment of the mid-1980s, Nolte's article was vehemently critiqued by Jürgen Habermas, one of the most prominent historians of the liberal Left. Habermas linked Nolte's arguments with the conservative turn in German politics and with the effort to construct a new German identity, relieved from the burden of Nazism. He hence saw such assertions as mostly political rather than scientific and expressed concern for revisionist and apologist tendencies in German historiography. He argued that political loyalty should be placed on postwar German institutions rather than on notions of common descent and hence called for "constitutional patriotism" devoid of harmful nationalist ideas (Maier 1988; Art 2006: 72–77).

[18] Another effort to relieve Germans of moral guilt came from Andreas Hillgruber, who presented the dilemmas faced by Nazi soldiers as they defended the Eastern Front against the Soviet attack, in *Zweierlei Untergang: Die Zerschlagung des deutschen Reiches und das Ende des europäischen Judentums*, (Berlin: Siedler 1986). See Maier 1988; Baldwin 1990.

[19] For example, Weizsäcker (CDU) argued that the "genocide inflicted on the Jews, however, has no precedent." In his speech, copies of which were later distributed in schools, he also blamed ordinary Germans for Nazi crimes: "Whoever opened his eyes and ears, whoever wanted to inform himself, could not escape knowing that deportation trains were rolling. The imagination of men is insufficient to encompass the means and the scale of the annihilation. But in reality the crime itself was compounded by the attempts of all too many people – my generation as well, we who were young and who had no part in the planning and the execution of the events – not to take note of what was happening." The German President also said that "the 8th of May was a day of liberation" but he was also careful to say that "we have really no reason to take part today in victory celebrations." He also said that apart from commemorating the "six million Jews who were murdered in concentration camps" and the "peoples who suffered in the war," "as Germans we commemorate in sorrow of our own countrymen, who lost their lives as soldiers, in air attacks in their homeland, during imprisonment and in their flight elsewhere." See Weizsäcker 1986: 43–60; here, 44–45, 47.

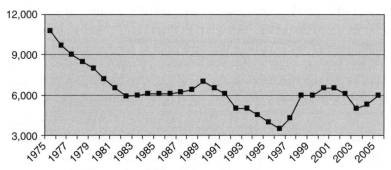

FIGURE 4.2. NPD membership, 1975–2005
Source: Baden Württemberg, Landesamt für Verfassungsschutz; data after 1990 also include the five eastern German states.

Immigration, History, and the Far Right. The political controversy over the Nazi past and the partisan disagreements over immigration enhanced the political prospects of the Far Right. The return of nationalist rhetoric in mainstream political discourse legitimated the Far Right's insistence on an ethnocratic view of politics, granting it an opportunity to leave the political wilderness in which it found itself for fifteen years. The most immediate effect of the mainstream parties' emphasis on German identity was on the Far Right's recruitment efforts: After 1982, the NPD encountered fewer problems in recruiting members. After a decade of continuous drop, its membership figures started rising (Figure 4.2), despite growing competition from the DVU. A right-wing extremist organization founded in the early 1970s by the Bavarian owner of nationalist publications, Gerhard Frey, the DVU witnessed a considerable membership expansion of its membership after the *Wende*. By 1987, when it was officially founded as a party, the DVU had almost as many members as the NPD.

Apart from giving a recruitment boost to the two Far Right parties, the *Wende* provided the impetus for the genesis of a third one, the Republicans (Republikaner, REP). The party was founded a few months after Kohl's election by two former CSU members, Franz Handlos and Ekkehart Voigt, and by Franz Schönhuber, a journalist who had hosted a popular Bavarian radio show before being fired for publishing his Waffen-SS memoirs. The founders resented Strauss's brokering of a big loan that a West German consortium granted to the German Democratic Republic in 1983. By 1985, Schönhuber managed to prevail over the other two to become the national party chairman. In the midst of the immigration disputes, the party stressed the importance of national identity and argued for the preservation of national culture. And as historical memory moved to the center of partisan politics, the party became a staunch defender of the "decriminalization of German history," rejecting its reduction to the Nazi era (Betz 1990: 52). Moreover, the party prioritized German unification. Throughout the *Wende*, the party's organizational strength grew from 2,400 members in 1985 to 8,000 in 1988, although it was primarily concentrated in Bavaria (Westle and Niedermayer 1992: 89). Using the compensation that the generous party financing law granted the REP from the Bavarian elections in 1986 (in which it got 3%), the party built organizational networks throughout the Federal Republic, and by 1987, it had organizations in all but one state (Betz 1990: 52).

By playing the nationalist card, the Christian Democrats furnished the Far Right with an opportunity to extend its organizational basis and to "tune in" to the mainstream debate. But as long as the Union parties kept the card on the table, the organizational growth of the Far Right and its well-timed nationalist rhetoric would not be sufficient to improve its electoral fortunes. Ahead of 1987 federal elections, the Christian Democrats stepped up their efforts to curb asylum applications. In June 1986 Kohl floated for the first time the idea of amending Article 16 of the Basic Law to restrict the applicants' Right of judicial review (Karapin 2002: 198). In a news conference he held in August he announced punitive measures for airlines that carried passengers without valid visas for West Germany. He also stated: "We are not a nation of immigration. And we do not want to become one."[20] Kohl's plans and rhetoric met stiff resistance from the opposition. Rejecting

---

[20] It has been argued that the strong reactions of civil society groups against Far Right parties have contributed to their electoral misfortunes in Germany (e.g., Art 2006). This might be true for the early 1990s, but in the mid-1980s, it appears that civil society did not always play such a role. At around the same time when Kohl was announcing stricter measures to curb a new rise in asylum applications, a group of 299 citizens of Mönchneversdorf, a village in the North German state of Schleswig-Holstein, formed a human barricade to block plans for the construction of a refugee center. According to the *New York Times*, they were swamped by congratulatory mail and telegrams from all over West Germany and urged to continue their action; James Markham, "Bonn takes steps against refugees" August 28,1987, p. A7.

the conservative efforts to restrict the right to asylum, the Greens turned the issue into one of their campaign themes. One of their 1987 electoral pamphlets read, "Democracy must be without borders: Asylum is a Human Right."

Despite pressures from their liberal wing, the Christian Democrats were also able to remain firm on their commitment to reorient historical memory away from the Holocaust. President Weizsäcker's speech in 1985 was taken by some to reflect a crack between the national and the liberal factions of the CDU, creating expectations for a change in the party's course. But by 1987, the "unabashedly patriotic" appeals of the CDU's Bavarian sister-party dashed such hopes.[21] A few weeks before the election, Zimmerman (CSU) unequivocally distanced himself from Weizsäcker's speech, stating that as a lieutenant of the German *Wehrmacht* he primarily saw "May 1945" as a defeat, not as liberation. He insisted that current politics must look to the future.[22] Strauss, the Bavarian CSU premier, was even more explicit during a campaign rally in his home state: "We have to end the attempt to limit German history to the 12 years of Hitler – the representation of German history as an endless path of Germans' mistakes and crimes, criminalizing the Germans. We must emerge from the dismal Third Reich and become a normal nation again." He further argued that West Germany needs a strong national identity and a "return to historical normality."[23] The national conservative overtones of the CSU appeals were not only evident in their leaders' statements but also on their campaign pamphlets. One of them simply printed the first verse of the Federal Republic's national anthem: "Unity and Justice and Freedom for the German Fatherland" (*Einigkeit und Recht und Freiheit für das deutsche Vaterland*).[24]

[21] It has been argued that the nationalist turn of the CSU was largely a response to the threat of the Republikaner, which received 3% of the vote in the 1986 Bavarian elections. This is only partly true: sensitive to the possibility of an electoral failure, the Republikaner did not even enter the race. The only Far Right competitor to the CSU was the NPD, which received 0.6% of the Bavarian vote, compared to 0.3% in the 1983 elections.

[22] "Das ist Terror der Straße" *Der Spiegel* 49, 1986, pp. 45–54; here, 52–53.

[23] James M. Markham, "An Unabashedly Patriotic Strauss Goes Stumping" *New York Times*, January 13, 1987, p. A4. See also Strauss's interview in *Spiegel*, "Es wird harte Verhandlungen geben" 4, 1987, pp. 24–29, esp. p. 25.

[24] In their analysis Kitschelt and McGann argue that "within less than two years after winning the 1983 elections" the Christian Democrats "would neither be able

The firm position of the Christian Democrats on national identity issues limited the political space to the Far Right. Apart from
the unfavorable opportunity structure, though, Far Right parties also
confronted the unwillingness of the media to give them exposure.
Despite his previous tenure in the media and his communication charisma, Schönhuber (REP) proved unable to rise above the "Chinese
wall" that the German press had erected against the Far Right. The
analysis of *Spiegel* articles from 1983 to 1987 only found one article
on the REP, shortly after its founding, and one on the NPD. Lacking
media exposure, the Far Right was unable to enter the mainstream
debate. The only Far Right party that ended up contesting the 1987
elections, the NPD, received a mere 0.6% of the national vote, despite
the support it received from Frey's DVU.

The Reversal of the Wende *and German Reunification.* The Pyrrhic
victory of the Christian Democrats in the 1987 elections provided
the impetus for the gradual moderation of their position on national
identity. Although the Union parties retained power and managed
to keep the Far Right out of parliament, they suffered considerable
defections to their liberal coalition partners, the FDP.[25] Their electoral slide strengthened the liberal faction of the party, which had
been apprehensive of the conservative turn. Christian Democratic
observers were quick to blame the electoral debacle of the CDU to its
unsuccessful attempt to "master the past" and to its failure to espouse

---

nor willing to engineer" the *Wende*. They hence suggest that by 1985, the Kohl
coalition returned to the "politics of centripetalism," continuing the policies of the
Schmidt government. This "policy convergence in the German party system created an opening for voter defections to the new left-libertarian (Green) and rightist
party alternatives" (1995: 213). The analysis is probably correct with regards to
economic policy but misses the partisan disputes over immigration, asylum and
history. The polarizing effect of these disputes might explain the perception among
voters that between October 1984 and December 1986 the CDU/CSU shifted to the
Right (from a 7.5 to a 7.9 on a Left – Right scale) whereas the SPD shifted to the
Left (from a 3.7 to a 3.5). See "Nur die Grünen haben keine Sorgen" *Der Spiegel* 52,
1986, p. 45.
[25] CDU support dropped significantly from 38.2% in 1983 to 34.5% in 1987. The
CSU's support in Bavaria also dropped from 59.5% in 1983 to 55.1% in 1987. The
combined result of the two parties was the worst since 1949. The main beneficiaries
in the elections were the FDP and the Greens; the latter at the expense of the SPD,
which dropped by 1%.

the course prescribed by president Weizsäcker. They urged Kohl to return to the "politics of the middle" rather than continue along the national conservative course that led to the CDU's electoral misfortunes.[26] Their analysis echoed the concerns of senior party members, like Heiner Geissler and Johann Baptist Gradl, that the conservative turn of the Kohl administration alienated its other two factions, the liberal and Christian-social one, putting at risk its catch-all profile.[27]

But while the electoral slide of the Christian Democrats exposed the need to reverse the conservative turn, the change took more than a year to materialize. Although the result weakened the national conservatives, they continued to have key posts in the government and the party, through which they exerted considerable influence. During the first few months after the election, they sought to exercise this influence to sustain the conservative turn. Their intentions were made obvious in both their writings and in their speeches. Analyzing the political consequences of the 1987 elections, for example, Heinrich Lummer wrote that many Germans wanted to see an end to their confrontation with the past. "One cannot always show a people their black marks and reduce history, for example [the history] of the Germans, to the time between 1933 and 1945. Eventually, people want to be proud of something again." Despite the electoral failure of the Far Right, the influential representative of CDU's national conservatives warned that unless conservatives could successfully integrate right-wing voters, "a new party [would] emerge." Similarly, Strauss (CSU) spoke in May 1987 of the "need for a new national identity." He insisted that "we must never allow German history to be reduced to the period between 1933 and 1945, or between 1914 and 1945. We must once again have more respect for our own history" (both quoted in Betz 1988: 149).

A new draft of the immigration law prepared by conservative minister of interior, Zimmermann (CSU), showed that Lummer's and Strauss's ideas were more than idle talk. The draft was leaked to the press in April 1988 and proved to be a political dynamite, as it sought to impose additional restrictions on immigration to Germany. Using

---

[26] See, for example, the analysis of the CDU theoretician, Warnfried Dettling, in *Der Spiegel* 6, 1987, p. 20.
[27] "Aufpassen in der Wahl der Begriffe" *Der Spiegel* 3, 1987, pp. 17–20; here 20.

ethnocultural arguments, the draft reasoned that if immigration were allowed to continue unchecked, it would lead to the "abandonment of societal homogeneity, which is primarily determined by membership of the German nation. Germany's common history, heritage, language and culture would lose their unifying and defining nature. The Federal Republic would develop little by little into a multinational and multicultural society, which would over time be weighed down by the resulting problems with its minorities" (Green 2004: 61; see also 59–63).

The draft created a political storm against Zimmermann. The reactions came from the SPD and the Greens, but also from the Union's coalition partner, the FDP. A leading FDP member, Klaus Kinkel, openly criticized the draft as one that left foreigners with no rights. The FDP's parliamentary spokesman on international affairs, Burkhard Hirsch, described it as "extraordinarily narrow-minded." More importantly, the proposal came under fire from within the CDU. The general secretary of the CDU, Heiner Geissler, disapproved the draft's denial that Germany is a country of immigration. The CDU's own interior affairs spokesman, Johannes Gerster, was just as critical of the draft in an emergency parliamentary debate held in summer 1988. There were also reactions from the Christian–social wing of the CDU that had earlier tabled liberal proposals for integrating immigrants. Influential interest groups, like the Christian Democratic Employees' Association, also dismissed the draft. Citing Germany's historical responsibility and Nazi past, they proposed a right to citizenship (Green 2004: 61–62; Murray 1994: 29–30).[28]

The reactions within the CDU marked the reversal of the *Wende* and the movement of partisan politics away from the ethnocultural direction that Kohl had drawn in 1982. The controversy over the immigration law and the bad publicity Zimmermann received made him a political liability for Kohl, who eventually moved him to a different ministry, in Spring 1989. This was yet another setback for the national conservatives, after Strauss's (CSU) sudden death in October 1988. Six years after their efforts to prioritize national identity issues, the national conservatives found themselves on the defensive. By late 1988, it was evident that the Christian Democrats were adopting a

[28] See also "Ausländerrecht: Bis an die Grenzen" *Der Spiegel* 23, 1988, pp. 34–38.

more moderate course on national identity issues. Their growing moderation cost Philipp Jenninger (CDU) his job, when he delivered a highly controversial and widely misunderstood speech to the German parliament on the fiftieth anniversary of the Nazi *Kristallnacht*. His attempt to expose the perverse rationale that led to the pogrom caused a walk-out by fifty opposition MPs and international criticism. Under pressure from Kohl and other CDU members, the president of the Bundestag resigned the following day (Art 2006: 82–84). By distancing himself from his close associate, Kohl signaled the failure of his earlier efforts (e.g. through Bitburg) to "master the past."

The reversal of the *Wende* changed the opportunity structure for the Far Right, setting the stage for notable breakthroughs in state and European elections in 1989. During the preceding years, the NPD, the DVU, and the REP had changed neither their leadership nor their appeals. Nor did they significantly increase their membership. Their modest organizational expansion was mostly the result, rather than the cause of their minor successes, as in Bremen, where the DVU won a seat in the 1987 elections with 3.2% of the vote.[29] What had really changed was the stance of the CDU on national identity issues. Throughout most of the 1980s, the Christian Democrats stood firm on national identity issues crowding the Far Right out of the competitive space. But the perceived weakening of the national conservatives toward the late 1980s created a political opening for the Far Right. The main beneficiary of this opening was the REP. Shortly before the January 1989 election in Berlin the party managed to temporarily break the unofficial embargo of local German media with a xenophobic television advertisement, which infuriated the political establishment and gave the party much-needed publicity. Although the publicity was negative, it was enough to lift the party

[29] Media exposure played a critical role in this minor breakthrough for the DVU – the first for a Far Right party since the 1960s. The leader of the party, Gerhard Frey, pumped 2 million Deutsche Marks into the campaign, for advertising. This was more than the advertising spending of all the mainstream parties combined. See "Rechtsextremisten: Was machen" *Der Spiegel* 39, 1987, pp. 50–51; "Dieses Altersheim auf Rädern" *Der Spiegel* 31, 1987, pp. 33–36. It is worth noting, though, that the electoral laws for the Bremen elections are different than elsewhere in Germany, in ways that lower the barrier to entry.

out of obscurity (see also Roth 1990: 27; Stöss 1990: 41–42). As a CDU parliamentarian in Berlin recalls:

There was a kind of agreement from the media not to give any forum to the extremist parties in this campaign. But due to electoral regulations, these parties are entitled to one TV spot. The Republikaner spot made a splash: all they showed was a Turkish woman with a scarf and Turkish children in the street. There was no text, just the tune from "Play me the song of death" (*Spiel mir das Lied vom Tod*). When the spot went on TV there was an outrage – there were long discussions on TV and in the newspapers, which blamed the Republikaner for racism. Basically, this was exactly what they needed. No one knew they existed before but the discussion put them on the electoral map.[30]

Indeed, an empirical analysis of regional newspaper coverage documents a notable spurt in references to the REP after the controversy over the TV spot and after reactions to a planned party function. In five Berlin newspapers the party was only mentioned eleven times before the spot went on the air and thirty-six times afterwards; the REP was mentioned sixty-seven times after its planned function. By the last phase of the campaign the party got more references in these newspapers than the Greens or the FDP. The vast majority of articles in these newspapers focused on the reactions to its TV spot and to its meeting. In fact, the controversy over the TV spot had made such a splash that 73% of those polled said that they remembered it, although a mere 6% actually saw it when it was first broadcasted (Friedrichsen et al. 1995).

The 7.5% the REP received in the Berlin state election did to the party what the Dreux breakthrough did to the French National Front (Kitschelt with McGann 1995: 99–101). Political commentators started discussing what the party's breakthrough meant for the Christian Democrats, pollsters began searching for the profile of the typical REP voter and concerned citizens initiated demonstrations against it. All these, inadvertently increased the party's exposure and amplified its message, temporarily making the REP the center of attention. A few weeks after the Berlin elections the party started appearing on

---

[30] Interview #25, member of CDU Fraktion in Berlin parliament, June 2004, Berlin. See also "Unser Endziel ist der Bundestag" *Der Spiegel* 28, 1989, p. 31; "Debatte über Wahlwerbespot von Wahlkampftönen bestimmt" *Tagesspiegel*, January 12, 1989; "SFB will ausländerfeindlichen Spot der Republikaner nicht ausstrahlen" *Der Tagesspiegel*, January 18, 1989, p. 11.

Spiegel's regular polls of the "political situation" and its leader, Franz Schönhuber, ranked among the twenty most popular German politicians. Party support originally stood at 3% but this was enough for political commentators to ask whether the REP would be the fifth party to enter the Bundestag in the 1990 elections. More than 40% of those polled thought so, while 13% stated they would welcome this development.[31] Since its founding, in 1983, German journalists avoided giving the REP publicity, but after the Berlin elections the party started receiving more attention. Even those who had been the most critical to the Far Right temporarily broke long-held taboos by opening their pages to Schönhuber. A few weeks before the European elections *Spiegel* put a picture of Schönhuber on its cover, albeit branding him as a right-wing "Führer." The REP rode on this unprecedented – though temporary – wave of media attention to get 7.1% of the vote.[32] The DVU got another 1.6%, adding 444,921 votes to REP's 2,008,629, marking the best electoral result for Far Right parties ever.

The REP's breakthroughs shook the Christian Democratic leadership and revitalized discussions about the course of the party. The Berlin debacle enhanced the political capital of the national conservative wing of the party, which blamed it on the leftward shift of the CDU. Dregger (CDU), for example, argued that REP copied the Union's program and argued that it would be "suicidal if we no longer represent a part of our program." The CDU, he argued, is not only a social and liberal party, but also a national conservative one. "We love Germany" he said. His views were amplified by the CDU's Bavarian sister-party, which launched a fierce attack against the liberal wing of the Union for pushing the party in the wrong direction, ignoring the public resonance of themes like immigration and asylum. The target of the Bavarian leadership was the general secretary of the CDU, Geissler, whom they blamed for making an opening of the party to the left of the political spectrum, especially on national identity issues.[33]

---

[31] "Fünfte Partei in den Bundenstag" *Der Spiegel* 9, 1989, pp. 44–53.
[32] The extraordinarily high percentage of the Republikaner is partly due to the lower participation rate in European elections. In the 1989 elections, it was 62% compared to 84% in the 1987 federal elections.
[33] "Rita Süssmuth: Die CDU nicht umkrempeln" *Süddeutsche Zeitung*, February 3, 1989, p. 2; "Spannungen zwischen CSU and CDU über den Kurs der Union" *Der Tagesspiegel*, January 31, 1989, p. 5.

Initially, Kohl sought to bridge the deep divisions in the party, defending Geissler and ignoring calls for his resignation. But by August 1989, Kohl gave in to pressures from the national conservatives and dismissed the long-standing party official. The signal was clear: Kohl sought to reclaim the political territory that the Union was perceived to be deserting through the liberals' reversal of the *Wende*.[34]

As parties grow, their electoral fortunes are less dependent on mainstream party maneuvering and more reliant on their own capacity to sustain the electoral momentum. Despite the new turn of the Union parties toward national conservatism, popular support for the REP did not wane. After the Berlin breakthrough, poll after poll showed party support to steadily stand at around 5%. Moreover, the party witnessed the rapid expansion of its organizational network, as its membership grew from 8,500 in December 1988, to 12,000 in March 1989, 21,000 in September 1989, and 25,000 by December 1989 (Backes and Jesse 1993: 112). Furthermore, the electoral advances in secondary elections improved the financial standing of the party. On account of its electoral breakthroughs the party collected nearly DM 17.4 million in campaign reimbursements, most of it for its support in European elections. Having spent less than a third of this, the party ended the year with a notable surplus. By October 1989, it was obvious that Christian Democratic efforts to curb the growth of the REP were largely ineffective, as the party continued to make electoral advances, this time in the Baden-Württemberg municipal elections. The party exceeded 10% in three key state cities and received 6.9% and several seats in the Stuttgart city council.

But within a month, everything changed. By December, support for the REP started fading and by early 1990 it dropped to 2% of those regularly polled by *Spiegel* (Figure 4.3; see also Roth 1990). What happened? The fall of the Berlin Wall and the decision to reunify Germany in late November 1989, allowed Kohl to reclaim the national conservative space and to credibly present the Christian Democrats as resolute defenders of German nationhood. The reunification, a long-standing demand of national conservatives such as

---

[34] "Kohl sacks Geißler to appease right wing" *Financial Times*, August 22, 1989; Ferdinard Protzman, "Kohl replaces party official after losses to the far right" *New York Times*, August 22, 1989.

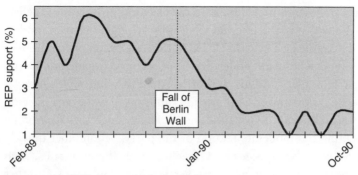

FIGURE 4.3. REP: Down with the Wall
Source: Adjusted from opinion polls in *Spiegel* 44/1990: 41; rounded to percentages.

Strauss, deprived the REP of an important programmatic demand. Through his fast-track unification plan Kohl turned Far Right words into deeds. Moreover, his appeals to the "unity of the nation," to "one German people," and to "the German fatherland" bolstered German national identity. The reunification revived earlier conservative efforts to revitalize national identity right when they seemed to be faltering. Amidst chants of "Germany united fatherland" in the East and prints of black-red-yellow newspaper titles in the West, Leftist calls for multiculturalism seemed to be out of place. To many, reunification made Germany, albeit indirectly, what Kohl had promised to make it in 1982: a normal, confident nation again, to be trusted by its current allies and its previous foes. In this euphoric climate, Kohl went a step further, questioning the legal status of the territory Germany conceded to Poland in 1945.

By the December 1990 elections, Kohl was able to capitalize on reunification to halt the electoral momentum of the REP, before it had the time to consolidate its organizational presence and to solidify its leadership structures. Indeed, despite its notable organizational growth after its 1989 advances and notwithstanding its improved financial resources, the party did not manage to build organizational strongholds outside Bavaria, and to a lesser extent, Berlin (Stöss 1990: 54). One example of its organizational shortcomings was that the REP was unable to contest every municipal election (e.g., in North Rhine-Westphalia). Lacking solid organizational roots, its membership quickly fell by 40% within a year, to 15,000 in 1990.

The most important impediment to the electoral prospects of the Far Right, though, was the internal leadership struggle between moderates and extremists. The struggle led to the resignation of Schönhuber in May 1990 who came under fire from regional organizations and other party leaders for his authoritarian leadership style. After a series of litigation moves, public insults and staged walk-outs, he won re-election in a highly divisive and chaotic party congress in Ruhrstorf. Representing the moderate faction of the party, Schönhuber quickly moved to expel his opponents. Other top party functionaries, such as European Parliament members Peter Köhler and Hans-Günther Shodruch, resigned voluntarily. Lacking solid leadership and organization, the party received a mere 2.1% in the 1990 parliamentary elections, largely due to its relative strength in Bavaria, where it received a third of its votes. Instead of using its previous breakthroughs as basis to grow its electoral strength, the party collapsed due to leadership and organizational failures that made it vulnerable to Christian Democratic co-optation strategies.

The Asylum Issue Returns

The reunification of Germany allowed the Union parties to reclaim the space temporarily lost to the REP but it presented the Kohl government with a series of socioeconomic challenges that, by the early 1990s, started undermining its popularity. One of the most important issues was the rapid growth of asylum applications, which reinforced the negative public attitudes toward foreigners and led to a number of hate-crimes, especially in the East. The government's insistence on the need to change the German constitution to tighten the asylum law, led to yet another partisan row over the issue, which lasted from 1991 to 1993. In the midst of the controversy about asylum, Far Rightists got a chance to revive their waning electoral fortunes and to achieve a number of electoral successes in state elections. But the firm position of the Union parties on the asylum issue, which eventually led to the revision of the German constitution, closed the window of opportunity for the Far Right facilitating its electoral demise.

Unlike a decade ago, the new controversy over the asylum issue was largely a response to the sharp increase in asylum applications, which, by the early 1990s, had exceeded all precedents. In 1987 the number of asylum applications was limited to 57,000 but by 1990 it reached 193,000. In 1991, 256,000 individuals arrived in Germany seeking asylum, and in 1992, the number of new asylum entrants reached 438,000. Along with the large flow of German re-settlers and the immigration of East Germans to West Germany, the continuous arrival of applicants created social tensions and, by 1992, it spiralled into deadly neo-Nazi violence against immigrants. The situation started getting out of control as early as September 1991, when extremist gangs began terrorizing foreigners causing them to flee the localities in which they were temporarily housed. In one of the best-known cases, in Hoyerswerda, a group of youngsters besieged two apartment complexes for nearly a week before the authorities boarded the foreign residents onto buses and escorted them to an army base. Jubilant residents of the impoverished eastern town got onto national television and proclaimed that their town was "foreign-free." There were tens of similar incidents across the country in that week, one of which had cost the life of a Ghanaian refugee.[35] Within the two years of the asylum controversy, the number of violent extreme-Right actions in Germany increased from 178 in 1990 to 1495 in 1992. Amidst this radicalized social environment, a number of polls recorded an alarming rise in antiforeigner sentiment and in anti-Semitism in the early 1990s. For example, the number of Germans who stated that they do not want a Jewish friend increased from 12% in 1987 to 22% in 1992 (Ignazi 2003: 76–78). There was also a strong public demand for a change: in early 1991, the vast majority of East and West Germans supported limiting the asylum right.[36] By September 1992, 61% of those polled ranked the asylum issue as the most important problem in Germany.

The public resonance of the asylum issue and the significant media attention it generated,[37] presented mainstream parties with pressures to address the situation. The national conservative faction of

[35] See "Lieber Sterben als nach Sachsen" *Der Spiegel* 40, 1991, pp. 30–38; Stephen Kinzer, "A wave of attacks on foreigners stirs shock in Germany" *New York Times*, October 1, 1991, p. A1.
[36] "Asylrecht beschränken?" *Der Spiegel* 6, 1991, p. 47.
[37] *Der Spiegel* devoted several of its cover stories on the asylum issue toward the end of 1991. One of them, in early September, pictured Germany as a boat full of people, echoing the conservative claim that the "boat is full." The magazine titled its cover story, "Assault of the Poor" (*Ansturm der Armen*), September 9, 1991.

the Christian Democrats, which was most sensitive to such pressures, became the most forceful proponent of tighter asylum laws. In early 1991, the CSU associated the asylum situation with CDU's drift away from its conservative basis and led a campaign for the revision of the constitution to stop the influx of refugees. The CDU soon followed suit. After a number of electoral setbacks in the Hamburg and Rhineland Palatinate elections and as the number of asylum applications grew, the CDU started realizing the political perils of ignoring the issue and the electoral rationale for exploiting it. The general secretary of the CDU, Volker Rühe, circulated an election strategy paper, which "advised party members to keep the asylum question at the forefront of the election debate in order to put the 'heat' on the SPD" (Young 1995: 67; Green 2004: 85–86). With the SPD being deeply divided over the tightening of asylum laws and the Greens being against it, the issue seemed to be an electoral "winner" for the CDU. In the Bremen elections in late September 1991, this strategy seemed to bear fruit: after a campaign dominated by the asylum issue, the CDU was rewarded with a 7% gain in the traditionally SPD-led state, while the Social Democrats suffered a 12% drop that broke their thirty-year majority. The other beneficiary of the SPD's electoral debacle, though, was the Far Right DVU, which got 6.2% of the vote, increasing its support by 2.8%.

The electoral losses of the Social Democrats along with the regional breakthrough of the Far Right exposed the need to take legislative measures to curb the flow of asylum seekers. But it did not help bring the two big parties closer to an agreement on the issue nor ease the political discord over the appropriate policy response. Pressed by its Left wing and by the multicultural approach of the Greens, the SPD proposed a number of measures to tighten the asylum law, but objected the Christian Democrat suggestion to revise Article 16 of the Basic Law. Since the Kohl government needed SPD's consent to master the two-thirds majority needed for constitutional revision, the issue continued to be bitterly contested for more than a year. As social tensions and discontent continued to mount, the political discussion over the asylum issue became intense pitting again liberal multiculturalists against national conservatives. The CDU insisted that the only way to limit the number of asylum applications was to change the constitution and put the blame on the SPD for refusing to accept this.

As CDU general secretary Rühe put it, "every asylum seeker come Friday is an SPD asylum seeker." The CSU went beyond mere anti-SPD rhetoric: it started publishing in Munich newspapers the names of SPD politicians who refused to change the asylum law.

The radicalization of political competition over the asylum issue and the seeming ineffectiveness of the political establishment to solve it helped the Far Right inject its antiforeigner rhetoric into the mainstream discourse. By identifying the asylum issue as a "problem" that needed urgent resolution, mainstream parties inadvertently legitimized Far Rightist claims that foreigners stole German jobs and caused crime. The antiforeigner violence in Hoyerswerda and, later, in Rostock, damaged the image of Germany abroad but helped boost the popularity of the Far Right at home. Even after the public outcry that the antiforeigner riots had caused, 27% of Germans stated that they "have understanding" for the "radical rightist tendencies" that the "foreigner problem" had unleashed.[38] As social tensions mounted, the high visibility of the issue seems to have benefited the Far Right. In October 1991, the REP started reappearing on *Spiegel*'s poll of the political situation after a long absence, and by September 1992, the party polled 7%. For as long as the issue topped the political debate, the Far Rightist appeals started becoming more legitimate. Asked in late 1991 which party had the "best concept" in the "foreigner policy," as many as 11% of those polled named the REP.[39] A year later, and after the murder of three Turkish immigrants in Mölln, 19% of the population agreed with the Far-Right slogan "Foreigners out."[40] The growing visibility of the Far Right started benefiting it at the polls. In April 1992, the DVU managed to get 6.3% in the Schleswig-Holstein elections, depriving the SPD its majority, and the REP stunned the CDU-held Baden-Württemberg with a 10.9% breakthrough. By December, most Germans thought that it was likely that the REP would enter the Bundestag, and 15% of the population stated they would welcome such a development.[41] For a second time within

---

[38] "Verständnis für Radikale?" *Der Spiegel* 48, 1991, p. 61.
[39] "Mit den Schönhubers gegen Ausländer?" *Der Spiegel* 38, 1991, p. 50; 13% named the CSU, 22% the CDU, 26% the SPD and 12% stated "no party."
[40] Before the Mölln murders, 32% of the population agreed with this statement. "Nach Mölln ein Volk im Schock" *Der Spiegel* 50, 1992, p. 58.
[41] "Republikaner in der Bundestag?" *Der Spiegel* 50, 1992, p. 61.

only a few years, the electoral prospects of the Far Right set off political and historical alarms.

As before, the alarms went off prematurely. The asylum controversy enhanced the political prospects of the Far Right but, beyond a few regional breakthroughs, the radicalization of the issue had a minimal impact on Far Right voting at the national level. Once again, the Christian Democrats were able to block the rise of the Far Right by remaining firm on their initial position that the asylum issue could only be resolved through a constitutional amendment. By late 1992, and as the SPD continued to reject the CDU proposals, chancellor Kohl hardened his position, threatening to declare a state of emergency to unilaterally amend the constitution. CDU efforts to block the entry of the REP into the Bundestag were not restrained to political rhetoric. The alarming signals sent by Far Right gains in regional elections provided the impetus for the organizational mobilization of the CDU's national conservative faction. Towards the end of the 1992, Lummer founded the "Germany Forum" to provide a "political homeland" to CDU members who wanted to replace the "multicultural utopia" and the "class-struggle rhetoric" with a renewed focus on the "German fatherland."[42] For the national conservatives, the emphasis on German identity was the only effective antidote to Far Right advances. Such convictions found considerable support among CDU leaders, like Wolfgang Schäuble, who argued that the CDU should use the "national element" to help stabilize democracy. The popular CDU interior minister reasoned that national identity constitutes a binding force that could give citizens a sense of belonging and help them confront the challenges of reunification. Stressing the emotional strength of national symbolism, Schäuble admitted that the emphasis on the "national" constituted a strategic weapon against the Far Right.[43]

In December 1992, the SPD caved in to the CDU's unwavering pledge to revise Article 16 of the German constitution. After a tense

[42] "Titanic auf dem Rhein" *Der Spiegel* 53, 1992, pp. 23–24.
[43] See, for example, his interview "Das Nationale Nutzen" *Der Spiegel* 38, 1994, pp. 30–34; the interview reflected the views published in Schäuble's book, *Und der Zukunft zugewandt*, Berlin: Siedler, 1994. The book received negative reviews from journalists, who "criticized his effort to play the national card." Discouraged by the reception of the book, he later decided not to have the book republished; Interview #16, *Die Zeit* journalist, Berlin, May 2004.

13-hour debate in the Bundestag, most SPD representatives joined the Christian Democrats to vote in favor of the constitutional amendment in May 1993. The rest joined ranks with the Greens voting against the amendment, as the ten thousand protesters that gathered outside the parliament building had demanded. Despite Social Democratic defections and Green opposition, the two major parties were able to get the two-thirds of the votes necessary to change the German constitution. The amendment limited the right to asylum to only those who came from countries that the German government listed as subjecting their citizens to political persecution. This excluded East European and many African countries from where a large number of the asylum seekers originated. With the new law, the latter group would be turned back at the border. This constituted a political triumph for the national conservative faction of the Christian Democrats that had rallied for this constitutional amendment since the early 1980s. After more than a decade, their alarmist calls about the dilution of German identity and the "overforeignization" of Germany had won the day. In this sense, the revision of the asylum law allowed the Christian Democrats to strengthen their credibility as the defenders of national identity against liberal multiculturalists who were accused of dragging Germany "toward a new global order with a grand common culture and, if possible, even a world government."[44]

The tightening of the asylum law closed the window of opportunity available to the Far Right (Minkenberg 1995: 222–223). Before the amendment of Article 16, the Far Right achieved a number of electoral breakthroughs in state elections and increased its membership base. But the constitutional amendment put a brake on the Far Right's electoral advances both at the state and at the national level. At the European elections in June 1994, where defections from mainstream parties are more common than in national elections, the REP received only 3.9% of the vote. Moreover, the party remained under the 5%-threshold in all eight state elections held during that year. By

---

[44] Norbert Gois, CSU member of Bundestag, on May 28, 1993, during debate of asylum law. Gois argued that aspirations for the creation of a common culture "is a fantasy. People will always separate themselves from one another." In addition, he warned about the threat of "overforeignization" that would bring a "catastrophe." "Our people are scared that one day they will no longer live in the Germany that they want to live" (Steiner 2000: 88).

TABLE 4.2. Television Exposure of German Politicians, 1994*

	ARD	ZDF	SAT1	RTL	Total	Total %
Helmut Kohl (CDU)	371	344	346	195	1256	39.5
Rudolf Scharping (SPD)	317	234	126	151	828	26.1
Klaus Kinkel (FDP)	140	271	68	76	555	17.5
Theo Waigel (CSU)	92	73	21	12	198	6.2
Joschka Fischer (Greens)	36	94	1	6	137	4.3
Gregor Gysi (PDS)	48	70	8	48	174	5.5
Franz Schönhuber (REP)	8	13	4	4	29	0.9
Total					3177	100.0

Gray shade, Far-Right parties.
* Jan–Oct 1994; minutes in television programs.
Source: Der Spiegel, 40/1994: 29, author's calculations.

the national election of October 1994, Far Right support returned to its 1990-levels of approximately 2%. The electoral misfortunes of the Far Right were partly due to the effectiveness of the new law. Within a year, the number of asylum seekers dropped from 323,000 in 1993 to 127,000 in 1994. This removed the asylum issue from the political limelight and turned public attention to other issues. Asked before the election, only 5% considered the "foreigner policy" to be the most critical electoral issue compared to 40% who thought that unemployment was most important.[45]

Apart from the decreasing political salience of the asylum issue, the Far Right confronted persistent visibility barriers. Despite the REP's earlier advances, during the 1994 electoral campaign the mainstream media avoided giving the Far Right much exposure. As Table 4.2 shows, the leader of the party, Schönhuber, only got 0.9% of all airtime in the four national TV channels during 1994. This limited exposure focused on the renewed infighting within the REP, after Schönhuber's flirtation with Frey's DVU that eventually cost him his position. An

[45] "Sargdeckel auf" Der Spiegel 40, 1994, p. 20. For an analysis of electoral issues during the 1994 electoral campaign see Klingemann and Lass 1996: 157–181.

official at the Office for the Protection of the Constitution, the agency
that systematically monitors extremist parties and organizations,
attributes the failure of the Far Right to get media exposure to "a
strong consensus among the German media – both newspapers and
television channels – not to give a forum to such parties."[46] "In other
countries," an experienced journalist suggested, "you will see such
people on your evening news. In Germany, you will not... As far as I
am concerned, I try my best not to give right-wing extremists a forum
in the *Tagesspiegel*. They often come to me telling me they want to
reveal something. I sit and listen to them. But I write nothing."[47] The
views of my interviewees are consistent with survey evidence showing
that German journalists consider themselves to be the guardians of
democracy. In one survey, more than 90% of journalists polled said
that they consider it their duty to combat a party that constitutes an
obvious threat to society (Müller 1996: 160).

Citizenship and Immigration since the Mid-1990s

Throughout the rest of the 1990s, the resurfacing of questions about
the Nazi past and the persistence of public concerns over immigration
ensured the continuation of identity politics. Yet, despite the public
resonance and political salience of such issues, Far Rightists failed to
make any noteworthy electoral advances in the 1998 and 2002 elections. This was largely due to the tactical positioning of the Christian
Democrats on national identity issues. The Christian Democrats
rejected efforts to broaden the circle of complicity for Nazi crimes
and the last Kohl administration successfully blocked leftist efforts
to change citizenship law. Once in opposition, the Union parties
sought to actively mobilize antiforeigner sentiments against Gerhard
Schröder's plans to grant dual citizenship to immigrants and, later,
against government efforts to change Germany's immigration policy.
Apart from positioning of the Christian Democrats, the Far Right
also confronted the persistent disregard of the major media, which
refused to give it publicity. Recognizing this deficiency, the Far Right

---

[46] Interview #22, High ranking official of Berlin branch of Office for the Protection
of the Constitution, Ministry of Interior, June 2004, Berlin.
[47] Interview #23, Field Journalist of *Tagesspiegel*, June 2004, Berlin.

sought to gain exposure through expensive advertising campaigns. The remaining of this section analyzes how partisan debates over national identity and how the lack of media exposure affected the electoral fortunes of the Far Right in the mid-1990s.

As before, political rows over German identity partly revolved around historical memory. The commemoration of various fifty-year anniversaries in 1995, the release of Daniel Goldhagen's *Hitler's Willing Executioners* and a wandering exhibition about the crimes of the Nazi's regular army (the *Wehrmacht*) helped bring historical memory back into center-stage. The resurfacing of the Nazi past in the public discourse is documented by analyses of news coverage. One such analysis shows a multifold increase in the frequency of references to the Holocaust in the conservative *Frankfurter Allgemeine Zeitung* (*FAZ*) between 1993 and 1998 (Langenbacher 2002: 120). The increase was steepest between 1996 and 1998, the period when Goldhagen toured Germany presenting his book and when the *Wehrmacht*-crimes exhibit created the most controversies. Like Goldhagen's book, the exhibit sought to widen the circle of complicity for Nazi crimes beyond the SS or the Waffen-SS by exposing the involvement of regular army soldiers in the execution of racially motivated policies. But unlike the book, the exhibit created a political uproar that revitalized divisions between national conservatives and liberal multiculturalists.

The political controversy peaked when the exhibit was put on display in Munich, in February 1997, causing a reaction among veterans and soldiers. Their case was taken up by the conservative media. The *FAZ* questioned the authenticity of the pictures and highlighted the organizers' past involvement in leftist causes.[48] The *Bayernkurier*, a CSU newspaper, called it "a campaign of destruction against the German people." The Christian Democrats followed suit. The leader of the Bavarian CSU, Peter Gauweiler, boycotted the opening ceremony of the exhibition, which was hosted by the Social Democratic council of Munich. He attacked the exhibition as a cheap attempt to tarnish the honor of ordinary German soldiers and carried his own

---

[48] Indeed, some of the photographs were mislabelled. The Hamburg Institute for Social Research, which created the exhibit to commemorate the fiftieth anniversary of the end of World War II, corrected and reopened the exhibit in 2001 (Eley 2000; Langenbacher 2002: 6–7; Art 2006: 90–91).

ceremony at the Tomb of the Unknown Soldier. Prominent members of the CDU also distanced themselves from the exhibit. Former German president and *Wehrmacht* soldier, Richard von Weizsacker, whose much-celebrated 1985-speech stressed German complicity in Nazi crimes, warned against "the self-righteousness of the successor generations."[49]

The political furore over the exhibit was carried over to the Bundestag, which devoted a session in March 1997, debating the exhibit. During the debate, the Christian Democrats remained firm on their position against the exhibit, accusing the Greens and the Social Democrats of propagating self-hatred. In turn, the two parties accused the Union of seeking to comfort and aid neo-Nazis by denying the evidence of German war crimes. In the end, the two sides failed to reach a common resolution about the exhibit because the Christian Democrats refused to accept any text that incriminated the *Wehrmacht* (Art 2006: 91). The final text passed by the governing coalition constituted a political victory for the Christian Democrats, who were able to sustain their firm position against the widening of the circle of complicity in Nazi crimes. It noted that, while parts of the *Wehrmacht* were involved in Nazi crimes, the majority of soldiers were not.

The unwavering position of the Union on national identity issues was not only evident in their rejection of the *Wehrmacht* exhibition but also in their successful blocking of changes to citizenship law. Based on a nationality code that dates back to 1913, "German citizenship law is based exclusively on descent, allowing immigrants and their descendants to remain indefinitely outside the community of citizens" (Brubaker 1992: 114). The Kühn memorandum of 1977 sought to change this but efforts to extend political rights to millions of immigrants ran against the opposition of the Christian Democrats, who had tried, instead, to repatriate them. In 1993, the Greens and the SPD sought to revive the debate over citizenship, with a nationwide signature petition and with the introduction of legislative bills in favor of dual citizenship. By permitting immigrants and their children to hold dual citizenships, both parties wanted to facilitate the

[49] Lucian Kim, "German Photo Exhibit Prompts Thousands of Angry Words," *Christian Science Monitor*, July 21, 1997, p. 7.

naturalization of more foreigners. But the Christian Democratic coalition blocked these efforts, by rejecting the bills in April 1994, a few months before the national elections. After the elections, and despite pressures from Catholic organizations and from the liberal wing of the party, the Union continued to reject *jus soli*[50] and dual citizenship. This was largely due to the objections of the CSU and the national conservative wing of the CDU, which were able to kill internal party proposals for liberal reforms. Under their strong opposition, the five parliamentary sessions that were devoted to the issue failed to resolve the gridlock. By the 1998 election, plans for revamping the nationality code were effectively shelved, as Christian Democratic objections made it impossible to build a political majority for reforming the citizenship law.

The building of such a majority became possible with Gerhard Schröder's victory in the election. Shortly after the election, the Red-Green coalition agreed to a plan for radical reform of the nationality code, accepting both dual citizenship and the *jus soli*. "As well as the strong symbolism of reforming a law which still dated back to the 'bad old days' of overt German ethnonationalism, something which was always going to go down well with the government's left-wing supporters, a reform had the added attraction of incurring relatively little financial cost" (Green 2004: 96). But exactly because of this symbolic nature of citizenship reform, the proposed plan soon came under attack by the conservative opposition. "German conservatives considered dual citizenship a threat to both the loyalty of immigrants to the German state and to the identity and integrity of German nationhood" (Minkenberg 2003: 231). The General Secretary of the CDU protested that with the plan "Germany would become a multicultural playground." And Rupert Stolz, a prominent Christian Democratic legal expert, cautioned that the reform would "transform Germany into a land of immigration, a land of unlimited immigration."[51] As usual, CSU politicians went even further in their rhetoric. The new CSU chief, Edmund Stoiber, contended that the plan would pose dangers equivalent to the Red Army Faction's terrorism in the 1970s,

---

[50] Citizenship based on birthplace, rather than descent (*jus sanguinis*).
[51] Roger Cohen, "The German 'Volk' Seem set to Let Outsiders in" *New York Times*, October 16, 2003, p. 4.

while Wolfgang Zeitlmann warned of Islamic parties in the Bundestag and new immigration of "limitless proportions" (Cooper 2002: 95). Given the minority status of the Union parties in the two legislative houses, such shrill rhetoric aimed at appeasing their voters, 81% of whom told pollsters they opposed the plan.[52]

With state elections in Hesse coming up in February 1999, the Christian Democrats were tempted to further radicalize the dual citizenship issue, by launching a petition drive against the governmental proposal. The idea was discussed in the higher echelons of the Christian Democratic party and taken up by the CDU candidate in the upcoming election, Ronald Koch. The tactical utility of this unusual[53] move was multifold. Shortly after their electoral defeat and lacking veto points in the political process, the Christian Democrats saw an opportunity to rally the support of their disgruntled voters. More importantly, they sought to block the rise of the Far Right, which achieved a small but alarming gain in the 1998 national legislative election (Cooper 2002).[54] To do so, though, they had to rely on the mobilization of latent xenophobia at the risk of being accused of antiforeigner populism. The new head of the CDU, Wolfgang Schäuble, was aware of the risk involved, but decided that the price was worth paying. As he recalls in his memoirs, "during an interview with two journalists from *Die Zeit*... I realized how difficult it would be to defuse the allegations of anti-foreigner populism. Nonetheless, I was more determined than ever to push ahead with the petition campaign" (Schäuble 2000: 86, quoted in Green 2004: 99).

Indeed, the radicalization of the double citizenship issue by the Christian Democrats proved effective. It allowed Koch to achieve a surprising victory in Hesse, upsetting the government majority in the

---

[52] This compares with 59% of FDP voters, 52% of PDS voters, 50% of SPD voters, and 30% of Green voters. See Green (2004: 101).

[53] Up until that time the CDU had made little use of this method of political mobilization. Out of 2000 petition drives reported in the leftist *tageszeigung* between 1986 and 1998, the Union parties participated in only 14 at the Land or local level (Cooper 2002: 90).

[54] The three Far Right parties that contested the federal election in 1998 received 3.3% of the national vote, compared to 1.9% in 1994. This was almost entirely due to the participation in the election of the DVU, which got 1.2% of the vote, and the NPD, which got 0.3% of the vote. This was the only time that the DVU participated in national elections.

upper legislative house, the Bundesrat. More than 60% of those who switched to the CDU in Hesse were primarily motivated by the dual nationality issue (Cooper 2002: 96). Moreover, during the petition public opposition to the issue strengthened from 63% in January to 68% in February 1999. The 5 million signatures collected nation-wide highlighted widespread public concerns and helped bring about a major shift in the government policy, away from dual citizenship. The amended bill included a lighter version of *jus soli*, to be made acceptable to the FDP, but entirely dropped dual citizenship, at the dismay of the Greens. The final bill, which marked the most impor-tant change in German citizenship law since 1913, was passed in May 1999 (Joppke 2001: 351–353). Holding firm to its stance for the pres-ervation of blood ties in the nationality code, the Union parties voted against the law and threatened to take it to the constitutional court.

The Christian Democrats unwavering opposition to the issue limited the political space available for Far Right mobilization. Although controversial, the petition reinforced the Union's credibil-ity as a resolute defender of German identity and deprived the Far Right of a potential rallying point in future elections. The Union's argument, that dual citizenship hinders the integration of immi-grants, was distinct from the antiforeigner rhetoric of the Far Right. But in the radicalized environment the petition created, the distinc-tion was lost on many, who erroneously considered the signature drive to be a referendum against foreigners.[55] The petition against dual citizenship hence restricted the political space left to the three Far Right parties, which were compelled to support the Christian Democratic initiative.

The radicalization of national identity issues can help mainstream parties block the Far Right, but it can also harm them if it cannot be sustained. Unconstrained by the burden of governing, the Union was able to sustain its firm stance on national identity issues until the 2002 elections. The government's efforts to change the country's immigration policy set a new focal point for partisan conflict over national identity, furnishing the Christian Democrats with several opportunities to present themselves as resolute defenders of German

[55] Some people were reported to had been asking where they could "sign up against foreigners" (Green 2004: 103).

nationhood. The first came in February 2000, when the Red-Green governing coalition unveiled plans to issue up to 20,000 five-year work permits for highly qualified IT specialists to fill up vacancies. Despite their close association with business associations, which had lobbied for this measure, the Christian Democrats initially dismissed these plans and sought to use it to rally support for elections in North Rhine-Westphalia in May 2000. The CDU candidate there, Jürgen Rüttgers, coined the term "Children, not Indians" (*Kinder statt Inder*) to trivialize the "Green Card" program and argue for child education, instead. His statements were later used in state election pamphlets by the REP. Soon after the work permits row, the "dominant culture" (*Leitkultur*) controversy gave the Christian Democrats another opportunity to score conservative points. The controversy arose when a top CDU legislator argued in an interview that nonethnic German immigrants should adopt Germany's dominant culture. But the most important partisan row occurred over Schröder's plans to revamp Germany's immigration law. Aware of the sensitivity of the issue for the CDU, the Red-Green government sought to avoid a confrontation with the opposition by setting up a cross-party commission on immigration. The CDU, though, established a different commission, which in May 2001 pre-empted the findings of the governmental commission by publishing its own. The commission maintained that "Germany is not a *classical* country of immigration," marking a slight departure from CDU's long-standing position. But it also stressed that all foreigners must adhere to the values of Germany's Christian culture, echoing the "dominant culture" arguments that stirred controversy in 2000.

The CDU proposals tilted the balance toward a much more restrictive law than the government had originally envisioned. In fact, the government's draft bill, published in August 2001, was closer to the CDU's proposals than to those of the government commission (Green 2004: 122, 121–127). Yet, the CDU continued to reject the government bill arguing that it would increase, not decrease immigration. To a large extent, the CDU position echoed public opinion. In June 2001, opinion polls showed that more than half of those asked wanted the new law to reduce immigration. In tune with such concerns, the Christian Democrats opposed the proposed bill in a heated legislative session in May 2002, in which conservative representatives staged a walk out, threatening to take the issue to the constitutional court.[56] They then made immigration a top campaign issue for the September elections. Their firmness on the immigration issue was signified by the choice of the conservative leader of the CSU, Edmund Stoiber, as the Union's candidate. During the campaign, the Christian Democrats accused the government of undermining the national security and the economy by letting in too many immigrants. Connecting immigration with unemployment, they argued that Germany could not make room for immigrant workers until it found more jobs for Germans.

The Christian Democrats' firm stance on citizenship and immigration left little breathing room to the Far Right. Unsurprisingly, the combined score for the REP and the NPD dropped to 1% in the 2002 elections, the worst Far Right result in fifteen years. But the electoral misfortunes of the Far Right during this period were not only due to the crowdedness of the political space, but also due to their persistent failure to get media exposure. Despite the salience of national identity issues, mainstream media refrained from giving the Far Right much exposure. To overcome this obstacle, the Far Right sought to gain exposure through violent street demonstrations and expensive advertising campaigns. In the late 1990s, for example, there was a marked increase in NPD's street action, "one of the few means" the party had at its disposal "for publicizing its opinion and getting media attention."[57] But despite pictures of right-wing extremist violence that frequently appeared on German television (Schellenberg 2005), the mainstream media had largely avoided covering NPD demonstrations. In those occasions that they did, they mostly treated them as events, refusing to host the Far Rightists' opinions. Apart from organizing street action, the German Far Right also sought to buy exposure by spending enormous amounts of money in advertising. In the 1998 election in Sachsen-Anhalt, the DVU received an impressive 12.9% of the vote after an expensive advertising campaign that cost more than those of the CDU and the SPD combined.[58] Unable to sustain

[56] Indeed, the court annulled the bill, because of irregularities in the upper house's voting procedure.
[57] Interview #26, Frank Schwerdt, NPD General Manager and Chairman of Thüringen NPD, Berlin, June 2004.
[58] The DVU spent 3 million Deutsche Marks versus the CDU's 1 million and the SPD's 1.5 million (Karapin 2002: 210–211).

such spending levels, the party did not even participate in the next Sachsen-Anhalt elections.

The media contributed to the loss of the DVU's publicity momentum by refusing to cover the activities of its parliamentary group. Indeed, even in those states where the Far Right *had* representation, the media was hesitant to give them exposure. As a DVU functionary complained, "raising public awareness for our party is our big problem. When you ask the common man in the street if the DVU is in parliament, he will tell you that we are not. How would they know we exist? They do not see us on TV; they do not read about us in the newspapers; they do not listen to us on the radio. They do not know us!"[59] Indeed, evidence from media monitoring agencies shows Far Right exposure to be very limited, even after important breakthroughs like the one in Sachsen-Anhalt in 1998. DVU's success in these elections, for example, initiated a loud debate about "right-wing radicalism" fed by polls which showed Germany's "extreme right potential" to stand at about 15%. During the 1998 legislative campaign, this was one of the major themes discussed in election programs of the main German television channels (Krüger and Zapf-Schramm 1999: 232). But even then, the debate about Far Rightists took place in their absence. As shown in Table 4.3, DVU appearances on German television constituted only 1.5% of all party appearances in the thirty weeks prior to the elections – the period that included the party's shocking advances in the Sachsen-Anhalt elections.

Throughout the 1990s, the German Far Right did not only fail to attract television spotlights but it also failed to gain exposure by the German press. Despite widespread concerns about right-wing extremism, which were particularly salient in the early 1990s, I only found three references to the three German Far Right parties in the December editions of the weekly *Spiegel* between 1988 and 2005 out of a total of 295 references to German political parties.[60] All three were for the REP – two in 1992 and one in 1994. My findings are consistent with those of other studies of newspaper coverage. Analyzing the content of *Süddeutsche Zeitung* and *Bild* two months before the 1994,

[59] Interview #21, Thilo Kabus, Press speaker of the DVU Brandenburg parliamentary group, June 2004, Berlin.
[60] These were references made in the index of the magazine. The data for 1991 and 2004 are missing.

TABLE 4.3. *Party Television Appearances in Election Programs, 1998 (% of Appearances)*

	Total (n = 1190)	ARD (n = 430)	ZDF (n = 487)	RTL (n = 119)	SAT1 (n = 112)	ProSieben (n = 42)
CDU	28.7	26.3	28.7	35.3	26.8	38.1
CSU	8.1	7.2	8.2	6.7	8.9	16.7
FDP	9.2	7.7	10.9	6.7	10.7	7.1
Greens	13.1	13	14	15.1	10.7	4.8
SPD	30.3	27	32	29.4	36.6	28.6
PDS	6.3	7.9	6	3.4	5.4	4.8
DVU	1.5	3.3	-	2.5	0.9	-
Others	2.9	7.7	0.2	0.8	-	-

Gray shade, Far-right parties.
Note: Analysis of all information and election programs between 17–01hrs in the 30 weeks prior to the 1998 legislative elections.
Source: Krüger and Zapf-Schramm 1999: 233.

1998, and 2002 federal elections, for example, one study finds that the German press gave absolutely no coverage to the policy positions of extreme right parties. Although the German media may often refer to the Far Right as a danger to democracy and while other political actors might make negative references to it, the study finds that "not a single sentence gives readers a hint of these parties' policy stances." The cross-comparative analysis of newspaper content shows that the degree of exposure granted to German Far Right parties contrasts sharply with that granted to such parties in Austria, Switzerland, and France (Bornschier 2008: 236–237).

In more recent years, the German mainstream media have continued to deny Far Right parties publicity. In 2002, for example, none of the three Far Right parties received enough exposure to merit special mention in the detailed television monitoring report of *Media Perspektiven* for the national election. In this report, the references to the NPD or the REP were included in the "others" category.[61] The eighteen parties included in this category received merely 4% of the 3,728 references all parties received in programs with election-related input (Krüger and Zapf-Schramm 2002: 618). Similarly, in the 2005

[61] The DVU only participated in the 1994 national legislative elections.

elections the NPD and the REP got 0% of all party appearances in all types of television programs, including news bulletins and election debates (Krüger et al. 2005: 608). Since the 2005 elections, the picture has not changed: Far Right parties continue to confront high visibility barriers, even after notable regional breakthroughs. According to the monthly TV monitoring reports of the *Institut für empirische Medienforschung*, which tracks the number of appearances of all German political parties in the main news bulletins, the Far Right has been getting less than 1% of all party appearances in all but two months since September 2005. Its highest level of exposure was in September 2006, after NPD's notable breakthrough in the state election of Mecklenburg-Pomerania, where it won six seats in the state parliament. Even then, when the election topped the political agenda for that month, the NPD only got 1.3% of all party appearances on news programs. Despite occasional advances in local or regional elections, the German Far Right remains on the sidelines of the mainstream debate, largely due to unwillingness of the mass media to give it publicity.

Conclusion

This chapter has sought to examine the trajectory of the German Far Right since the late 1970s. The task was twofold, to account for temporal variation in Far Right support and to explain the overall failure of the Far Right in Germany. The analysis has mostly focused on the former but the findings can also help account for the electoral misfortunes of the German Far Right.

Based on the evidence presented in this chapter, the failure of the Far Right is largely due to the Christian Democrats' positioning on national identity issues. In the early 1980s, the Union parties politicized national identity issues creating a new political space in German politics. Initially, they managed to sustain their position in this new space at the expense of the Far Right. But towards the late 1980s, this proved to be a risky strategy: Kohl's *Wende* alienated key constituents and compelled the CDU to moderate its positions on national identity issues, thus furnishing the Far Right with opportunities for an electoral breakthrough. Notwithstanding their experience in the 1980s, the Christian Democrats continued to play the nationalist card in the

1990s. This time, though, they confronted significantly less pressures to retract the card. In part, this was due to an overall shift in the system toward the Union's positions, marked by the SPD's vote for the tightening of the asylum law in 1993 and by the Free Democrats flirtation with liberal nationalism in the mid-1990s. Toward the late 1990s, pressures for de-radicalizing national identity issues were further deflected by the CDU's opposition status, which reduced the need for accepting pragmatic solutions to Germany's pressing immigration problems. It remains to be seen how CDU's assumption of power and how its coalition with the SPD will affect its strategy for combating the Far Right. Given these constraints, playing the nationalist card can backfire. If the Christian Democrats become compelled to retract it, they will furnish the Far Right with an opportunity for electoral advances.

The analysis of the German case, though, has also demonstrated that mainstream party positioning is not the only obstacle for aspiring Far Right legislators. Entrance into the electoral market requires media visibility. Whereas in Austria the media granted enormous exposure to the Jörg Haider, in Germany the Far Right confronted a prohibitively high publicity threshold. A strong journalistic ethos and a widespread media consensus made it hard for the Far Right to get much exposure in the mainstream press and on television. Does this make the German media exceptional? The examination of the Greek case will help provide some answers.

5

Greek Nationalists: From Mainstream to the Margins?

Walking in the crowded streets of Athens a few days before the national parliamentary elections of March 2004, one could barely miss a bizarre pamphlet of the Far Right Popular Orthodox Rally (Λαϊκός Ορθόδοξος Συναγερμός, LAOS) that shows a flying pigeon and strangely reads "The pigeon concurs." The pigeon is a Christian reference to the Holy Ghost and as the flamboyant leader of LAOS, George Karatzaferis, explains on his marginal television channel, Teleasty (Τηλεάστυ), by sitting on his head during his visit to the Orthodox Patriarch in Constantinople, the pigeon "anointed" him the next Greek prime minister. He insists that this has only happened twice in two thousand years, the previous time with Jesus Christ. Although Karatzaferis rejects the Far Right label, his ethnocentric rhetoric bears more similarities with the German Republikaner and the Austrian FPÖ than with the "popular Right" he sometimes claims to represent. His party is the new face of the Greek Far Right, which has fully embraced nationalism in its search for ideological distinctiveness and has discarded the rusty appeals of its postauthoritarian predecessors. This chapter traces the trajectory of the postauthoritarian and the contemporary Greek Far Right since 1974. It seeks to demonstrate that despite marked historical, cultural, and institutional differences between Greece and Austria and Germany, the trajectory of the Greek Far Right has been shaped by processes similar to those affecting the fortunes of its Austrian and German counterparts.

The transformation of the Greek Far Right has been met with inter-mittent successes at the polls. Apart from a few short-lived advances, the Greek Far Right has yet to become a permanent force in Greek party politics. This might explain why it has largely escaped scholarly attention. The voluminous literature of the Far Right includes only sporadic references to the Greek case, paralleling it with those of Spain and Portugal. Concentrating on the period of democratic transition, casual observers attribute the failure of the Far Right to the unpleasant memories of authoritarianism. But while the undesirability of dictator-ship goes a long way to account for the failure of the *postauthoritar-ian* Far Right, it is too static to account for the varied performance of the *contemporary* Greek Far Right. So is the emphasis on the majori-tarian attributes of the Greek electoral system. Although reinforced proportional representation favors bipartisanship, it has not inhibited the appearance of smaller Greek parties during the past decades. To explain the varied fortunes of such parties, it is important to go beyond the institutional constraints they confront. One must also look deeper than broad socioeconomic conditions: Like Germany, Greece has one of the highest unemployment rates and immigration levels in Europe, but this has not led to persistent Far Right support.

This chapter employs the theoretical framework developed earlier to understand the trajectory of the Greek Far Right. To do so, it uti-lizes information from original party documents and from interviews with Far Right leaders. Unlike earlier accounts, the study differentiates between the postauthoritarian and the new Far Right and focuses the explanatory analysis on the latter, which is more comparable with the European Far Right. To account for the trajectory of the contemporary Greek Far Right, this chapter examines how Socialists and conserva-tives have dealt with national identity questions since the early 1990s and how the media have treated the Far Right. The analysis docu-ments the creation of political opportunities for the Far Right after the 1990s, when national identity issues took increased prominence in Greek politics. Confronted with issues such as the Macedonia crisis in 1992 or identity cards after 2000, the Greek conservative party, New Democracy (Νέα Δημοκρατία, ND), chose to play the national-ist card. But it was later compelled to retract it, as the issues proved too divisive for the party and its electorate. Conservative oscillation on national identity issues led to ND splintering and to the formation of new parties challenging its monopoly on the Right of the political spectrum. Confronted with favorable opportunity structures, the nascent parties needed media attention to become known. Whenever they got it, they staged notable electoral breakthroughs. The Political Spring (Πολιτική Άνοιξη, PS) capitalized on its nationalist position on the Macedonia issue to stage an important breakthrough in 1993 before falling into political oblivion. Similarly, LAOS benefited from the fallout from the identity cards controversy to build its initial basis of support and achieve a breakthrough in the 2002 local elections. A much more radical and populist party than the borderline case of the Political Spring, LAOS capitalized on divisions within ND over national identity issues to make a breakthrough in the 2007 elections, winning 3.8% and ten seats in the Greek parliament.

The first part of this chapter sketches the electoral trajectory of the Greek Far Right since 1974, highlighting the differences between the postauthoritarian and the contemporary Far Right. This section documents the gradual transformation of the Far Right through the adoption of a nationalist ideological platform. It also examines the ideological platform of the modern Greek Far Right, pointing to the similarities and differences of the various groupings competing with ND on the Right of the political spectrum since the early 1990s. The second and lengthier section of this chapter seeks to account for their sporadic successes – and sudden failures – by examining patterns of party competition over national identity and media exposure. The first part of this section seeks to account for the minor but important breakthrough of the Political Spring in 1993 by looking at the partisan row over the Macedonia issue. The second part examines the sudden collapse of the Political Spring in the mid-1990s, using it as basis for understanding "flash" party phenomena. The last part examines how the political controversy over identity cards in 2000 created opportunities for the subsequent rise of LAOS. In light of LAOS's recent breakthrough in the 2007 legislative elections, this chapter concludes with an assessment of the future of the modern Greek Far Right.

The Trajectory of the Greek Far Right

Unlike its European counterparts, the Greek Far Right has defied systematic treatment. Apart from a few brief analyses of earlier Far

Right groupings (Dimitras 1992; Kapetanyannis 1995) and some sporadic references to it in comparative studies (e.g., Mudde 2007), the Greek Far Right has largely been ignored. As a quick glance at Table 5.1 suggests, this lack of academic interest is largely because of its dismal electoral performance. With only one exception, the various Far Right parties participating in national legislative elections in the 1980s and 1990s failed to attract more than 2% of the vote. More successful parties, such as the dubious case of the Political Spring, have largely been treated with scholarly indifference, as outliers to the overall trajectory of the Greek party system that defy standard typological distinctions.[1] Only recently has interest in the subject grown, largely because of the electoral advances of the LAOS. So far, though, this interest has been limited to descriptive analyses that tend to lack an appreciation of the West European experience with the Far Right.[2] Missing this comparative perspective, such analyses sometimes avoid the categorization of LAOS as "Far Right" because the party has limited or no direct association with the postauthoritarian Far Right or with fascism. Using the minimal definition explicated in Chapter 1, though, LAOS is not dissimilar from the West European Far Right. While the party has few direct links with authoritarianism, it shares with its European contemporaries an ideological preoccupation with "national" issues and a nationalist conception of politics. It is in this view that the Political Spring has some similarities with LAOS. The analysis will underline these similarities but also the differences between LAOS and the Political Spring. Given the dearth of scholarly accounts on the Greek Far Right, this section will examine its trajectory with more detail than that awarded by the earlier chapters to its Austrian and German counterparts.

The Postauthoritarian Far Right. As in Germany and Austria, the transition of Greece to democracy in 1974 left behind a segment of the population that was still attached to the old regime and refused to accept the new political realities. This group, composed of ex-army officers, ex-junta officials, and diehard anti-Communists,

---

[1] The only article the author came across on the Political Spring is Mihas 1998.
[2] One noteworthy exception is Kolovos (2005), who tries to integrate the study of the Greek and the European Far Right.

TABLE 5.1. *Results in Greek Parliamentary Elections, 1974–2007*

	1974	1977	1981	1985	1989J	1989N	1990	1993	1996	2000	2004	2007
New Democracy	54.4	41.8	35.9	40.8	44.3	46.2	46.9	39.3	38.1	42.7	45.4	41.8
PASOK	13.6	25.3	48	45.8	39.1	40.7	38.6	46.9	41.5	43.8	40.5	38.1
Communist Party*	9.4	9.4	10.9	9.1				4.5	5.6	5.5	5.9	8.2
Coalition of the Left					13.1	11	10.3	2.9	5.1	3.2	3.3	5
National Dem. Union	1.1											
National Camp		6.8										
Progressives' Party			1.7									
Nat. Pol. Union (EPEN)				0.6	0.3							
National Party							0.1	0.1	0.2			
Political Spring								4.9	2.9			
Party of Hellenism									0.2	0.1		
Front Line										0.2		
Hellenic Front											0.1	
Popular Orthodox Rally											2.2	3.8
Others	21.5	16.7	3.5	3.7	3.2	2.1	4.1	1.4	6.4	4.5	2.6	3.1

* 1974: EDA, KKE, KKE Interior.
Source: Greek Interior Ministry, Athens (Ελληνικό Υπουργείο Εσωτερικών, Αθήνα).

became the core of the various Far Right parties that appeared in the late 1970s and 1980s. They were largely led from older politicians who belonged to the pre-1967 political establishment, such as Petros Garoufalias, Stefanos Stefanopoulos, Spyros Theotokis, and Spyros Markezinis. Rooted in the historical cleavages that shaped modern Greek party politics, the programmatic appeals of the postauthoritarian Far Right were largely a reaction to the policies set in place after 1974, especially those relating to the treatment of the Communist party, the king, and ex-junta officials. Unlike the contemporary Greek Far Right, which is more directly comparable with the European, the parties representing the postauthoritarian Far Right were not explicitly nationalist. Their programs included implicit nationalist references but mostly as a reaction to leftist internationalism than as a positive identification with the Greek nation.

The first party that came to be associated with the postauthoritarian Far Right was the National Democratic Union (Εθνική Δημοκρατική Ένωση, NDU). It was formed in 1974, right after the transition to democracy, as a reaction to the way the prime minister, Constantine Karamanlis, handled the Turkish invasion of Cyprus, the Communists, and ex-junta officers. Unlike most contemporary European Far Right parties, the party supported Greek membership in international organizations. It was critical of the decision to withdraw Greece from NATO, and it supported Greece's entry into the EEC. Like the VdU in postwar Austria, which rejected the government's de-Nazification efforts, the NDU rebuffed the "indiscriminate persecution of large number of nationally-minded citizens as well as the ruthless staining of reputations and the humiliation of the armed and security forces" (Dimitras 1992: 261). Like all Far-Right parties during this period, the NDU was also morally conservative, pledging to protect the Helleno-Christian tradition. Although the leader of the party, Garoufalias, was quickly branded as a Far Rightist by his political opponents, he insisted that his party was against any form of dictatorship and stressed his democratic credentials. Overall, his party rallied for the support of the "nationally minded," one of the three important camps in Greek politics associated with the pre-1967 National Radical Union (Εθνική Ριζοσπαστική Ένωσις, ERE). But in the November 1974 elections the party received only 1.1% of the national vote, as the majority of the Greek populace rallied behind Karamanlis's New Democracy.

It was only after 1974 that reactions against Karamanlis started to gain electoral momentum. Such reactions intensified after the Greek populace voted overwhelmingly against the monarchy in 1975, causing the consternation of many conservative supporters. Along with Karamanlis's legalization of the Communist party and the handling of Turkish provocations in the Aegean,[3] dissatisfaction with government policies led to the creation of another Far-Right party: the National Camp (Εθνική Παράταξη, NC). The party proved much more successful than the NDU, presenting a considerable challenge to the conservative ND. Apart from its fervent anti-Communism, the party pledged to free jailed junta leaders, to achieve Greek membership into the European Community, and to rid the economy from state interventionism. Capitalizing on popular dissatisfaction with Karamanlis, the NC managed to get 6.8% of the 1977 vote.

By 1981, though, most of the National Camp's members returned to the conservative ND. The remaining members took refuge in the Party of the Progressives (Κόμμα Προοδευτικών, PP), a conservative grouping that managed to receive 1.7% in the 1981 national election and 2% in the European elections, receiving a seat in the European Parliament. Like its two predecessors, the party demanded the release of jailed junta leaders and emphasized the importance of Classical and Christian education for the revival of the Great Idea.[4] Moreover, the party rejected the government's social and nationalization policies, pledging instead to limit state intervention in the economy and to strengthen private initiative. The party was replaced by the National Political Union (Εθνική Πολιτική Ένωση, EPEN), a party nominally led by the imprisoned colonel and former dictator George Papadopoulos. Fiercely anti-Communist and socially conservative,

---

[3] In August 1976, the Turkish government sent a survey ship, *Sismik*, to an oil exploration mission in an area the Greeks consider to be part of their continental shelf. The leader of the Pan-Hellenic Socialist Movement (PASOK), Andreas Papandreou, called for the sinking of the *Sismik* and criticized the conservative government of Constantine Karamanlis for choosing to take the issue to the United Nations instead.

[4] A reference to older irredentist claims.

the party centered its programmatic appeal on the release of its jailed leader. Unlike all previous parties, EPEN contested several elections, those of 1985 and June 1989, and it won a seat in the European Parliament in 1984. But its dismal results led to mass defections from the party and to the formation of a new one: the National Party (Εθνικό Κόμμα, NP).

The Contemporary Far Right. The founding of the National Party in 1989 by a thousand EPEN members set the stage for the ideological shift of the Greek Far Right.[5] The most distinctive characteristic of this shift was the emphasis on nationalism.[6] Realizing the need to broaden its appeal beyond the historical claims of the postauthoritarian predecessor, the new Far Right discarded its earlier programmatic fixation on the release of imprisoned junta leaders.[7] Instead, it

[5] Even before the appearance of the National Party, the United Nationalist Movement (Ενιαίο Εθνικιστικό Κίνημα, ENEK) attempted to make nationalism the most distinctive characteristic of the Greek Far Right. The party clearly identifies itself as nationalist and seeks to turn Greece into a nationalist state through revolutionary action. See next footnote for reference.

[6] This finding is based on the examination of the following party programs: Εθνική Δημοκρατική Ένωση (National Democratic Union), «Εργασία – Εθνική ισχύς – ευημερία οι πρωταρχικοί στόχοι της Ε.Δ.Ε.» *Ελεύθερος Κόσμος*, 23 Οκτωβρίου 1974, σελ. 3, 7; Εθνική Παράταξη (National Camp), «Διακήρυξις της Εθνικής Παρατάξεως προς τον Ελληνικόν Λαόν», *Ελεύθερος Κόσμος*, 9 Οκτωβρίου 1977, σελ. 3; Κόμμα Προοδευτικών (Party of the Progressives), «Αι Θέσεις της Πολιτικής του κ. Σπύρου Μαρκεζίνη και η Ανασύστασις του Κόμματος των Προοδευτικών», *Εστία*, 5 Νοεμβρίου 1979, σελ. 6; ΕΠΕΝ (National Political Union), «Η Πολιτική μας Πρόταση: ΕΠΕΝ, Έφτασε η Ώρα!», 1989; Ενιαίο Εθνικιστικό Κίνημα, ENEK (United Nationalist Movement), «ENEK: 15 Ιδεολογικές Αρχές», unknown date; Εθνικό Κόμμα (National Party), «Εθνικό Κόμμα: Πολιτικές Αρχές», unknown date; Ελληνικό Μέτωπο (Hellenic Front), «Πολιτικό Πρόγραμμα: Αποφάσεις Ιδρυτικού Συνεδρίου», Αθήνα 9–10 Απριλίου 1994; Πρώτη Γραμμή (Front Line), «Τι είναι και τι θέλει η Πρώτη Γραμμή», unknown date; ΛΑ.Ο.Σ. (Popular Orthodox Rally), «Γιατί; Ομιλία του Προέδρου του ΛΑ.Ο.Σ. Γιώργου Καρατζαφέρη», 14 Σεπτεμβρίου 2003. I am thankful to Ioannis Kolovos for making some of these available. I supplemented the analysis of party programs with interviews with Far Right leaders, especially with leading figures of LAOS and the Hellenic Front.

[7] As the leader of the Hellenic Front's youth group put it, "In 1977, the demand for the release of Papadopoulos and for the return of the King was socially appealing. There were approximately 3,000 people military officers that got fired from the army after the junta and another 3,000 that got kicked out of the police. They rallied against Karamanlis because they felt that what happened to them was unfair. But by the early 1980s, the social force that created those demands started fading away especially after many members of the National Camp joined New Democracy

fully embraced nationalism as the supreme value and the essence of its ideology. One of the most fervent advocates of this change was the leader of EPEN's youth group (and, since 2007, a LAOS MP), Makis Vorides, who considered nationalism to be the missing link between the party and society. As he recalls:

Towards the late 1980s, I realized the need to change the demands of our movement (EPEN). We had demanded the release of the army officers who were involved in the junta, the return of the King, and the rehabilitation of the anti-Communist fight of 1946–9. All these smelled like mothballs to me! The King himself did not want to return! More importantly, our demands were historical, not social. I told EPEN that we must move on. The legal discussion of whether General Papadopoulos should be in prison or not is interesting but it does not really concern the society in general. The demands about the past blocked our future.[8]

The ideological shift of the Far Right was evident in the program of the National Party, which called for the subordination of individual rights to the interest of the nation, from where they are supposedly derived. The party asserted the right for "self-determination" for Greek populations abroad and advocated the secession of "non-liberated" Greek homelands. More importantly, the party paid close attention to developments in the rest of Europe, where Far Rightists started making significant electoral advances by capitalizing on anti-foreigner sentiment. Following the example of the French National Front, with which EPEN was affiliated, the Greek Far Rightists gradually extended their nationalist appeals to immigration.[9] The National Party introduced anti-immigrant statements into its 1990 program, calling for the repatriation of foreign workers. Moreover, blending the moral traditionalism of its predecessors with anti-Semitism, the party blamed "world Zionism" for corrupting "Helleno-Christian traditions."[10]

Initially, the transformation of the ideological profile of the Greek Far Right did not alleviate its electoral misfortunes. Despite its

for the 1981 elections. After the 1981 elections, there was a period of decline for the patriotic front." Interview #7, February 2004, Athens.
[8] Interview #11, Athens, February 2004.
[9] Several interviews with leaders of the National Party's successor party, the Hellenic Front, Athens, February–March 2004.
[10] National Party program, p. 2 [in Greek].

ideological turn to nationalism, the National Party failed miserably in the 1990 election, receiving 0.1% of the vote. It was only in the early 1990s, when the Macedonia issue broke out, that nationalists got new opportunities to revive their waning political fortunes. Amid the nationalist fervor that swept Greece over the Macedonia issue, Political Spring, an ND splinter party that adopted a maximalist position on the matter, staged a significant breakthrough in the 1993 elections. Avoiding the traditional emphasis of the Greek Far Right on "Helleno-Christian" values, the party built its credibility by insisting that the name "Macedonia" is exclusively Greek, but by the mid-1990s, it collapsed. Its early success revitalized Far Rightist efforts to gain electoral prominence. In 1994, Vorides and former members of earlier Far Right groupings formed the Hellenic Front (Ελληνικό Μέτωπο, HF), identifying themselves as Greek nationalists and seeking to fight "national decadence" and illegal immigration.[11] Initially, the party was inactive, and it was only in 2000 that it started participating in national elections. Along with the Front Line (Πρώτη Γραμμή, FL), a party headed by the unrepentant Holocaust-denier Constantine Plevris,[12] the Hellenic Front received 0.2% of the vote. The two parties faced competition from Sotiris Sofianopoulos, a former host of a local television program in Argolida and fervent nationalist. Initially founded in 1981, his Party of Hellenism (Κόμμα Ελληνισμού, PH) called for a return to "Hellenic roots" and presented "Hellenism" as a substitute of capitalism, socialism, and communism.[13] Sofianopoulos

---

[11]   The party was initially dormant but began functioning in 1997.

[12]   Plevris is a historian and the theoretician of the Far Right. He is the founder of the Party of the 4th of August (the date of the Metaxas dictatorship in 1936), the only party that existed during the seven-year junta. He is probably the most outspoken apologist of Nazism and of the Greek dictatorship. His books include *Let's Talk about Jews! Goebbels*, and *Ioannis Metaxas*. His last book, *The Jews: All the Truth*, reprints the "Protocols of Zion" and presents a grand apologia of the Nazi regime. He argues, for example, that "Hitler was enormously sensitive and due to his character, he refused to sacrifice civilians, even in exchange for victory. The history of humanity will blame Adolf Hitler for the following: 1. He did not rid, albeit he could, Europe from the Jews and 2. He did not use the special chemical weapons that only Germany possessed to achieve victory" (p. 882). See http://www.iospress. gr/mikro2006/mikro20060715.htm (last accessed: October 2007). Ios is a group of investigative journalists working for the Greek daily Eleftherotypia who have written extensively on the Far Right and who have been interviewed by the author.

[13]   In February 2004, the author observed a meeting of members of the Party of Hellenism in a remote neighborhood in Athens. Throughout the meeting,

revived the dormant party in 1996 and ran in the national legislative elections, receiving 0.2% of the vote. In 2004, the Party of Hellenism and the Front Line joined LAOS, lured by the access Karatzaferis could grant them to Teleasty and to his weekly newspaper, *Alpha 1*.

LAOS. Founded in 2000, LAOS made an impression on political pundits with its performance at the 2002 municipal elections, receiving 13.6% in the most populous Greek prefecture of Athens-Piraeus. The party got 2.2% in the legislative elections in March 2004, 4.1% in the European elections in June 2004, and 3.8% in legislative elections of September 2007. Most observers consider the last result to be an important breakthrough for LAOS because it granted the party ten seats in the national legislature, as many as the Political Spring had won in 1993.[14] Like the Political Spring, LAOS came into being after its leader's departure from ND, with which he was voted MP in Athens in 1993, 1996, and 2000. Both LAOS and the Political Spring have held maximalist views on "national" issues and have sought to profit from the mobilization of nationalist sentiments. The political

Sofianopoulos tried to convince the participants about his "theory of intentionality," insisting that Greece's economic misfortunes are because of intentional efforts by the Karamanlis and the Papandreou governments, who are obeying orders from the Americans and the Jews. Another member, who claimed to be a former attaché of the Greek embassy in the United States, told the group that the "president was right" and went on to explain to the author his theory of the Siamese Twins: "I can attest to what the President says. I am the one who discovered the Policy of the Siamese Twins, which the US established to manage Greek–Turkish relations. This policy started almost immediately after the Second World War. Supposedly, the policy intended to treat equally Greece and Turkey in order to prevent a war between them, because otherwise, the Soviets would get access to the Aegean. At least this is the argumentation the Jewish lobby tried to project. The truth is that the Jews did not want either Turkey or Greece to become too powerful and dominant in the region because they would overshadow the power of Israel. To implement the plan, Turkey (which fought against the Americans in the First World War and did not lose a single soldier in the Second World War) had to be made richer and Greece, which was already richer than Turkey, poorer. This was the basis of the Siamese Twins policy. In order to make Greece poorer, they allowed the growth of PASOK. In line with their thinking, a socialist party would scare foreign capital away and destroy the industrial production of the country. Nothing happens without a cause!" As the meeting continued, a member of the party came in and started shouting that they should "set the parliament on fire!"

[14] The number of seats won by LAOS was partly because of changes in the Greek electoral system, which limited the disproportionality of reinforced proportional representation in favor of smaller parties.

residue of this mobilization is what attracts some former PS members to LAOS, especially in northern Greece.[15]

But while both parties have built their electoral fortunes on the waving of Greek flags, they also differ in substantial ways. First, they differ in rhetorical style. Unlike the Political Spring, LAOS uses radical populist rhetoric, making direct appeals to the "common man" and distancing itself from the political establishment. Karatzaferis has popularized the term "Athens junta" to refer to the Socialist government and has claimed that the Greek dictatorship compares favorably with the Papandreou (PASOK) government. Such positive references to the dictatorship are common in the political rhetoric of the party but were absent from that of the Political Spring.[16] This marks a second distinction between the two parties: While LAOS seeks to court support from the postauthoritarian Right, the PS tried to distance itself from it. This explains why, unlike the PS, LAOS is often viewed as a direct descendant of the postauthoritarian Far Right. The presence of older EPEN members in LAOS highlights some continuity between the postauthoritarian and the contemporary Far Right, which was absent in the case of PS. The third and most important difference is ideological. The PS established its political reputation by tactically adopting a nationalist position on the Macedonia issue but did not fully embrace nationalism. As discussed later, right after its initial success in the 1993 elections, the PS quickly turned to more moderate appeals seeking to squeeze into the political space separating PASOK from ND. Its liberal views on economic issues can go a long way to explain why Greek voters viewed the party as being on the Left of ND, despite its hard-line position on national ones.[17] By contrast, LAOS has a comprehensive nationalist worldview through

[15] Xenokratis Saklas, for example, a candidate of LAOS for the 2007 elections, says that he had joined PS in the 1990s for the same reason he joined LAOS: He believed in its stance on national issues, especially the Macedonian one. See http://www. laosver.gr/news/local/12886.html (LAOS, local newspaper in Imathia; 5 September 2007; last accessed November 2007).

[16] In his first appearance in the Greek parliament with LAOS, Karatzaferis stirred controversy by referring positively to the agricultural policy of the Greek junta. He asked the government to "write off the agricultural debts. The dictatorship did it. If the dictatorship can do it then so can democracy, because we are wider and of better quality than dictatorship." Official parliamentary minutes, "Continuation of the discussion on the Programmatic Statements of the Government," September 30, 2007, p. 426 [in Greek].

[17] According to an exit poll for the 1993 elections, voters' placement of PASOK on the Left-Right axis averaged 5.1. Political Spring's 7, and ND's 8.7. More than

which it filters its programmatic positions on both foreign policy and domestic issues. This worldview explains its frequent resort to anti-immigrant and anti-Semitic rhetoric. While the PS flirted with the idea of turning into a Greek reincarnation of the French National Front, this remained a minority view within the party.

An examination of party documents and newspaper reports as well as interviews with LAOS's top officials will further illuminate certain aspects of its ideology, leadership, and organization. Unlike the PS, LAOS is explicitly nationalist, seeking to protect "the Nation, the Genus, the Faith, the History and the cultural identity" of the Greeks. Given the historical association between the Greek nation and Greek religion, "faith in Orthodoxy" constitutes one of the "founding stones" of its ideology. In his televised speeches and public appearances, Karatzaferis makes frequent references to Orthodoxy and to the Greek Church, which he considers the "mother of the modern Greek state."[18] He is known to have had a close relationship with the late Greek Archbishop Christodoulos, with whom they agreed on issues such as the name of the Former Yugoslav Republic of Macedonia (FYROM) and the revision of history books. Because of the status and role of the church in Greek politics, Karatzaferis often uses this relationship as a source of legitimacy for his ideas. The explicit appeals to Greek Orthodoxy make LAOS different not only from the PS but also from most of its European counterparts, which are not as explicit on religious issues. Religious appeals also bring LAOS closer to the postauthoritarian Far Right, which made explicit appeals to Helleno-Christian values.

Like all European Far Right parties, LAOS makes xenophobic appeals, calling for the expulsion of illegal immigrants. According to LAOS, illegal immigration is the biggest "wound" in Greek society, undermining national security, increasing unemployment, and causing crime.[19] Angrily replying to questioning about her views on

---

half of PS voters placed themselves on positions 7–10 on the scale, while a fifth self-placed at 9 and 10; Γιάννης Μαυρής, «Το 'Προφίλ' της Πολιτικής Άνοιξης» *Καθημερινή*, 24 Οκτωβρίου 1993, σελ. 14 (Yiannis Mavris, "The 'profile' of the Political Spring" *Kathimerini*, October 24, 1993, p. 14).

[18] Program of the Popular Orthodox Party (2001), "LAOS: For a Greece that belongs to the Greeks." Athens: LAOS [in Greek].

[19] *Ibid.*

immigration, a candidate of the party for the 2004 national legislative elections put this quite succinctly: "I do not want an Albanian neighbor, but a Greek one. I prefer neighbors who will enter my house through the door at 6pm, not those who break into my house through the windows at 3am. If this makes me a far rightist, then I am!"[20] In his rhetorical outbursts, the leader of the party reinforces such xenophobic claims by asking: "Compare and pick: Greece of Greek Christians?[21] Or, Greece of Albanian illegal-immigrants?"[22] The anti-immigrant profile of the party has been bolstered by the absorption of the Hellenic Front, which was the most vocal opponent of immigration. But in recent years, LAOS has largely avoided earlier rhetorical excesses, in part because the issue has stayed on the sidelines of the mainstream debate. In its 2007 program, the party rejected "the solution of the multi-cultural society" and the welfare policies that "benefit Muslims and Gypsies by allowing them to live without the need to work." LAOS argues that Greece should use its cultural heritage and Greek education to make immigrant children "to be Greeks in soul and in spirit."[23]

The party is not only against immigration, but it is also suspicious of foreign powers, especially the United States. Its first program maintained that the "party was founded because foreign powers want to impose a new situation to our people, foreign and extraneous to the traditions of our race." Seeking to tap into widespread anti-American sentiments among the Greek populace, Karatzaferis accuses the two main parties for "slave-like" behavior toward the United States, which is leading the country "into a situation that is going to be worse than Nazism." Not surprisingly, the party is sympathetic to those who stand against the United States. Karatzaferis boasts to have a picture with Fidel Castro in his office and to be an admirer of Hugo Chávez. He is also sympathetic to China, "the only power that can pose a credible bulwark against American hegemony."[24] As he reassures his followers, "I have not suddenly become a Communist but Fidel is the symbol of resistance

---

[20] Interview #5, Athens, February 2004.
[21] This was one of the slogans of the Greek junta (Ελλάς Ελλήνων Χριστιανών).
[22] http://www.iospress.gr/ios2002/ios20021020a.htm (last accessed: September 28, 2007).
[23] LAOS, "Framework of Positions," August 2007, Athens [in Greek].
[24] Discussion with the author; Limassol, Cyprus; July 2006.

against the Americans, and the Americans are those plotting every-thing against Greece."[25]

The party's suspicion of Western powers is connected with its fer-vent anti-Semitism. Its proclamation asks the party's supporters to say "no" to "the puppets of foreign and domestic Zionism" and warns that Greeks "live in a country run by Jews." Such views are consistent with those of its leader, who in 1996, as a ND MP, tabled a formal query in the Greek parliament about the Jewish descent of the deputy foreign minister, Christos Rozakis. In May 2000, he claimed on his television show: "The prime minister is of Jewish descent. His grand-father was Aaron Avouris. George Papandreou has his grandmother, Mineiko, who was Polish-Jew. The entire government is run by Jews."[26] In private discussions, members of the party go even further than their leader: "Six million deaths. This is overblown! Hitler, a Jew, surely persecuted the Jews. But such numbers are exaggerated."[27]

---

[25] Λ. Σταυρόπουλος, "Ο 'κόκκινος' κ. Καρατζαφέρης" *Το Βήμα*, 4 Νοεμβρίου 2007, σελ. Α22 (L. Stavropoulos, "The 'red' Mr Karatzaferis" *To Vima*, November 4, 2007, p. A22).

[26] Ιός, "Ο Αγών του" *Ελευθεροτυπία*, 20 Οκτωβρίου 2002 (Ios, "His Kampf" *Eleftherotypia*, October 20, 2002).

[27] Interviews in the party's office with a high-ranking party official and a self-identified historian; Athens, February 2004. It is worth reciting in full this part of the discussion:

Party Official: We have nothing against Jews, and I want to really emphasize this. At a personal level, we have absolutely nothing against them. We are against Zionism, though. Jews and Zionism are two different things. In fact, Jews have been persecuted by Zionists.

[A self-proclaimed historian enters the room and sits with us; I take notes and let them continue the discussion among themselves].

Party Official: Six million deaths. This is overblown. Hitler, a Jew, surely perse-cuted the Jews. But such numbers are exaggerated.

"Historian:" The Jews live under a tragic dictatorship. You know they cannot even marry foreigners. Now tell me, is this democratic?

Party Official: [unclear name], a Jew, said himself that the Jews that died during World War Two were not six million. There were no six million Jews. The cre-matoria existed, the torturing took place, all this happened but not in the extent people think.

"Historian:" There were no crematoria!

Party Official: Yes, but if you say that, you are going to jail! I agree with you, but we cannot really say that. But let me ask Mr. Ellinas who comes from the United States: Why was there not a single Jew on the Twin Towers? Was it a coincidence that the Jews were the ones that filmed the planes hitting the towers?

"Historian:" And don't forget Joseph Isaac Jahuda, a Jewish historian. He argued that Hebrew has roots in ancient Greek. Have you ever heard him again? He simply disappeared. And let me tell you, it is the Jews that killed Kapodistrias

Like most of its European and Greek counterparts, LAOS rejects the term "Far Right," insisting that the placement of parties on a Left-Right scale is outdated. Karatzaferis rarely misses an opportunity to stress that "the party is on the Right on national issues and on the Left on social issues."[28] Indeed, the party makes a significant effort to appeal to leftist voters, especially workers, through fierce populist attacks on globalization, foreign chains, and commercial banks. During the party's first congress, in 2001, Karatzaferis associated Carrefour, a French-owned hypermarket, with totalitarianism. He also drafted a legislative bill to place ceilings on salaries based on a multiple of the minimum wage. Encapsulating the programmatic mix of social and nationalist policies, the third party congress, in February 2006, convened under the slogan "National and Popular" (Εθνικά και Λαϊκά). The emphasis the party places on social issues is sometimes reminiscent of left-wing or anti-plutocratic populism. In his first appearance in the Greek parliament in September 2007, the leader of LAOS asked the government to combat banks, which record the "biggest profits" in Europe. "This is not the product of labor but the product of theft. Bankers are thieves, Mr. Prime Minister, and you must send the attorney in to check" on the banks, he said.[29]

The organizational structure of LAOS revolves around the leadership of the party's president, both on statute and in practice. According to the party's Memorandum of Association, the president represents LAOS in all domestic and foreign functions, convenes and determines the agenda of the congress, expresses the party's ideology, appoints officials in key organizational posts, and establishes certain committees.[30] In practice, the party is under the firm control of Karatzaferis, who rarely convenes the Executive Office and who runs it with the help of close associates and employees from

[head of Greek state after 1827] because they did not want him to revive Greece, just as he did in other countries.

[28] Brief discussion with the author, February 2004, Athens.

[29] Official parliamentary minutes, "Continuation of the discussion on the Programmatic Statements of the Government," September 29, 2007, p. 195 [in Greek].

[30] The party's congress elects forty out of the ninety members of the Central Committee, which, in turn, elects ten out of the eleven members of the Executive Office. Apart from the Executive Office, there is also a Political Council, which is organized into thematic committees, paralleling those of the Greek Parliament. The party also has youth and student organizations, some with regional offices.

his small television station, Teleasty. As a member of the Executive Office suggested:

There is no organization in LAOS. There is a Central Committee, made up of 90 people and an Executive Office, made up of elected members and selected members (I am one of them). But the committee only met twice in the past two years. Mr Karatzaferis runs the show by himself. I believe he purposefully keeps the party so disorganized.[31]

What the party lacks in organization, it makes up through the television exposure Teleasty grants to party executives, by regularly having them on talk shows or by letting them host their own. Karatzaferis gains considerable visibility on his own daily show, in which one of his closest associates takes the role of the interviewer, asking Karatzaferis what appears to be a pre-agreed set of questions.[32] Teleasty does not only grant Karatzaferis recognizability and publicity, but it is also a major weapon for establishing the party's dominance among the various Far Right groupings. Karatzaferis has been using the channel as a means to lure competing Far Rightists to join forces with LAOS. The Front Line's founder, Constantine Plevris, for example, who was a party candidate for the 2004 legislative elections, has regular appearances on Teleasty. Access to Teleasty also convinced the leadership of the Party of Hellenism to join forces with Karatzaferis. "We realized from previous experience that regardless of how organized a party is, there needs to be a medium through which to project its ideas. The alliance with LAOS offered this medium."[33] Lacking such access, the leaders of another Far Right party, the Hellenic Front, spent most of their campaign time in 2004 on the road, addressing small crowds, disseminating pamphlets, and sticking posters. As a member of the Front complained, "when you do not have a medium, like Mr. Karatzaferis, then you have to rely on pamphlets, posters, and placards. Since this is the only means to become known, we have better results where we are organized enough to perform these basic activities."[34] Recognizing the importance of having access to Karatzaferis's small television station, the party suspended its operation in May 2005 and joined forces

[31] Interview #10, Athens, February 2004.
[32] The author observed one of the shows in the studios of Teleasty in Athens in March 2004.
[33] Interview #9, February 2004, Athens.
[34] Interview #7, February 2004, Athens.

with LAOS. Makis Vorides, its former leader, joined the Executive Committee of LAOS, and a number of other party functionaries became members of LAOS's Political Council. In 2007, he became an MP after more than two decades spent in the political wilderness.

Explaining the Trajectory of the Contemporary Far Right

While the contemporary Far Right has failed to establish a permanent presence in Greek politics, this quick sketch of its trajectory has high-lighted its brief spurts of electoral support. Analyses of the Greek Far Right that average its electoral performance over time tend to miss these spurts, treating them as outliers to an overall story of electoral failure. This section will show, however, that the electoral break-throughs of the Greek Far Right are not outliers but rather the result of processes similar to those identified in Austria and Germany. The remaining of this chapter will demonstrate how partisan competition over Greek identity created opportunities for the rise of ND splinter parties. And it will show how the varying treatment of these parties by the media helped or prevented them from turning these opportunities into electoral capital. The first part of this section will look at partisan competition and media coverage during the Macedonia crisis, which led to the rise of the Political Spring. The second part explores the sudden collapse of the Political Spring. The third part examines party and media behavior during the controversy over identity cards and investigates the impact of the controversy on the trajectory of LAOS.

The Macedonia Issue. Few issues have received as much scholarly attention in Greece as the country's dispute with the FYROM over its claim to what the Greeks considered to be an inseparable aspect of their national identity: the name "Macedonia." This attention is well justified, as no other issue has managed to raise nationalist and xenophobic fervor at such high levels as the Macedonia issue did. This section recounts the row over Macedonia, highlighting the role of political actors and media outlets in mobilizing public opinion. Because so much has been written on the events themselves, the study focuses on their impact on electoral change.[35] It shows how

---

[35] For an analysis of how political elites framed the issue, see Loizides 2005.

the conservatives played the nationalist card over Macedonia before international pressures compelled them to retract it. The perceived backpedaling of ND on the issue opened a window of opportunity for the rise of a splinter party, the Political Spring, which established a reputation for its hard-line, nationalist position. Aided by considerable media attention, the PS managed to stage a breakthrough in the 1993 elections.

The dispute over Macedonia broke out in late 1991 when the small former Yugoslav republic declared its independence from Belgrade and sought international recognition. Using its leverage within the EU, Greece made the recognition conditional on the name of the new entity and on its denouncement of territorial claims against Greece. The Greek government was most concerned about the references in the new state's constitution to a "Macedonian" nation, as it could create a minority problem in northern Greece, where a small number of Slavic Macedonians reside (Danforth 1995: 147–149; Roudometof 2002: 132–137). Although Greek apprehensions concentrated on the minority issue, the Greek foreign minister, Antonis Samaras, swiftly placed the "name" issue at the top of his foreign policy agenda (Skylakakis 1995). The basic claim of the Greek government was that "Macedonia" is a cultural and historical property of Greece, which cannot be claimed by its northern neighbor. Hence, Samaras demanded that the name of the new republic would not contain the word Macedonia or any of its derivatives.

To strengthen the Greek position, Samaras sought to mobilize public support for it. In February 1992, as diplomatic negotiations carried on, he engineered a huge rally for the "Greekness" of Macedonia in Salonica. With the help of the media, which gave wide coverage of the planned event, the rally drew more than a million people, one of the largest ever.[36] The unexpectedly high participation rate was a sign of the nationalist fervor that started sweeping the country over

---

[36] The media gave extensive coverage to the "pan-Macedonian" rally, heralding it as the largest gathering in northern Greece ever and encouraging citizens to participate. All mainstream newspapers ran front-page stories providing details for the planned rally, all public schools closed to let students attend it, and buses offered free transportation to it. Major television channels hosted a two-hour pre-show of the rally, which began with the national anthem and Greek flag graphics. For an insightful account of the way the Greek media covered the Salonica rally, see Toumbas 2001: 121–171.

the Macedonia issue. Many of the participants were covered with Greek flags, others were dressed with traditional Macedonian costumes, and a number of them carried banners reading: "Macedonia is, was and always will be Greek!" "Real Macedonians are Greek," "Macedonian History is Greek History." In his address to the rally, the mayor of Salonica and main organizer, Constantine Cosmopoulos (ND), captured the nationalistic momentum that was quickly spreading across the country:

> History is not an object of exchange. And of course it is not an object of theft because it belongs to us. It belongs to all of us Greeks. ... This government in Skopje [the capital of FYROM] has circulated currency with our symbols, even maps showing Salonica as their capital. They refer to Alexander the Great as a Slav, how dare they? This aggressive behavior can only be stopped by the strength of the Greeks. We Greeks are here. ... It is only logical that this little weak country will only get more aggressive as it gains strength. ... All this action taken by the Skopians [the citizens of FYROM] is ending up at one thing, it is uniting the Greeks. They led us to this historic gathering today and we are focusing on one thing, the preservation of our national identity. (cited in Toumbas 2001: 145)

The nationalistic outbursts of the organizers and the participants were amplified by extensive television coverage of the rally and by highly opinionated reports from journalists who acted more as participants than observers. Their biased reports fed the evening news bulletins, which went as far as arbitrarily using military jets as background to their coverage of the rally. Overall, the rally helped to mobilize public opinion against the small northern state: In 1992, pollsters found that 94% of those asked thought that the Greek government should not recognize the new state. Interestingly, more than a third advocated military action against FYROM (Toumbas 2001: 151).

The enormous popular resonance of the problem gave mainstream politicians incentives to enhance their political capital by radicalizing the Macedonia issue. In Germany or in Austria, the radicalization of national identity issues pitted the Left against the Right. But in Greece, radicalization followed a different pattern: public concerns encouraged mainstream parties to try to outbid each other on the preferred outcome of the row with FYROM. Both major parties adopted hard-line positions over the name of the new state, refusing to accept the compromises tabled by the European interlocutors. Conservative efforts were spearheaded by Samaras. Armed with pictures from the massive rally in Salonica, the Greek foreign minister warned his European counterparts that no Greek government can recognize the new state with the name Macedonia. His position was not fully shared by the prime minister, Constantine Mitsotakis, and many moderates within the conservative camp, who thought that the name issue was negotiable (Skylakakis 1995; Tziampiris 2000: 96–102). Aware of the divisions within the government party, the Socialist opposition sought to profit from the issue by outbidding the conservatives. In a time of national crisis, this issue presented the Pan-Hellenic Socialist Movement (Πανελλήνιο Σοσιαλιστικό Κίνημα, PASOK) with an opportunity to present itself as the true defender of the Greek nation (Keridis 1998: 206–208). Going further than Samaras, then, Socialist leader Andreas Papandreou (PASOK) put the issue on the legislative agenda and criticized the government for mishandling it. More importantly, he argued that the issue posed "threats against the nation and against our territorial integrity," insisting that Greece "cannot recognize the name Macedonia" in the new state. He welcomed the "reawakening of the nation" brought about by the rally and proposed the establishment of a "Legislature of Hellenism" composed of Greeks from the diaspora.[37] His views echoed those of his nationalist MP, Stelios Papathemelis, who repeatedly warned against dire consequences of compromise and called for the "reawakening of the whole Nation" and a counterattack against Greek enemies (Papathemelis 1992: 17–21).

The hard-line position of the foreign minister and the Socialist efforts to outbid him boxed Greek diplomacy into a position that was difficult to sustain internationally. The adverse international environment became evident when the European interlocutor tabled a proposal in April 1992 for naming the new entity "New Macedonia" despite Greek objections. Realizing the difficulty in convincing the international community about the name issue, the Greek prime minister entertained the idea of a negotiated solution, but his foreign minister adamantly refused any compromise. His insistence cost him his

---

[37] Official parliamentary minutes, "Discussion under the initiative of PASOK president on the Government's foreign policy course and the consequences on our National issues," February 24, 1992, pp. 4160–4181.

job in April 1992, yet, interestingly, the conservative prime minister continued to play the nationalist card, adopting the ousted foreign minister's intransigent position. So, in summer 1992, when FYROM applied to the UN for recognition and when its parliament endorsed the "Star of Vergina"[38] as its flag, Greece responded by blocking the delivery of oil to the landlocked state.

The insistence of the Mitsotakis government on the name issue was mostly because of domestic considerations, as repeated polls showed that Macedonia was becoming one of the top political concerns among the populace. After the Salonica rally, the media continued to flood public opinion with biased reports and to stir nationalist passions against the neighboring state. A characteristic example of how the media dealt with the issue was a call by a radio host, George Trangas, to boycott Danish, Dutch, and Italian products because of the unfavorable positions these countries held toward the Macedonia issue. His call led to a spontaneous nationwide boycott by both retailers and consumers that reportedly shrunk demand for Italian and Dutch products by 25% (Tziampiris 2000: 112–113).[39] Mainstream newspapers fed this xenophobic frenzy by presenting Greece as the righteous victim of a world conspiracy against the Greek nation. Some of the titles of Greek dailies are indicative of the way the Greek press handled the Macedonia issue: "We and the barbarians of Europe," "The Europe of idiots," and "Athens is a victim of a German Plot." In the seventeen months after the outbreak of the issue, in December 1991, the five largest Greek newspapers printed 1,883 stories in their Sunday editions related to Macedonia (Demertzis et al. 1999: 32–33). Their biased reporting caught the attention of the Union for Athens Dailies, which noted "instances of inexact reporting and unjustified editorializing" that is "foreign to the traditions and ethics of the journalistic world" (Toumbas 2001: 151).

The mobilization of public opinion on the Macedonia issue became a political liability for the conservative government when international pressures compelled it to moderate its intransigent position. By 1992, Greece confronted the specter of international isolation

---

[38] This is the emblem of the ancient Macedonian dynasty, found in northern Greece in the tomb of Philip the Second, the father of Alexander the Great.

[39] Although the government did not support the boycott, the then foreign minister, Samaras, described it as a "spontaneous, pure and patriotic" move.

not only in the United Nations, where it had limited political leverage, but also in the European Community. In a meeting of the New
Democracy's parliamentary group in October 1992, the new Greek
foreign minister, Michalis Papaconstantinou, signaled his intent to
moderate the Greek position when he warned that "unless we achieve
a solution on this issue we will then have to confront our own isolation" (cited in Tzampiris 2000: 148). He was largely responding to
pressures from moderate conservatives who argued that Greek insistence on the name issue was isolating Greece and damaging Greek
foreign policy. A number of them had already sent Mitsotakis a letter
criticizing his foreign policy adventures. When PASOK motioned a
no-confidence vote against the government in March 1993, one of the
most prominent members of the ND, former prime minister George
Rallis, gave up his parliamentary seat in protest against the nationalist
turn in Greek foreign policy (Rallis 1995: 40–43). But moves toward
a compromise also alienated the national conservative wing of the
party. Another prominent member of ND and its subsequent leader,
Miltiades Evert, threatened that he and his political friends would
stop supporting the government if Greece accepted any solution that
included the word "Macedonia" in the name of the new state (Keridis
1998: 226). The radicalization of the Macedonian question inadvertently split the party and threatened its slim majority. The final blow
for the government came in September 1993, when Samaras called
on ND MPs to withdraw their confidence from the government and
bring it down because it had become dangerous for the country. Only
two MPs did so, joining Samaras's newly founded Political Spring.
Having lost his parliamentary majority, Mitsotakis dissolved the parliament and called for new elections to be held in October.

   A single-issue party that sprung out of its leader's hard-line position
on Macedonia, Political Spring hoped to capitalize on Samaras's issue
credibility to fill the political space deserted by the conservatives. Its
plans confronted two main obstacles. First, the party had to compete
for the same space with PASOK, which had, in the meantime, increased
its nationalist rhetoric. Accusing the government of betraying national
interests, Papandreou pledged several times before the elections that
a Socialist government would never recognize the new state under a
name that includes the word Macedonia or its derivatives. He promised
to set in motion "a great patriotic movement ... to restore the dignity of

Greece, Epirus, Macedonia, Thrace, the Aegean and Cyprus all united
in a non-negotiable line of defense" (cited in Toumbas 2001: 170).
Earlier, the party had aired television commercials that were critical of
the conservatives' handling of the Macedonia issue, showing the lower-
ing of the Greek flag. Second, Political Spring had to overcome the challenge of organizing an electoral campaign at such short notice and with
so little organizational experience. Short campaigns pose significant
organizational challenges for all parties, but they are most taxing for
new parties that lack sophisticated organizational infrastructure.

To overcome its organizational shortcomings, the party relied on
the outsized media exposure Samaras enjoyed. Along with his intransigent position on Macedonia, Samaras's previous tenure in the foreign
ministry granted him considerable visibility in the mainstream media.
This increased after his highly publicized call on ND parliamentarians to bring the government down. Moreover, Political Spring made
up for its organizational deficiencies by spending significant resources
for television advertising. At a time when television started dominating the political information market, the newly founded party got as
much as 6% of the total advertising airtime political parties bought for
the 1993 campaign.[40] This was substantially higher than the combined
advertising airtime of the other two small parties: the Communist
Party and the Coalition of the Left (Συνασπισμός της Αριστεράς και
της Προόδου). More importantly, though, the PS received a lot of
favorable coverage from the mainstream media, such as the influential conservative daily *Kathimerini*. The coverage of PS contrasted
with that received by the ND leader and prime minister, Mitsotakis,
who ended up accusing the owner of *Kathimerini* for bribing Samaras
with a billion drachmas to form the new party in order to bring his
government down. Three days before the elections, Mitsotakis went
a step further, arguing that several media owners gave exposure to
the PS and were critical of his government because it denied them
lucrative media licenses and public contracts.[41] With the help of this

[40] According to Papathanassopoulos (2000: 48), in 1992, seven out ten Greeks (69%)
indicated that television was their source of daily information, compared to 15%
who got their information from the evening press and 11% who received it from
radio stations. The dominance of television in the Greek information market is also
confirmed by more recent data in Hallin and Mancini 2004: 23, 25.
[41] «Το κατάντημα ενός πρωθυπουργού» *Καθημερινή*, 6 Οκτωβρίου 1993, σελ. 1
("Come-down of a prime minister," *Kathimerini*, October 6, 1993, p. 1); «Και νέο

significant media exposure, Political Spring managed to surpass the institutional barriers posed by the majoritarian aspects of the Greek electoral law. Staging an important breakthrough, the party received 4.9% of the vote and became the third largest Greek party overnight. Nearly three-fourths of its voters, or 3.6%, defected from ND, while 0.8% came from PASOK and 0.5% from the Coalition of the Left.

Beyond Macedonia: The Collapse of the Political Spring. Political Spring managed to change the Greek electoral terrain overnight, but after another brief spurt in support in the 1994 European elections, the party fell out of favor with the Greek populace. In the 1996 national legislative election, PS support dropped to 2.9%, depriving the party of legislative representation. Its life cycle was almost identical with that of the Macedonia issue: As long as the issue topped the political agenda, the party managed to sustain its initial electoral gains. But once the issue became less salient – especially after the 1995 interim accord with FYROM that resolved all issues but the name – Political Spring, along with the Macedonia issue, disappeared from television screens and newspapers columns.[42] In part, its precipitous fall was because of its failure to develop the necessary intraparty structures to overcome the visibility obstacles the party now confronted. Having relied on the media for communicating with voters, the party had not set in place the organizational mechanisms to sustain voter and member support. An example of the negligence of standard organizational functions was that the party did not have a national congress for more than four years after its founding. This left the PS vulnerable to New Democracy, which sought to destabilize the political newcomer by recruiting PS members and officials. In January 1996, for example, ND announced the recruitment of four prominent PS members, two of whom had important organizational roles within

---

ατόπημα Μητσοτάκη» *Καθημερινή*, 7 Οκτωβρίου 1993, σελ. 1–2 ("A new foul from Mitsotakis," *Kathimerini*, October 7, 1993, pp. 1–2).
[42] Throughout the 1996 electoral campaign, Samaras complained several times that his party got no airtime. After the elections, he said: "I know we are alone. Without a newspaper, radio station or television that even smiles at the Political Spring"; Ντίνα Βαγενά, «Σαμαράς: Η χώρα μπαίνει σε γύρους υποχωρήσεων» *Ελευθεροτυπία*, 23 Σεπτεμβρίου 1996 (Dina Vagena, "Samaras: The country is entering a round of concessions," *Eleftherotypia*, September 23, 1996).

the new party.[43] The deficiencies of intraparty structures did not go unnoticed by the leader of the party, who attributed its electoral misfortunes to "organizational weaknesses."[44] But by the time the party leadership sought to address these weaknesses, its electoral fortunes had already waned.

Apart from organization, the most fundamental problem of PS was its inability to successfully extend its initial appeals beyond the Macedonia issue. During its first years of existence, the PS found itself in a similar position to that of the Austrian FPÖ during the Waldheim affair: By maintaining a maximalist position on the Macedonia issue, the PS managed to establish itself as a credible defender of Greek identity and to capture a significant part of the "national" space. But unlike the Haider FPÖ, the party failed to use this credibility to extend its appeals to related issues. For some party members, such as Nikitas Kaklamanis, the issue of immigration constituted an obvious programmatic extension. The rising number of immigrants and widespread Greek xenophobia seemed to make this issue an electoral winner. In the first party congress, Kaklamanis argued that the party should make a more decisive turn to the "patriotic" right by protecting Greek jobs and the Greek minority in Albania. He stated that Greeks should have priority over foreigners in the job market – "first the Greek, and then the foreign workers" – and called for the autonomy of the Greek minority in Albania. But his views were only supported by a small minority of party members. The majority supported the "centrist radical" course to which Samaras had stirred the party after its electoral breakthrough in 1993.[45] Unfortunately for the PS, its position in the competitive space was already "overcrowded" by the two main parties, dooming the party to political irrelevance. Far from being

---

[43] Μπάμπης Παπαπαναγιώτου, "Μάχη στην πασαρέλλα του εκσυγχρονισμού" *Ελευθεροτυπία*, 28 Ιανουαρίου 1996 (Babis Papapanayiotou, "Battle on the catwalk of modernization," *Eleftherotypia*, January 28, 1996).

[44] This was at the first party congress held in late May 1997; "Ναι σε επαφή, αλλά όχι να πάει σε γάμο" *Ελευθεροτυπία*, 31 Μαΐου 1997 ("Yes to contact, but no to marriage," *Eleftherotypia*, May 31, 1997).

[45] «Αυτόνομη πορεία και ακροδεξιά αμφισβήτηση» *Τα Νέα*, 31 Μαΐου 1997 ("Autonomous course and Far Right challenge," *Ta Nea*, May 31, 1997); «Ναι σε επαφή, αλλά όχι να πάει σε γάμο» *Ελευθεροτυπία*, 31 Μαΐου 1997 ("Yes to contact, no to marriage," *Eleftherotypia*, May 31, 1997).

distinctive, the Political Spring's vague appeals for state modernization echoed those of the liberal wing of New Democracy from which Samaras had originated. Such appeals pushed the Political Spring away from the "national" space in which it had thrived in the 1993 elections, thereby limiting its ability to sustain and extend its initial support.

The turn of the PS toward the political center coincided with an effort by ND to recapture the political space lost to the political newcomer through a hardening of its stance on foreign policy issues. The ND supported the controversial trade embargo that the new Socialist government imposed on FYROM in 1994 and the new pan-Macedonian rally organized against international reactions to the embargo. Moreover, the new conservative leader, Miltiades Evert, criticized the government for its failure to resolve the name issue in the 1995 interim accord. But it was a new confrontation with Turkey over the territorial status of the uninhabited Imia islets that allowed the conservatives to reclaim its credibility on "national" issues and to regain the political space lost to Samaras in 1993. The death of three Greek marines during a brief military encounter with Turkish warships in January 1996 rekindled nationalist fervor, putting considerable pressure on the newly elected Socialist Prime Minister Costas Simitis. Evert called the handling of the crisis "an act of treason" and staged an ND walkout from the parliamentary discussion of the Imia incident. The PS also walked out but avoided the vitriolic attacks of the conservative opposition. In the run-up to the 1996 elections, the conservative leader skillfully turned Imia into one of the most important campaign themes. By playing the nationalist card, he was able to regain most of the votes lost to the Political Spring in 1993. This proved insufficient for winning the elections because many PASOK deserters chose the newly founded Democratic Social Movement instead of ND. Led by Demetris Tsovolas, the party mixed national with social populist rhetoric, which further complicated the Political Spring's electoral efforts.

Simitis's victory in the 1996 election led to the partial de-escalation of foreign policy tensions and to the de-mobilization of nationalist fervor (Kazamias 1997). Whereas in the 1980s his predecessor had used Greco-Turkish tensions to mobilize latent nationalist sentiments,

Simitis adopted a more moderate policy toward Turkey.[46] Despite the nationwide outcry over the Öcalan affair and the mobilization against the Kosovo war in 1999, Simitis tried to stir Greek foreign policy away from national populist excesses. He was helped by two factors. The first was the leadership change in ND. The young Costas Karamanlis seemed to consent to this more moderate handling of national affairs, avoided nationalist rhetoric, and toned down conservative criticism of foreign policy. The most powerful factor, though, was the compassionate response of Greek and Turkish citizens to the earthquakes that shook the two countries in 1999. The earthquakes dissolved public perceptions of national antagonism and replaced them with feelings of mutual solidarity. This sudden shift in public attitudes removed the biggest obstacle to foreign policy moderation and reinforced the 180-degree change in the Greek position toward EU membership for Turkey. The growing moderation in Greek foreign policy transformed the political climate, removing much of the nationalist rhetoric from the mainstream political debate. Unlike the 1996 elections, in which national matters such as Imia dominated the campaign, the 2000 elections were preoccupied with domestic issues, especially with the sharp fall of the stock exchange.[47]

Identity Cards and New Political Opportunities. While the de-escalation of foreign policy tensions eliminated a major issue from partisan competition, in April 2000, a different issue emerged over a regulatory decision to remove references to religious affiliation from Greek identity cards.[48] The decision led to a protracted political row

---

[46] Simitis represented the modernists within PASOK, who were critical of its national populist excesses. In the late 1980s, he had criticized PASOK's draft of a new declaration of principles for its ethnocentrism and parochialism (Dimitras 1992: 251–252). In his prologue to his 1992 book, he warned against "the wind of nationalist populism that blew into the country" and about the "nationalist outburst that distorted our understanding of international developments" (Simitis 1992: 9).

[47] During the month before the elections, more than half the top stories in *Eleftherotypia*, for example, were about the stock exchange crash. During the televised debate between the two candidates, national identity issues were not discussed at all. Out of the many questions that were asked, there was only a question about relations with Turkey. Γιώργος Καρέλιας, «Ισοπαλία υπέρ Σημίτη», *Ελευθεροτυπία*, 31 Μαρτίου 2000, σελ. 1 (George Karelias, "Draw in favor of Simitis," *Eleftherotypia*, March 31, 2000, p. 1).

[48] For identification purposes, a Greek identity card is equivalent to an American driver's license.

over Greek identity between the Socialist government and the conservative opposition. The debate furnished Karatzaferis with an opportunity to enter the mainstream debate, gain media visibility, and legitimize his ethnocentric claims. When the conservatives sought to de-radicalize the issue, Karatzaferis capitalized on his enhanced media visibility to stage a notable breakthrough in the 2002 municipal elections. Initially, the Far Right's advance in this secondary election failed to improve its electoral standing at the national level because of the lack of media visibility. But in the past few years, the party has successfully overcome its visibility obstacles and staged an important breakthrough in the 2007 elections.

The event that triggered the radicalization of Greek politics over national identity was a seemingly unimportant decision of a regulator in April 2000 to remove religious affiliation from identification cards because it was considered personal information. This outraged many Greeks, who thought that the decision questioned the "indissoluble links between Orthodoxy and the nation" (Prodromou 2004: 70). The decision gave way to sizable rallies organized by church hardliners with the tacit support of conservative politicians.[49] The issue received a lot of media coverage for days, which increased its public resonance. The leftist daily *Eleftherotypia*, for example, printed thirty of its sixty top front-page stories on this in the two months that followed the decision. And there was at least one article about identity

---

[49] To understand how the seemingly unimportant issue about identity cards raised concerns about national identity, it is important to appreciate the relation between Greek Orthodoxy and Greek nationalism. Since the initiation of the Greek War of Independence in 1821, religion has been one of the most important national demarcation lines, and it continues to serve as a point of reference for the Greek nation (Mavrogordatos 2003: 128). Upon independence, Orthodoxy gained constitutional stature that gave it institutional autonomy and laid the ground for its tight relationship with the state. This close connection of the church with the state proved too sacred for any government to tamper with. In the past thirty years, both Socialists and conservatives have avoided dealing with the separation of the state from the church and comfortably bypassed the issue in the 1998 constitutional revision, although 48% of the population was supportive of the separation – compared to 39% who were against it (VPRC 2000: 234). Because of the traditional role of the church in state affairs, priests have always found it natural to discuss political matters, especially foreign policy. Church intervention in state affairs became even more evident after the accession of Archbishop Christodoulos in 1998, whose energetic rhetoric and fashionable style afforded him a lot of media attention. He died in 2008.

cards in forty-six of its sixty cover pages.[50] In the weeks that followed the announcement of the decision, tens of thousands of angry demonstrators took to the streets with Byzantine emblems and national flags, while clerics themselves threatened taking up arms against the government. Three months after the issue came out, only 31% agreed with the governmental decision, whereas 60% disagreed.[51]

As with the case of Macedonia, the public resonance of the identity cards issue encouraged the conservatives to politicize it. Tempted by the broad appeal of religion in society and constrained by the over-representation of churchgoers in the conservative ranks, ND probably saw a chance to enhance its electoral capital.[52] Hence, ND launched an attack against the government, questioning the legal grounds of the decision and seeking to undermine efforts to separate the church from the state. The leader of ND was among the first signatories during a signature drive organized by the church to demand a referendum on the issue – an authority reserved for the legislature.[53] Moreover, ND took the issue to the Greek parliament drafting a bill that accommodated the church's position. The 10-hour debate of this bill in July 2000 soon turned into a battle between the government and the opposition about the definition of "Greekness." The conservatives rejected efforts to discard references to religious affiliation from Greek identity cards because Orthodoxy is closely tied with Greekness. As Eleftherios Papanikolaou (ND) put it:

The identity of Greeks is intimately related through the ages with Orthodoxy. They are the two interrelated constituents of our historic identity. Orthodoxy and Hellenism are the two powerful elements of our historical continuity and coherence. ... The Greeks owe their freedom to their faith in Christ and their

---

[50] Author's analysis of newspaper covers of *Eleftherotypia* in April and May 2000.
[51] Γιώργος Λακόπουλος, «Η απόρρητη έρευνα Σημίτη για την Εκκλησία», *Το Βήμα*, 2 Ιουλίου 2000 (G. Lakopoulos, "The confidential report by Simitis for the Church," *To Vima*, July 2, 2000).
[52] According to a poll by Metron Analysis, conducted in May 2000, opposition to the decision increased with frequency of church attendance. See http://www.metronanalysis.gr/gr/polls/pub4311/index_files/frame.htm (last accessed: January 3, 2008).
[53] According to a Metron Analysis poll, conducted in October 2000, 33.2% of ND voters in the 2000 elections had already signed the church's signature list, compared to 6.6% of PASOK voters and 10.2% of other voters. See http://www.metronanalysis.gr/gr/polls/pub4483/index_files/frame.htm (last accessed: January 3, 2008).

identity was formed in the Orthodox Church. The Greek Orthodox mind gave birth to freedom fighters. The fighters and heroes of 1821 accomplished the miracle because they fought for the holy faith of Christ and for the freedom of the homeland.

Similarly, Panayiotes Psomiades (ND) argued that the identity cards raised the issue of the preservation of Greek identity: "We say 'yes' to globalization, but we should not sell our cultural heritage, this powerful element of our national conscience. I believe that in Europe there is also place for Orthodoxy, this pure, 24-carat jewel, which some of you want to throw away and to mix with mud." Highlighting the link between Greek Orthodoxy and Greekness, conservatives rejected efforts by "leftist internationalists" to undermine the influence of the church.[54]

By contrast, the Socialist government viewed the issue as part of efforts to integrate the growing number of foreigners to Greek society by transforming old state structures and adjusting them to match the new demographic realities. As Stavros Benos (PASOK) noted in parliament: "Our country, due to its growth, has become a regional power. The price, though, is this volume of economic migrants which – let us not fool ourselves – will grow in the years to come. Hence, the biggest challenge is the creation of a true multicultural society, where the rule of law will protect all citizens in their civic activities." Moreover, PASOK related the issue with the need to separate the church from the state.[55]

Previous chapters have suggested that the radicalization of national identity issues provides the impetus for the genesis of new Far Right parties and for the revitalization of older ones. In Germany, for example, the *Wende* facilitated the founding of the Republikaner, which had splintered from the CSU. And in Austria, the controversy over the Nazi past increased the political capital of Jörg Haider, revitalizing the nationalist flank of the FPÖ. The controversy over Greek identity cards had a similar impact in Greek party politics, leading to

---

[54] Yiannis Marinos, an ND member of the European parliament, made this argument in Γιάννης Μαρίνος, «Τώρα επωφελείται η κυβέρνηση », *Το Βήμα*, 27 Αυγούστου 2000, σελ. 59 ("Now the government benefits," *To Vima*, August 27, 2000, p. 59).

[55] Parliamentary minutes, July 6, 2000.

the genesis of LAOS. Founded in September 2000, the party sought
to profit from the radicalization of the issue, positioning itself as the
defender of Greek Orthodoxy.

At first, the appearance of LAOS did not seem threatening for
the conservatives, who were able to sustain their firm position on
the cards issue, despite some internal disagreements.[56] But as the
municipal elections of 2002 approached, the conservatives realized
the need to moderate their position in order to extend their appeal
to the centrist voters. Their main efforts concentrated in the Greater
Athens "super prefecture," which was the most visible of the many
municipal confrontations between the government and the opposition because of the size of the electorate – a third of Greek voters. In
line with such efforts, the ND candidate for Greater Athens was the
journalist Yiannis Tzannetakos, who was very critical of the church
and Archbishop Christodoulos when the identity cards issue broke
out in 2000. The centrist strategy of ND furnished the Far Right with
an opportunity to capture the political space New Democracy was
perceived as deserting. The backpedaling of the ND allowed the Far
Right candidate for the Greater Athens elections and leader of LAOS,
Karatzaferis, to present himself as the only true defender of Greek
Orthodoxy.

To do so, Karatzaferis relied on outsized media publicity granted to
his candidacy by the mainstream media. During the six weeks of the
electoral campaign, there were many newspaper references to the Far
Right candidate. Exposure of the Far Right did not only come from
leftist newspapers, such as *Ta Nea* and *Eleftherotypia*, but also from
the conservative *Kathimerini* (Table 5.2). Moreover, television channels
would give Karatzaferis prime time, hosting him on their main evening
news bulletins, on talk shows, and on television panels. Furthermore,
Karatzaferis would also appear daily in his two-hour television program hosted by his own nationwide albeit marginal channel, Teleasty.
Television appearances would generously give Karatzaferis what most
politicians pay fortunes to get through advertising: recognizability. By

---

[56] Moderate conservatives and liberals, like Marieta Yiannakou and Stephanos
Manos, disagreed with the stance of the party and with the mass mobilization
organized by the church. Σοφία Γιαννάκα, «Ο Αρχιεπίσκοπος ενώνει τη ΝΔ», *Το
Βήμα*, 25 Ιουνίου 2000, σελ. 16 (Sofia Yiannaka, "The Archbishop unites New
Democracy," *To Vima*, June 25, 2000, p. 16).

TABLE 5.2. *Newspaper Coverage of "Greater Athens" 2002 Elections**

Newspaper Articles	Kathimerini	Eleftherotypia	Nea	Total
Karatzaferis (LAOS)	39	89	49	177
Gennimata (PASOK)	57	130	62	249
Tzanetakos (ND)	97	163	133	393
Total	193	382	244	819

* September 1, 2002 to October 13, 2002; references to main candidates in major newspapers.
Source: Author's analysis.

the end of the campaign, so much was the airtime allotted to the Far Right candidate that his rivals had to complain that he got more television minutes than all of them combined.[57]

Socialist tacticians helped boost the exposure of LAOS in the media by skillfully and purposefully highlighting New Democracy's links to the Far Right. Just ten days before the election, PASOK accused ND of shady dealings with Karatzaferis and managed to turn the extreme Right into the major theme of the campaign. By highlighting ND's Far Right links, PASOK tried to scare away leftist votes and block New Democracy's centrist turn. At the same time, PASOK saw an opportunity to split New Democracy and to prevent an alliance between the conservatives and the Far Right in the second and most crucial round of the elections. The analysis of newspaper coverage during the campaign demonstrates the impact of Socialist tactics on the Far Right's exposure. While during the first four weeks of the campaign three of the top Greek dailies (*Ta Nea*, *Eleftherotypia*, and *Kathimerini*) mentioned the phrase "Far Right" only 7 times, in the last two weeks, they mentioned it 130 times. In the last few days, the Far Right issue almost monopolized the debate, boosting the exposure of Karatzaferis. *Kathimerini*'s main headline on the day of the election – "The Karatzaferis Construct" – epitomized the success of PASOK's tactic: It transformed the previously unimportant LAOS

[57] This is what Manolis Glezos, a Leftist leader, stated in an interview and a press conference during the last days of the electoral campaign for the municipal elections. Χριστίνα Κοραή, «Δικομματισμός, κανάλια επωάζουν το αυγό του φιδιού», *Ελευθεροτυπία*, 12 Οκτωβρίου 2002 (Christina Korai, "Bipartisanship and TV channels hatch the snake's egg," *Eleftherotypia*, October 12, 2002).

into a highly visible political force. With the help of the media, then, Karatzaferis was able to capitalize on the favorable opportunity structure and achieve a notable breakthrough at the municipal elections.

For new parties, advances in secondary elections can be a stepping stone for breakthroughs at the national level. Local breakthroughs are usually amplified by the media, conferring unproven parties with prominence and respectability (Kitschelt with McGann 1995: 99–100). Indeed, the immediate aftermath of the municipal elections put media spotlights on LAOS and gave rise to alarmist accounts about the rise of a Le Penist Far Right in Greece. Such alarmism was reinforced by surveys carried out in 2002, which showed that one out of five Greeks thought the country had room for a party like the French National Front. Moreover, almost a third of Greek voters thought that Greece needed a party that aimed at the deportation of illegal immigrants (Kolovos 2005: 39–41). Realizing the importance of the immigration issue for the Greek electorate, LAOS gradually extended its nationalist rhetoric to include immigration. In its pamphlets for the 2004 national legislative elections, the party argued that the flow of illegal immigrants to Greece is the "most serious wound afflicting Greek society." During the 2004 campaign, its candidates sought to profit from widespread Greek xenophobia, arguing that the country is facing a grave security threat from Albanian immigrants who are involved in criminal activities and who steal Greek jobs.[58] The timing of antiforeigner appeals was opportune, as the conservatives' centrist turn limited their ability to address the immigration concerns LAOS raised. But this time, mainstream media refused to give the party a forum to disseminate its messages. An analysis of official data shows that during the campaign, major television channels granted to LAOS only 215 minutes, a mere 0.5% of the total coverage given to Greek political parties (Table 5.3).[59] Unable to sustain the visibility it had earlier enjoyed, LAOS relied almost entirely on the exposure granted

---

[58] Several interviews with LAOS candidates, February 2004, Athens.
[59] The council published data for the first phase of the campaign, from January 7 to February 10, 2004. The author was unable to find data for the latter phase (the elections were held on March 7, 2004), despite several official requests. LAOS got disproportionate – and almost exclusive – coverage from Karatzaferis's Teleasty, but the channel is very marginal. The channel does not even rank on the list of AGB Hellas, the rating agency for television stations.

TABLE 5.3. *Television Airtime of Greek Parties**

Channel	PASOK	ND	KKE	SYN	DIKKI	LAOS	Journalists	Other
NET	3,901	2,598	670	720	78	35	358	147
ET1	60	60	9	35	0	0	0	0
ET3	1,619	1,163	288	259	71	11	10	0
MEGA	2,611	1,880	213	256	19	10	353	178
ANT1	2,257	1,832	269	95	55	59	179	67
ALPHA	4,122	3,596	474	526	102	16	657	113
STAR	2,599	2,162	200	299	96	48	212	146
ALTER	2,790	2,295	192	372	105	36	534	66
Total	19,959	15,586	2,315	2,562	526	215	2,303	717
Total (%)	45.2	35.3	5.2	5.8	1.2	0.5	5.2	1.6

* January 7 to February 10, 2004 (in minutes).
Source: National Council for Radio and Television, printed in Eleftherotypia, February 26, 2004.

to it by Karatzaferis's marginal channel. In the elections, the party received 2.2% of the national vote, below the 3% threshold necessary for legislative representation.

While the failure of LAOS to win legislative representation became the source of doubt for its future survival, the return of ND enhanced the structure of opportunity available for its future growth. When in opposition, the conservatives had more flexibility to maneuver on the issues that feed Far Right support. But once in government, they became compelled to balance their electoral motivations with their governmental responsibilities. The tension between the two became obvious only weeks after the new government took office, in April 2004, over a UN plan for the reunification of Cyprus. Whereas the Socialist PASOK was unambiguously supportive of the plan, ND avoided taking a clear stance on the issue, leaving LAOS as the most vocal defender of a "patriotic" no to the UN proposal.[60] This allowed

[60] The Greek Communists also rejected the UN proposal, albeit for different – anti-American, anti-imperial – reasons. On the day of the referenda in Cyprus over the UN plan, on April 24, 2004, the newspaper of LAOS, *Alpha 1*, proclaimed that the [Greek] Cypriots "stamp with their NO the refusal of Hellenism to unconditionally surrender to the plans and the demands of Americano-Zionists." See "Υπάρχουν ακόμα Έλληνες" *Αλφα 1*, σελ. 1 ("Greeks still exist," *Alpha 1*, p. 1).

the party to capitalize on the divisions created within ND over the UN plan, ahead of the June 2004 European elections. Aware of these potentially costly divisions, the governing party sought to limit defections to LAOS by recruiting back the former leader of Political Spring, Samaras, and giving him a visible spot on ND's European ballot. But despite these tactical maneuvers, LAOS managed to win 4.1% of the national vote in the European elections, gaining 90,000 additional votes and one seat in the European parliament.

The minor breakthrough in the European elections helped to dispel doubts about the viability of the party and give it the institutional legitimacy it was lacking. Karatzaferis used his Strasbourg seat to present LAOS as a legitimate player in Greek politics and enhance its visibility in the national media. To do so, he frequently bombarded the European Commission with questions on Greek "national" issues, promoting his views through the Eurosceptic Independence/Democracy Group in the European Parliament. During the first couple of years, though, the efforts to improve the public profile of LAOS did not yield the expected results. Major Greek television channels avoided giving LAOS much exposure, ignoring their institutional obligation to do so.[61] According to the data published by the Greek media regulator (Table 5.4), the party got less prime-time exposure than the 2.2% it received in the 2004 national elections. Although bipartisanship makes all small parties suffer from limited media attention in Greece, the exposure the other two parties – KKE and SYN – enjoyed exceeded their results in the last legislative elections. Among small parties, only the prime-time coverage of LAOS was systematically lower than its result in the last national vote.

In the period prior to the September 2007 legislative elections, two main issues furnished LAOS with opportunities to overcome the visibility problems it faced. The first was the resurfacing of the Macedonia issue because of the application of the country for entry into NATO and into the EU. Greece being a member of both organizations, the application confronted the conservative government with a new international crisis because of the name issue. While a growing number of

---

[61] According to directives 5/8.7.2003, 6/16.2.2004 and 1/12.2.2007 of National Council for Radio and Television, television channels have to give coverage to all political parties represented in the Greek and European parliament in approximation with their electoral support in the previous national legislative elections.

TABLE 5.4. *LAOS: Exposure on Major Television Channels,*
2005–2006
(Major News Bulletins, %)

Channel	Sep '05**	Oct '05	Nov '05**	Mar '06	Jul '06	Sep '06*	Oct '06	Nov '06	Dec '06
NET	0	0.28	0.77	0.26	0	0.32	1.08	0.07	0.26
MEGA	0	1.11	2.55	0	1.05	0	0	0.17	0.33
ANTι	0	1.28	0	1.54	0	0	0.76	0.60	0.39
ALPHA	1.02	0.66	0	4.24	0	0.44	0.78	0.13	0.17
ALTER	0	1.28	0	0.54	0	0	0.62	0	0.89
STAR	1.61	1.22	0	0.28	0	0	0.33	0.48	0.19

* First half; ** second half.
Source: Newspaper reports; National Council for Radio and Television data. I am grateful to Yiannis Kolovos for making these available.

countries recognized FYROM as the Republic of Macedonia, Greece continued to object to the use of this name and insisted that its northern neighbor use a derivate of Macedonia. Because Greece has a veto in both organizations, the conservative government could increase its domestic political capital by blocking the application process. But this risked the possibility of international isolation, similar to the one the country confronted in the mid-1990s. To avoid this, the conservatives sought to moderate public expectations by stressing the need for a "realistic" solution to the problem, hence preparing the ground for political compromise. Unlike the mid-1990s, they also refrained from the mass mobilization through public rallies. This left LAOS defending a maximalist position with a relatively high public resonance, especially in northern Greece. The party's 2007 program insisted that the new name should not include the word "Macedonia" at all and that Greece should veto FYROM's EU accession if this condition is not met.[62] As negotiations between the two countries and the UN mediator continued, the firm position of LAOS on the Macedonia issue boosted its visibility in the national media.

But the most important boost to the party's visibility was the controversy that broke out in 2007 about a new history textbook

---

[62] LAOS, "Framework of Positions," August 2007, Athens, pp. 21–22 [in Greek].

for twelve-year-olds. Introduced in September 2006, the new text-book sought to eliminate the nationalist overtones of the previous textbook, especially in its references to Turkey. But the textbook soon came under fierce attack by the church and by some conserva-tives for minimizing the suffering incurred by the Greeks under the Ottomans and during the flight of the Greeks from Smyrna (modern day Izmir, in Turkey) in 1922. The critics considered the revision-ist views presented in the textbook to be unpatriotic and pointed to historical inaccuracies, questioning the credentials of its authors. The issue divided the conservative camp between those who demanded the immediate withdrawal of the book and those who rejected this on institutional grounds. Among the former were prominent members of New Democracy, such as the Salonica prefect, Panayiotis Psomiades, and the ND MP, Yiannis Ioannides. Responding to this criticism, the conservative government asked various academic bodies to send comments to the drafters of the textbook to be taken into consider-ation for future revisions. But the ND education minister, Marieta Yiannakou, refused to give in to pressures for the withdrawal of the book. "The book will not be withdrawn," she said in the Greek par-liament in March 2007. While accepting that the book "has many problems," she insisted that these could be fixed by the next academic year through the normal institutional procedures.[63] Her insistence gained Yiannakou sympathy among the Left but aggravated certain members of her party, who felt that the government was supportive of an unpatriotic view of history.

The politicization and divisiveness of the issue boosted the vis-ibility of LAOS in the national media, which joined the church in demanding the immediate withdrawal of the textbook. During the protracted controversy over the textbook, the party was invited to the various panels to discuss the issue and was regularly hosted on prime time television news programs. So much was the attention granted to LAOS, that it raised suspicion among political commentators that the party was patronized by Socialist-controlled media. This suspi-cion was later vocalized and reinforced by the Greek Communists, who accused the Socialists of "directing" certain media to give LAOS

[63] Official parliamentary minutes, March 15, 2007, pp. 6616–6617.

excessive exposure.[64] While the Communists did not present any evidence at the time to substantiate these claims, subsequent data show that the national media gave much more attention to LAOS than its electoral standing would have justified. In the last month of the 2007 campaign, Karatzaferis received 9% of all television and radio references to political leaders; in the last week, Karatzaferis got 11% of all references, more than the leaders of SYRIZA and KKE.[65] Unlike before, in the 2007 campaign, the party managed to overcome previous visibility barriers, becoming a vocal contender in Greek politics, especially on national identity issues.

The increased visibility of LAOS complicated conservative efforts to prevent defections of ND voters. During the 2007 campaign, Karamanlis made last-minute attempts to appeal to potential defectors by hardening his stance on the Macedonia and textbook issues. In his last campaign rallies, he appealed to the "new patriotism" created after the destructive wildfires that shocked Greece in August, asking voters to raise only the Greek flag rather than party flags.[66] Moreover, the conservatives gave Rightist politicians a visible role in the campaign, especially in northern Greece, where LAOS enjoys disproportionately high support. For example, the ND leader campaigned in Salonica with the ND prefect, Panayiotis Psomiades, whose nationalist positions are very similar to those of Karatzaferis. It was thought that people such as Psomiades could facilitate the return of disillusioned ND voters, especially in non-urban districts, where it was easier to track them. In addition, the governing party sought to benefit from the presence of a new party, the Democratic Renaissance (Δημοκρατική Αναγέννηση), by helping it get exposure. Founded by the maverick ND MP and former PASOK minister and MP Stelios Papathemelis, the party had very similar positions with those of LAOS, especially on the Macedonia and textbook issues and sought to actively recruit former LAOS members.[67] Despite the novelty of the

[64] See footnote 4 in Chapter 1.
[65] Media Metrix, "Political Thermometer," September 25, 2007 [in Greek].
[66] Έλλη Τριανταφύλλου, "Μήνυμα για 'καθαρή εντολή'" *Καθημερινή*, 14 Σεπτεμβρίου 2007 (Elli Triantafyllou, "Message for 'clear mandate'," *Kathimerini*, September 14, 2007).
[67] The Democratic Renaissance was originally founded in 2003 but remained dormant until 2007, when it had its first congress. It is a national populist party, which, like LAOS, seeks to promote Greek Orthodox values. Papathemelis was

party, ND agreed to its participation in the highly publicized "political leaders' debate" a few days before the elections.[68] This helped give the party much more exposure than it would have received otherwise. Indeed, in the four weeks before the election, Papathemelis received 5.4% of all television and radio references to political leaders, largely because of exposure by publicly owned media.[69] At the election, the party received 0.8% of the national vote, getting considerable support in Salonica, where Papathemelis has his base. Despite these defections to the Democratic Renaissance and despite ND efforts to reclaim the political space lost to Karatzaferis, LAOS managed to stage a significant breakthrough by receiving 3.8% of the national vote and winning ten seats in the national parliament. Drawing most of its strength in urban areas where it received 5% to 6% of the national vote, the party elected six MPs in the broader Attica basin and two in Salonica.[70]

Conclusion

Given the recency of these developments, one can only speculate about the future of LAOS. Will it follow the fate of the Political Spring and vanish from the electoral map in the next few years? Or will it be able

a member of the Greek parliament between 1974 and 2007, a government minister under PASOK, an author, and a regular contributor to major Greek dailies. Throughout the campaign, he sought to distance his party from LAOS by calling Karatzaferis a "Greek Le Pen." Unlike LAOS, the Democratic Renaissance considered the possibility of a post-electoral alliance with ND.

[68] The "debate" is the most highly televised campaign event in Greece. Participation in the debate is subject to inter-party negotiation rather than specific rules, allowing major parties to determine the visibility granted to smaller parties. In 2004, for example, Karatzaferis was excluded from the debate because his party had no national or European parliamentary presence. But this same condition did not prevent the participation of his rival, Papathemelis, in the 2007 debate.

[69] «Καραμανλή 'έπαιξαν' τα ΜΜΕ», *Παρόν*, 16 Σεπτεμβρίου 2007 ("The media 'played' Karamanlis," *Paron*, September 16, 2007).

[70] About 40% of its voters had voted for ND in 2004, 11% had voted for PASOK, and 32% had voted for LAOS. According to the biggest exit poll, by VPRC (N=7.498), LAOS voters are overrepresented among young males with secondary education and among small business owners, professionals, managers, or private sector employees. There is no distinction among employed and unemployed LAOS voters (4% of each group voted for LAOS). LAOS attracted 18% of all protest votes, as many as SYRIZA and less than the Communist Party but slightly more than PASOK. VPRC/Kathimerini, special edition, September 18, 2007 [in Greek].

to sustain and extend its initial electoral gains? The framework developed here suggests that the future of LAOS will largely depend on factors endogenous to the party. The analysis of the Political Spring's collapse suggests that the survival of LAOS will depend on its capacity to broaden its appeals and to build its organizational infrastructure. Unlike the Political Spring, LAOS espouses a comprehensive nationalist ideology that allows it to make broad appeals on an entire range of issues beyond "national" ones. The most important of these other issues is immigration, one of high public resonance.[71] If LAOS uses its legislative and media presence to politicize this issue, it might be able to establish credibility on an issue that mainstream parties will have enormous difficulty addressing. An equally important factor for the future trajectory of LAOS relates to its organizational capacity. So far, the party has relied on the media to communicate with voters, setting aside the important task of organizational growth. Seven years after its founding, the party still lacks the necessary structures to mobilize voters and disseminate its newly gained resources. It also lacks the mechanisms to resolve intraparty conflicts. Unless the party builds its organizational capacity, it will become vulnerable to conservative co-optation strategies and fall victim to infighting between its radical and moderate members. Without solid organizational roots, LAOS might simply replicate the short trajectory of the Political Spring.

If the fate of LAOS largely lies in its own hands, what does this mean for mainstream parties? The question is most pressing for ND, from which LAOS draws most of its support. Should the conservatives try to reclaim the political space lost to LAOS by becoming tougher on issues such as Macedonia, EU membership for Turkey, or immigration? Or should ND combat the Far Right agenda and remain focused on making further inroads into the political center at the expense of PASOK? The new Karamanlis government seems to be inclined to co-opt rather than combat the agenda of the political newcomer. For example, one of the first decisions of the new government was to withdraw the controversial history textbook, as LAOS had demanded prior to the elections. The analysis here suggests that

---

[71] Greece has one of the highest levels of xenophobia in Europe. Almost seven out of ten Greeks think that immigrants are a threat to their way of life, by far the biggest percentage among the EU15. See Eurobarometer 199, 2003, p. 28.

this strategy is likely to be ineffective or, even, counterproductive. Rightward shifts on the national identity axis are likely to further legitimate the nationalist agenda of LAOS. Moreover, such shifts can pose significant problems for the conservatives, who, unlike LAOS, lack the flexibility to maneuvre in the competitive space. As long as LAOS remains in opposition, it can afford to move farther to the Right whenever ND seeks to regain ownership of its signature issues.

ND insiders are likely to disagree with this part of the analysis. They seem to be convinced that the "Sarkozy strategy" of co-optation is the most effective strategy to regain the votes lost to LAOS. Their assessment, though, seems to rely on a superficial analysis of French electoral politics that ignores two decades of failed conservative co-optation efforts. It is now the time, then, to examine in more detail French party politics and the rise of the best-known Far Right party.

6

The Growth, Persistence, and Fall of the French National Front

To develop its theoretical framework, this book carefully analyzed the two "most similar" cases of Germany and Austria and compared them with the "most different" case of Greece. It showed that despite marked differences between the Greek and the other country cases, a similar process shaped the electoral trajectory of the Far Right. To probe the generalizability of this framework, the last empirical chapter of this book examines the case of the French Far Right. There are important empirical and theoretical reasons for choosing France as a test case for the theory developed in the earlier chapters. Empirically, this is one of the most important cases in Europe because in the past few decades, the National Front (FN) has become a potent and permanent force in French politics. Despite the strong majoritarian qualities of the French electoral system, the party has averaged more than 9% in all but the most recent national legislative elections since 1986. Jean-Marie Le Pen, who failed to collect the 500 signatures necessary to run for the 1981 presidential elections, staged the biggest upset in modern French politics by making it to the second round of the 2002 presidential elections.

Apart from its empirical significance, the French case is also important for theoretical reasons: It offers a great opportunity to go beyond the particularities of the Austrian case and further examine the effect of party-specific variables on the electoral performance of the Far Right. The analysis of the FPÖ showed that such variables cannot sufficiently account for its initial breakthrough. But because of the particularities of the Austrian case, the impact of party-specific attributes could not be thoroughly examined. First, the constant – albeit minor – presence of the FPÖ in the Austrian party system reduced the visibility obstacles that many of its less successful counterparts confront. Its legislative presence since the 1950s granted it media access, financial resources, and organizational infrastructure that most Far Right startups lack. Second, the ideological appeal of the FPÖ varied considerably from that of its less successful German counterparts. While nationalism has been a central theme of the Far Right, it is less pronounced in Austria than in Germany. Third, the rise of the FPÖ is often associated with the "Haider phenomenon" (Sully 1997) – with a leadership change that brought to the fore a charismatic individual that led the party to its 1986 breakthrough. This raises questions about the degree to which this charisma itself, instead of other factors, can account for the success of Far Right parties (e.g., Immerfall 1998; Eatwell 2002; 2005; Kitschelt 2007: 1193–1195; van der Brug and Mughan 2007). It is worth wondering, then, how these particular characteristics of the FPÖ relate to its trajectory. The analysis of the French case can help dispel any remaining doubts about the effects of party-specific variables because the FN was a marginal rather than a minor party before its breakthrough and because it put forth a much more extremist appeal than its Austrian counterpart. Moreover, the party has had the same leader since 1972, a fact that limits the explanatory scope of scholarly accounts attributing its sudden electoral spurt to leadership charisma. Consistent with the framework developed and applied in this book, this chapter will show that the French FN achieved an electoral breakthrough in the mid-1980s because of factors that are largely exogenous to the party.

On account of this empirical and theoretical significance, the FN has attracted considerable scholarly attention. Some works focus on the party itself (e.g., Birenbaum 1992; Fysh and Wolfreys 1992; Ignazi and Ysmal 1992; Marcus 1995; Camus 1996; Simmons 1996; Ivaldi 1998; Davies 1999; DeClair 1999), while others seek to identify the determinants of its rise. The explanatory emphasis is on socioeconomic variables, especially postindustrialism, unemployment, and immigration (e.g., Mitra 1988; Bréchon and Mitra 1992; Lewis-Beck and Mitchell 1993; Gaspard 1995; Veugelers 1997; Perrineau 2000). As discussed in Chapter 1, such factors go a long way to account for the increased public demand for cultural protectionism but are inadequate to explain the timing, scope, and pace of electoral change. The big and abrupt breakthrough of the FN in the mid-1980s cannot be understood without a consideration of the political context within which it occurred. This chapter, then, seeks to extend the findings of earlier work on the supply factors that facilitated the rise of the French Far Right, focusing on the political opportunities made available to the FN by mainstream parties (Schain 1988; Husbands 1991; Schain et al. 2002). It departs from previous work in breaking down the rise of the French Far Right into phases and in viewing it through the prism of partisan competition over national identity. Moreover, it examines how the French media environment allowed the FN to capitalize on the political opportunities that mainstream parties created in the mid-1980s.

The first section of this chapter briefly describes the electoral trajectory of the postwar French Far Right. The second part examines the factors that facilitated the initial breakthrough of the FN in the early 1980s. It demonstrates how established parties helped create a new political space, furnishing the Far Right with an opportunity to enter the mainstream debate. And it shows how the French media environment helped the party enter the political mainstream. The third section documents the growth and consolidation of FN support after its initial breakthroughs and its impact on partisan competition. This chapter ends with some concluding remarks about the substantial drop in FN support in the 2007 presidential and legislative elections.

The Postwar Trajectory of the French Far Right

The trajectory of the French Far Right displays considerable similarities with that of its Austrian, German, and Greek counterparts. In all three countries, the transition to democracy met resistance from certain segments of society who remained attached to the old regime. In France, ex-Vichyites joined forces under the leadership of Jacques Isorni, the lawyer of Marshal Pétain, to form the National Union of Independents and Republicans (Union Nationale des Indépendants et des Républicains, UNIR). Their main demand was the rehabilitation of the honor of Pétain, who died in 1951 shortly after his release from prison. With the help of Le Pen, who joined Isorni's campaign, UNIR received 280,000 votes in the national legislative elections of 1951 and sent four deputies to the National Assembly. But the party did not escape the fate of many postauthoritarian extremist formations in Western Europe. Unable to survive the defections of its deputies to the major political parties, it soon collapsed.

Reactions to the economic modernization of the French economy and dissatisfaction with the unstable Fourth Republic gave rise to a new party in 1954, the Union for the Defense of Shopkeepers and Artisans (Union de Défense des Commerçants et Artisans), under the leadership of Pierre Poujade. An antitax protest movement that enjoyed the support of small shopkeepers and farmers, Poujade's party became the archetype of von Beyme's second "wave" of right-wing extremism (1988). The Poujadists bore some similarities with the contemporary Far Right such as their antisystemic, antipolitics, and anti-Semitic rhetoric. Campaigning under the slogan "Throw the rascals out," the party staged a major breakthrough in the 1956 parliamentary elections, receiving 11.6% of the vote and sending fifty-two deputies to the legislature, including the twenty-seven-year-old Jean-Marie Le Pen. But the success of the Poujadists proved short-lived, in part because of their failure to build the organizational infrastructure necessary to sustain their initial electoral gains. Lacking an organizational basis and split over the Algerian question, the party witnessed sudden collapse in the first parliamentary elections of the Fifth Republic in 1958.

During the first years of the Fifth Republic, de Gaulle's flip-flopping on the Algerian question created new opportunities for the Far Right. Although the French populace massively approved Algerian independence and the end of the Algerian War in the two referenda held in the early 1960s, a small minority of French voters felt betrayed by de Gaulle. Some of them, such as Le Pen, sought political refuge in the presidential candidacy of Jean-Louis Tixier-Vignancour. Focusing his 1965 campaign on telling "the truth about the loss of Algeria," Tixier-Vignancour sought to mobilize anti-Gaullist sentiments by presenting his candidacy as the "national opposition" standing "between de Gaulle and Moscow" (Simmons 1996: 55). His anti-Gaullist message convinced 5.2% of the electorate but fell short of the 25% he originally predicted, frustrating Le Pen's efforts to forge a single Far Right movement.

Undeterred by repeated electoral and organizational failures, Le Pen tried to revive his political fortunes as leader of the newly founded *Front National* (National Front, FN) in 1972. The party sought to unite the somewhat heterogeneous groupings of the Far Right under the banner of nationalism, realizing that this was probably the only idea they had in common. As Le Pen put it in May 1973, "the justification for the National Front is to be a point of assembly, a point of convergence for all national and nationalist opinion" (quoted in Simmons 1996: 65). Hence, the FN positioned itself as the "national opposition" that defended the "national culture" campaigning in the 1973 elections under the slogan "Defend the French." The poor performance of the party at the polls – it received 0.4% of the vote – triggered the defection of the more radical activists, who formed the Party of New Forces (Parti des Forces Nouvelles, PFN). Faced with competition for the extreme-right milieu, the FN performed miserably in the 1974 presidential elections (0.8%) and in the 1978 legislative elections (1.3%). Toward the late 1970s, Le Pen turned immigration into the single-most important issue of the FN's platform (Fysh and Wolfreys 1992: 321), but he failed to receive the 500 signatures necessary to run in the 1981 presidential elections, and the party only got 0.2% in that year's legislative elections. By 1983, when the party achieved a minor breakthrough in a local by-election in Dreux, most political analysts had written the FN off the political map. What can account, then, for the sudden reversal in the electoral fortunes of this failing party? The next section documents the process that gave rise to one of the most successful Far Right parties in Europe.

FN: From the Margins to the Mainstream

Competition over National Identity. To understand the breakthrough of the FN in the mid-1980s, it is important to examine the evolution of partisan competition over French identity. Identity politics remained on the sidelines of party competition in the 1970s but started gaining political prominence toward the turn of the decade, when immigration began generating public concerns. Public apprehension with immigration was evident as early as 1973, when anti-immigrant riots broke out in Paris suburbs and in Marseilles. Although the riots took place in a few communities with high unemployment and immigration rates, the unease about the presence of foreigners was broader. Pollsters showed that a clear majority of the French populace thought that the number and inflows of immigrants were too high. Until the mid-1970s, public concerns over immigration did not lead to the politicization of the issue: In the 1973 legislative elections and in the 1974 presidential elections, immigration was not a major campaign theme. But Giscard d'Estaing was well aware of the public resonance of the issue. Hence, one of the first measures he took after becoming president was to put a halt to immigration through executive decrees, regulations, and circulars. Unlike in Germany, the policy was effective, reducing the incoming number of alien permanent workers from 204,702 in 1973 to 67,415 in 1975. By the late 1970s, the inflow of permanent workers dropped even further (Figure 6.1). But by that time, the capacity of the government to treat immigration "as an almost private affair in which parliamentarians had no rightful role" (Hargreaves 2007: 170) was limited by a series of legal rulings against the immigration controls. The rulings pushed the issue to the fore, exposing deep partisan divisions on how immigration should be addressed. Thus, whereas in Germany the asylum debates largely followed spurts in the number of asylum-seekers, in France, the immigration issue gained national political prominence despite a marked drop in the immigration inflows (Money 1999: chapter 5).

The turn of French mainstream parties toward national identity preceded the rise of the Far Right. As in the previous cases examined in this book, this new political space was created by mainstream politicians who sought to profit from growing public demands for sociocultural protectionism. Toward the late 1970s, all mainstream parties started taking positions on a new axis of political contestation that was gradually supplementing the traditional competition of the Left and the Right over economic issues. But unlike the other country cases, in France, the decisive turn toward national identity largely came from the Left through the radicalization of the immigration issue by the French Communist Party (Parti Communiste Français, PCF) in the early 1980s. The Communists were preoccupied with the impact of immigration on their constituencies as early as the 1960s, but initially, the issue was only dealt with at the local level. Toward the late 1970s, Communist mayors took drastic measures to reduce

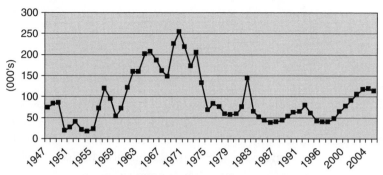

FIGURE 6.1. Inflow of permanent alien workers in France, 1947–2005
Source: The data for 1947–1993 were adjusted from Money 1999: 113; the data after 1977 include temporary workers, and the data for 1994 are missing. The figures for 1995–2005 were compiled from various official sources.

the number of immigrants in their localities by refusing them housing and benefits. In the early 1980s, the issue was gradually taken up by the national organization of the Communist Party. Confronted with electoral setbacks in traditional "bastions" of the PCF, the national leadership searched for new niches of support, and by the 1981 elections, it fully embraced the cause of its local branches (Schain 1988: 603–605; Kitschelt with McGann 1995: 97–98). The party called for the repatriation of immigrants and rejected proposals to grant them voting rights for local elections. The leader of the party, George Marchais, went a step further, associating immigration with unemployment. The event that came to symbolize the Communist stance on immigration was the protest march led by a Communist mayor against an immigrant dormitory in Vitry. In December 1980, the dormitory was attacked with a bulldozer, its water and electricity supplies were cut off, and its immigrant residents were asked to leave the city. In a letter to the Communist daily *L' Humanite*, Marchais gave his "unreserved approval" of the raid and led a march of 10,000 through Vitry against immigrant "ghettoes."[1] During the last phases of the presidential campaign, the local branches of the Communist party linked immigrants with crime and drugs. The Communist

[1] Sophie Fisher, "French Communists wage racist campaign," *Globe and Mail*, March 3, 1981, p. 12.

mayor of Montigny led a demonstration against a Moroccan family, erroneously accusing it of drug trafficking.[2] "For the first time, a major national party attempted to use issues of race and immigration to mobilize support for the presidential candidate" (Schain 1988: 605).

The radicalization of the immigration issue created a new and promising political space, but the Communists were ill-positioned to exploit it. Its stance in the 1981 elections caused tensions within the PCF, especially among many intellectuals who thought that the party was betraying its multiculturalist and humanist morals. Along with the electoral slide of the PCF at the 1981 polls, internal tensions set the basis for the de-radicalization of the issue. The PCF's coalition with the Socialist government of François Mitterrand provided an additional impetus for de-radicalization. As soon as they took office, the Socialists, who prided themselves on their liberal social attitudes, sought to regulate the status of illegal immigrants and immigrant organizations. Whereas the PCF had previously advocated the repatriation of illegal immigrants, the new coalition government offered amnesty to about 130,000 illegal aliens. Moreover, it granted formal recognition to immigrant organizations. By the time of the twenty-fifth party Congress, in 1985, the PCF further moderated its earlier position and started supporting grassroots demonstrations against racism. In addition, in June 1985, the Communists officially declared that they now favored the participation of immigrants in local elections (Schain 1988: 606–607). Having taken a tough stance on immigration, the Communists were gradually compelled to back down, presenting the National Front with an opportunity to capitalize on their retreat.

Party Appeals, Organization, and the Mass Media. In terms of ideological appeal, the FN was well positioned to benefit from the turn to cultural politics but lacked the necessary resources to disseminate its anti-immigrant message. The party included immigration into its electoral platform as early as the 1970s. In 1973, Le Pen led a campaign "for a tough regulation of foreign immigration and in particular

[2] Richard Eder, "Communist Party shatters fraternite of French Left," *New York Times*, March 7, 1981.

of immigration from outside Europe" (Simmons 1996: 64). By the end of the decade, this had become his signature issue, popularized by the now oft-cited FN slogan "One million unemployed is one million immigrants too many." As the ethnocultural ideas of the Nouvelle Droite and GRECE started gaining traction through the publication of *Le Figaro Magazine* (e.g., Shields 2007: chapter 6), the FN was ideally positioned to gain from the intellectual legitimation of its anti-immigrant platform. In 1978, the party campaigned for the legislative elections under the slogan "France for the French first," calling for the repatriation of 2 million immigrants.

Throughout this period, though, the programmatic emphasis on immigration did not yield electoral returns because the party lacked media access. To some extent, this was because of the failure of the party to attract media curiosity. But the most important reasons for the lack of visibility were the obstacles that French media practice imposed on startup parties. Since 1969, the rule of "three thirds" restricted television exposure to the government, the parliamentary majority, and the parliamentary opposition (Hallin and Mancini 2004: 109). This meant that new parties that lacked legislative representation did not get much exposure on French television. Apart from the few television slots granted by law to the FN prior to elections, the "three thirds" rule deprived the FN of a national platform for publicizing its anti-immigrant appeals. In the 1973 elections, the exposure given to the party through such free slots amounted to merely seven minutes (Durand 1996: 24).

Absent easy access to the mainstream media, new parties have to rely on their organizational apparatus to make their positions known. Throughout the 1970s, the FN set up a central committee, regional organizations, a party newspaper, and a youth organization, but this formal organizational setting did not grant the party the critical mass of loyal activists necessary to publicize party views. The fratricidal competition with the PFN not only undermined the ability of the FN to attract new members, but it also led to the defection of key members and loyal activists. When Jean-Pierre Stirbois joined the party in 1977, he "had imagined that the Front was a powerful organization, but quickly discovered that even if it had a leader, some ideas, as well as some quality volunteers, it lacked organization and an entrenched core of party militants" (1988: 27; quoted in DeClair 1999: 42). The new secretary-general quickly realized the need to strengthen the party's organizational structure, but his efforts in his home city, Dreux, were met with questionable success. As the Socialist mayor of the city, Françoise Gaspard recalled, in the early 1980s, "the extreme right had no headquarters in the city, only two or three known activists. The *Front National*'s office was no more than a mail drop, actually a post-office box rented by a plant manager" (Gaspard 1995: 118). Characteristic of this organizational weakness was the failure to collect the signatures necessary for the 1981 presidential elections. In the subsequent legislative elections, the party only fielded 74 candidates to contest the 491 seats, compared with 156 in 1978 and 115 in 1973. And in 1982, it contested only 65 of the 1945 cantons (Perrineau 1996; 1997). On account of these organizational weaknesses and electoral misfortunes, political analysts struck the party off the political map. As one put it, "this impotent coterie of phantoms survives only as a historical residue" (quoted in Mitra 1988: 49).

Two main factors helped the FN gain media access and, hence, to benefit from the "ethnicization" of party politics. The first related to the political maneuvering of the Socialist-led government, which, amid mounting economic problems and growing popular dissatisfaction, sought to use the FN in order to weaken the moderate Right. After the first years of the Socialist administration, the National Front started enjoying increased visibility from the mainstream French media. In part, this was because of the legitimization of its ideas by the Communists, which helped push xenophobia into the political mainstream. But more importantly, the increased publicity came after Mitterrand urged the presidents of three public television channels to grant Le Pen airtime after receiving complains from him in May 1982 that his party was boycotted by the media.[3] While the French Socialist president claimed to be defending media pluralism, some political

---

[3] In 1982, the national press and the public broadcasters ignored the sixth congress of the FN (coinciding with the FN's tenth year of existence). On May 26, Le Pen contacted Mitterrand to demand greater access to the media (television was still at this point directly controlled by the state). In a letter to Le Pen, Mitterrand assured him that the party will now receive due consideration: "It is unfortunate that the congress of a political party should be ignored by the radio and television. They should not ignore their obligation of pluralism. The incident to which you draw my attention should therefore not occur again. I have already asked the minister of

observers thought that the intervention aimed to empower Le Pen at the expense of the moderate Right. Shortly after Mitterrand's intervention, in June, Le Pen was invited to several news broadcasts; and in September, a party festival received broad media coverage (Durand 1996: 47–48).[4] Furnished with communication resources that small French parties usually lack, the increased access of the FN to the mainstream media was an important boost to its public profile. At a time of organizational weakness and electoral impotence, French television helped the FN overcome its decade-long visibility problems. By 1983, when the party achieved a breakthrough in the municipal elections in Dreux, Le Pen had become a sought-after guest for various talk shows. As in the case of Jörg Haider, "the media rise of Jean-Marie Le Pen preceded his electoral success" (Faux, Legrand, and Perez 1994: 20, cited in Simmons 1996: 77).

The second factor that helped the FN overcome its earlier visibility problems was its success in secondary elections. Such elections offer minor parties important opportunities for electoral success because they often revolve around different issues than those debated in national elections and because "they mobilize nationally unrepresentative distributions of voter preferences" (Kitschelt with McGann 1995: 99). The FN already had some success in the 1982 cantonal elections, especially in the small town of Dreux: Its general secretary, Jean-Pierre Stirbois, and his wife received 12.6% and 9.5% of the vote, respectively, compared to the 0.2% the FN received nationally. And in the 1983 municipal elections in a Paris district, Le Pen received 11.3% of the vote in the first ballot campaigning on the anti-immigrant slogan "Paris to the Parisians." These minor successes were largely overshadowed by the overall results in these elections, which showed growing popular discontent against the Socialist government. It was only a few months later that an isolated victory of the FN in a by-election in Dreux granted the party a national audience. In the first round of these elections, Stirbois received 16.7% of the vote; in the second round, the FN list joined that of the centre

Communication to notify the representatives of the media and radio of the breach you point out" (Durand 1996: 47–48).
[4] In France, as in southern Europe, public broadcasting is politicized, and it is often used as a tool for political propaganda by the government of the day (Humphreys 1996; see also Kuhn 1994). This explains why an intervention such as Mitterrand's can be so effective.

Right Rally for the Republic (Rassemblement pour la République, RPR) and Union for French Democracy (Union pour la Démocratie Française, UDF) to unseat the Socialist mayor. Four FN candidates, including Stirbois, secured seats in the town council. Because the Dreux by-election was the only one held at the time, the FN's victory drew national media attention, amplifying the anti-immigrant message of the FN (Gaspard 1995: 118–30; Marcus 1995). Along with the politically motivated exposure that public broadcasters gave the FN, the Dreux victory helped the party gain visibility and establish itself as a viable political force.

The Far Right's victory at Dreux also led to loud debates among the moderate Right on how they should deal with the rising party. The ambiguity about the preferred strategy of the moderate Right further boosted the FN's visibility and helped legitimize its agenda (Schain 1987). A few months before the European parliament elections, in February 1984, Le Pen appeared on one of the most popular and sought-after French television shows, *The Hour of Truth*. As Le Pen recalls, the decision of Antenne 2 to host him on this show suddenly transformed him into a respectable political leader and pushed him into the political mainstream (DeClair 1999: 74; see Chapter 2 here for full quote). Indeed, a survey carried out after the broadcasting of the program showed that voting intention for the FN doubled, from 3.5% to 7% (Durand 1996: 52–53). Another opinion poll, carried out in May, showed that 18% of the electorate had some degree of sympathy for Le Pen. Moreover, over 20% of respondents agreed with the proposition that Le Pen was a legitimate opposition leader, as were the leaders of the UDF and the RPR (Marcus 1995: 56). At the European polls, the party staged its first national breakthrough, receiving 11.2% of the vote and electing ten deputies to the European Parliament. An exit poll showed that there was a good match between the party's appeal and its voters' motivations: FN voters were overwhelmingly concerned with law and order and with immigration, and they were less concerned than the average voter about unemployment and the economy (Schain 1987: 237–238; see also Mitra 1988: 52).

Secondary breakthroughs can improve the electoral fortunes of minor parties not only by boosting their visibility but also by enhancing their recruitment efforts. Contrary to scholarly assertions about the electoral impact of party organization, the national breakthrough of the FN in the European elections seems to have been made possible

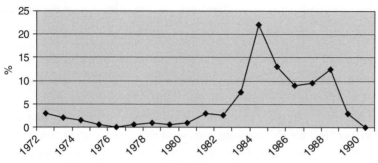

FIGURE 6.2. Recruitment rate of FN delegates, 1972–1990
Source: Reproduced from Birenbaum 1992: 354.

without a strong national or local base. At the time, the party lacked both members and money. As Guy Birenbaum points out, "the FN obtains its first electoral gains without really benefiting from an appropriate organization" (1992: 12). It was only after the party's secondary breakthroughs that party membership started growing. Birenbaum's survey of the FN's officials at the 1990 party congress is suggestive of the impact of secondary breakthroughs on the capacity of the party to recruit new members (Figure 6.2). Three-fourths of party delegates joined the party after its electoral success in Dreux, and almost a fourth joined the ranks of the FN in 1984 after its electoral spurt in the European elections. The enhanced organizational capacity of the party was also shown in its membership figures. At a time of growing recruitment difficulties for established parties, the FN was reported to have increased its members from a few thousand in the early 1980s to 65,000 in 1986 (Perrineau 1997: 46). In part, the new recruits came from the ranks for the RPR and the UDF and brought with them considerable organizational experience.

While in the 1970s the FN was a lose association of extreme-Right networks, toward the late 1980s, it grew into a "centralized machine with a strong pyramid-like organization" (Marcus 1995: 47). Under the organizational leadership of Stirbois – and, after 1988, of Carl Lang – the party set up parallel structures in all French departments and created numerous local sections across the country. To ensure its grip on the regional and local branches, the national leadership appointed departmental and local officials on the basis of co-optation, whereby officials at higher levels appoint those at the lower levels

(Simmons 1996: 187–191). Mirroring the organization of the French Communists, the regional and local branches formed the crucial links between the party and its growing number of voters. The strong local presence of the party prevented the co-optation of its agenda from the two parties of the mainstream Right in the mid-1980s and blocked their efforts to regain the political space they lost to the FN. Moreover, in the 1990s, the organizational density of the party proved critical for the communication of the party with voters, as the mainstream media were less willing to publicize its views. Despite its organizational expansion, the party remained highly centralized and efficient. Intraparty mechanisms granted Le Pen near absolute discretion in appointments to the political bureau and to the central committee of the party. And party statutes ensured direct control of the periphery from the center by preventing contact between the various regional and local branches. The organizational strength of the party was reinforced by associated organizations, such as the Institut de Formation Nationale, which was formed in 1985 to organize training functions across the country. The themes of the conferences and seminars organized by the Institute included party ideology and principles as well as electoral organization and public speaking. The Institute also issued a multivolume manual with checklists for how to set up a local branch, deal with the press and design party posters. The organizational apparatus of the party was further reinforced by the establishment of approximately twenty other associated organizations that sought to recruit farmers, women, entrepreneurs, veterans, and workers to the party; by the creation of a think tank; and by the production and circulation of a series of publications. The organizational spread of the party increased its capacity to contest local elections. In the 1985 cantonal elections, the party presented 1,521 candidates to contest seats in the 1945 cantons, compared to 65 three years earlier. In those cantons that the FN contested, party support exceeded 10%. Throughout 1985, the French Far Right polled approximately 10%, alarming the moderate Right and inducing Mitterrand to change the electoral law to proportional representation to split the center Right opposition in parliament.[5]

[5] The 1986 breakthrough of the National Front is sometimes attributed to this change in the electoral law. A closer examination of the sequence of events, though, allows

Mainstream Party Responses to the Rising Threat. The rise of the National Front changed the parameters of partisan competition over national identity, exacerbating the dilemmas of mainstream parties on how to deal with immigration. Pollsters repeatedly showed that by the mid-1980s, the ideas of the FN had wide appeal. In a 1985 poll, two-thirds of the respondents agreed that "if nothing is done to limit the number of foreigners, France risks losing its national identity." In another poll, 58% of respondents found the presence of immigrants in France "too much" (quoted in Feldblum 1999: 47). The high resonance of the immigration issue forced mainstream parties to address it. The pressures were particularly intense for the moderate Right, which witnessed the biggest defections to the FN. After its breakthroughs and because of its high media visibility, the FN managed to establish itself as a point of reference for partisan competition on immigration, and mainstream party positions came to be assessed by comparison with those of the Far Right (Ysmal 1984). The moderate Right had to take a firm stance on immigration in order to reclaim this political space from the new contestant and to win disgruntled leftist voters who were dissatisfied with the liberal opening of the Mitterrand government toward immigrants.

Between 1983 and 1985, then, there was a programmatic shift of the moderate Right on cultural politics. Signs of this shift were first evident in the campaign for the 1983 local elections. In response to the vitriolic campaign of the Far Right against immigrants, the moderate Right also started to toughen its stance. Candidates from both the UDF and the RPR – and even from the Socialists – pledged to stop the "invasion" of foreigners and linked immigration with unemployment and crime. In Toulon, for example, the UDF mayor stated that France refused to become the "dustbin of Europe."

considerable room for reverse causality. Mitterrand's decision to change the electoral law was in anticipation of the FN's electoral breakthrough, which was shown in the European and cantonal elections and in repeated polls in 1985, *before* the Socialist president changed the electoral law. Interestingly, despite a switch back to the pre-1986 plurality system, the FN got the same percentage in the 1988 elections as in the 1986 elections. A careful analysis of the 1997 election is suggestive of why voters continue to support the party despite the obstacles the plurality system raises to legislative representation. It shows that three-fourths of the FN's first-round voters stuck with Le Pen for the second round of the elections, even in those districts that the FN had absolutely no chance of winning (Givens 2005: 123).

After the alarming rise of the FN in the elections, immigration concerns became louder among moderate Right politicians. In summer 1983, the Gaullist mayor of Paris, Jacques Chirac, led an immigration clampdown, noting that the "threshold of tolerance" had been passed and that France no longer had the means to support those who "abused her hospitality." He argued that municipal services and welfare benefits should only be given to legal immigrants and proposed grouping immigrants of the same nationality into a given area (Marcus 1995: 79). In an interview in *Libération*, in October 1984, Chirac sought to co-opt the message of the FN by stating that "with less immigrants, there would be less unemployment, less tension in certain towns and areas, and a lower social cost" (Ysmal 1984: 18). The apprehension of the Gaullists about the handling of the issue went beyond its core leadership. In 1984, Alain Griotteray published a book titled *Immigrants: The Shock*, in which he put forth a stark defense of French identity against multiculturalism. And in 1985, Club 89, a political club affiliated with the RPR, argued in a strategy paper that immigrants threaten to dilute cultural identity and that the French had a duty to preserve it.

The turn of the moderate Right toward immigration crystallized in calls in 1985 to reform the French nationality code. The proposals were largely echoing those suggested in late 1984 by the FN and were part of the moderate Right's attempts to recapture the political space occupied by the Far Right ahead of the 1986 legislative elections. The UDF and RPR proposed to eliminate the automatic attribution of citizenship to those born on French soil by requiring them to apply for citizenship. The proposed changes drove to the heart of nationality laws by questioning the French tradition of citizenship, which is based on territorial (*jus soli*) rather than blood connection (*jus sanguinis*). For the moderate Right, the issue was one of defending French identity. Rightist politicians argued that the "voluntarist" elements of the proposed reform would strengthen French identity. Alain Mayoud, a UDF politician, argued that his proposal would help "preserve our national identity" (Feldblum 1999: 63). The issue was a theme at the spring congress of the RPR, which called for the introduction of voluntary elements in the naturalization procedure. A report published by the UDF in 1985 similarly argued that the acquisition of citizenship should be accompanied with cultural assimilation and with the conservation from other cultures of only those elements that are compatible with the French culture. This was anathema to the Left and to immigrant organizations; they associated the arguments of the moderate Right with the nationalist agenda of the FN.

The reform of the nationality code and the general theme of immigration featured prominently in the campaign for the 1986 legislative elections. The RPR and the UDF ran on a joint platform, which cited citizenship reform as one of its policy objectives. It was considered as a means to strengthen national identity and to make the national community more confident of its identity. The center Right was also explicit about the need to control immigration. In a major advertisement campaign, the RPR stated:

> The French people want to remain one nation. They want those who live on our soil to have certain rights, but also equivalent duties. That means: frontier control, the expulsion of illegal immigrants and delinquents, social rights reserved for persons legitimately present and family support to encourage population growth given only to nationals. The franchise belongs exclusively to the French. The acquisition of French nationality does not come through automatic mechanisms but must be requested and accepted. (cited in Husbands 1991: 186)

The electoral breakthrough of the National Front in 1986 elections showed the limitations of the moderate Right's strategy to reclaim this political space from the Far Right. The FN received 9.8% of the vote, and with the help of proportional representation, it sent 35 deputies to the national legislature – as many as the Communists (Table 6.1). As in the 1984 European elections, exit polls showed that immigration and security were the most important concerns for FN voters. Almost half of FN voters (46%) considered immigration to be the most important issue motivating their vote, while another 18% were primarily concerned with the feeling of insecurity. This compared with only 8% of all French voters that were preoccupied with either immigration or insecurity. Pollsters were also able to sketch the profile of the typical FN voter. As the UDF and the RPR, the FN was overrepresented among small business owners; and like the Communists and the Socialists, it was overrepresented among workers (Mitra 1988: 53–55).

TABLE 6.1. *FN Electoral Results, 1973–2007 (% of valid votes)*

1973 Legislative (1st round)	0.4
1974 Presidential	0.8
1978 Legislative (1st round)	1.3
1981 Legislative (1st round)	0.18
1984 European	11.08
1986 Legislative	9.80
1986 Regional	9.60
1988 Presidential	14.61
1988 Legislative (1st round)	9.73
1989 European	11.80
1992 Regional	13.85
1993 Legislative (1st round)	12.68
1994 European	10.61
1995 Presidential	15.27
1997 Legislative (1st round)	15.23
1998 Regional	15.27
1999 European	5.74
2002 Presidential (1st round)	16.86
2002 Presidential (2nd round)	17.79
2002 Legislative (1st round)	11.34
2004 Regional	14.7
2004 European	9.08
2007 Presidential	10.44
2007 Legislative (1st round)	4.29

Sources: Journal Officiel, Ministère de l'Intérieur; Ignazi 2003.

Several factors can account for the failure of the moderate Right to successfully co-opt the agenda of the Far Right. The first was its initial ambivalence on the issue, which allowed the FN to use its growing media exposure and its organizational entrenchment to establish issue credibility. The ambivalence is well documented by the moderate Right's legislative record. In July 1984, for example, the moderate Right voted in favor of a liberal proposal tabled by the Socialist government automatically granting renewable ten-year work and residence permits to the majority of legal immigrants settled in France. Signaling a reversal of the repatriation policy that had been encouraged by the moderate Right in the late 1970s, its support for the Socialist legislation left the FN as the only defender of mass deportations (Hargreaves 2007: 179–180). It took almost two years after the Dreux breakthrough before the moderate Right presented comprehensive proposals for addressing immigration. The delayed response of the moderate Right was partly because of internal divisions. The divisions were exposed in the 1984 European elections, when UDF and RPR candidates ran under a joint list headed by Simone Veil against a dissenting Gaullist list. Veil was responsible for the liberalization of abortion during Giscard d' Estaing's presidency and was considered too liberal for traditional conservatives (Marcus 1995: 55). The choice of such a liberal candidate to head the European elections at a time of growing FN popularity highlighted the ambiguous positioning of the moderate Right in the transformed competitive space.

Apart from its ambiguous programmatic signals, the moderate Right was also ambivalent in its dealing with the FN. Between 1983 and 1988, the UDF and the RPR oscillated between collaboration with and isolation from the FN. In Dreux, Chirac had initially denounced the prospect of collaborating with the FN as an alliance "against nature," but later, he accepted the collaboration as necessary to defeat the Left:

There are not 17 per cent dangerous extremists in Dreux. ... It is now much more dangerous to support a coalition that includes Communists than to support a coalition, at the level of municipal councils of moderate importance, that includes members of the National Front, which has relatively little importance. (quoted in Schain 1987: 240)

The Dreux alliance proved divisive for the moderate Right. Veil immediately condemned it, saying that if she were a voter in Dreux, she would abstain. Her condemnation received some support from a few centrist politicians, but for the most part, the top leadership and the voter base of the moderate Right approved the collaboration.[6] It was only after the electoral success of the FN in the European elections and once the moderate Right realized that the FN threat was likely to

---

[6] As Claude Labbe, the president of the RPR's group in the National Assembly, put it: "Le Pen exists, it is one of today's political realities. We have to take into account a political formation that exists, to work together, to act in concert with them, and not say 'I do not recognize you'" (quoted in Marcus 1995: 135).

be permanent that the leadership of the opposition started distancing itself from such alliances. By the 1985 cantonal elections, the moderate Right sought to erect a *cordon sanitaire* against Le Pen's party. Amid growing leftist mobilization against the FN and its ideas, the RPR issued a proscription opposing any alliances with the extreme right. Yet, although the top leadership of the rightist parties rejected any collaboration with Le Pen, until the late 1980s, local party function-aries continued to strike second-round deals with the FN in closely fought constituencies. The discordant strategy of the moderate Right weakened its claims about the dangers posed by the extreme right and helped legitimate its opponent (Schain 1987; Marcus 1995: 133–143). This undermined the efforts to win back FN voters by co-opting its anti-immigrant agenda.

Competing with the FN after Its Breakthroughs

One of the major arguments of this book is that as parties grow, they are better able to shape their electoral destinies. The analysis of the FN's subsequent development serves to highlight the difficulties mainstream parties confront in dealing with a Far Right party after its initial successes. The sequence of electoral breakthroughs between 1983 and 1986 helped the FN consolidate its position in the French party system as the most credible defender of national identity. This frustrated the attempts of the more established parties to win back the FN electorate. The next twenty years witnessed the gradual growth of the FN despite repeated efforts by the moderate Right to trespass its programmatic terrain.

The first of such efforts was undertaken by the new Chirac govern-ment in 1986. To reclaim the political space lost to Le Pen, the cen-ter Right government introduced tough immigration laws. This new policy approach was spearheaded by the interior minister, Charles Pasqua, who argued that the only way to win back FN voters was to adopt more muscular immigration policies. The centerpiece of his approach was a new immigration law – the so-called "Pasqua Law" – that introduced more restrictions for the entry and stay of foreigners in France (Fysh 1987). The most controversial aspect of the Law – the one that placed expulsions in the hands of administrative instead of judicial bodies – stirred considerable controversy in late 1986, when a number of Malian immigrants were rounded up and summarily expelled under false pretenses. The Chirac government was also keen to move ahead with its proposal to change the nationality code. As soon as the new government took office, it reaffirmed its pre-electoral pledge to eliminate the automaticity of the naturalization process and to replace it with a voluntary procedure (Brubaker 1992: 151). The legislation drafted by the government required individuals between the ages of sixteen and twenty-three to file a formal application and excluded those with serious criminal offenses. Moreover, it imposed restrictions on the right to earn citizenship through marriage with a French national in order to limit marriages of convenience.

The effort of the Chirac government to outbid Le Pen on national identity issues soon ran into trouble, as the proposed nationality code proved far too controversial and divisive than the moderate Right had anticipated. The reform was fiercely criticized from the Left and from President Mitterrand, who thought that the discussion about the nationality code threatened to divide French society and to increase the alienation felt by foreigners in France. Immigrant groups joined the Left in defending the republican tradition of the French state against the conservative efforts to do away with *jus soli*. In March 1987, some two hundred civil society groups staged a big demonstration in Paris against the reform. The reactions were not confined to the Left. "By the autumn of 1987 it was increasingly clear that there were growing divisions within the Government's own ranks – differences both within the RPR, as well as opposition from leading UDF politicians" (Marcus 1995: 83). The intensity of the reactions was too high a price to pay for the Chirac administration, which was still recovering from its confrontation with students over its planned education reform. In December 1987, the government withdrew the reform from the legislature and assigned the examination of the issue to a committee of experts. After a highly visible consultation process, the committee published its findings in January 1988. Its report sought to strike a middle ground between the government and the opposition, disappointing hardliners in the moderate Right. Ahead of the presidential campaign, Chirac quickly shelved the proposals of the committee and pledged to put the issue to a referendum should he be elected president. The flip-flopping of the moderate Right on the issue did not go unnoticed by Le Pen, who accused the government of yielding to the pressures of the

Left. Two years after the moderate Right's rightward shift, its strategy to outflank the Far Right and to recapture the space lost to Le Pen ended in failure (Marcus 1995; see also Feldblum 1999: chapters 5 and 6). On run-up to the presidential elections, the FN was able to present itself as the only credible defender of French identity.

During this period of governmental backpedaling over the nationality code, the FN continued to benefit from the considerable exposure it received from the mainstream French media. In part, this was because of the legislative presence of the FN, which gave it easier access to the media because of the "three thirds rule." As Le Pen put it, "the best period for the relationship with the media was from 1986 to 1988, when the FN had some deputies" (Le Pen quoted in Birenbaum and Villa 2003: 52). The media visibility of the FN was also because of the protracted controversy caused by the immigration and citizenship policy of the government. The media identified the FN with immigration and hence invited its leaders to offer their views whenever the topic was salient, either to refute them or simply to present the full spectrum of political commentary on the issue. Le Pen was frequently a guest on talk shows about immigration and featured on magazine and newspaper covers. Moreover, Le Pen managed to stir controversy with his anti-Semitic, revisionist, or xenophobic remarks. In one of the best known incidents, in September 1987, he referred to the Nazi gas chambers as a "detail in the history of the Second World War." The visibility of the FN in the mainstream media was also because of the publicity given to demonstrations against the Front held by pro-immigrant or other civil society groups. Such activities inadvertently helped to focus public attention on the FN and its ideas. Le Pen's growing presence in the mainstream media coincided with a turn of French broadcasters toward sensational journalism, imposed by the commercial criteria of newly privatized stations. The commercialization of French broadcasting rewarded Le Pen's unconventional behavior and theatrical skills. When asked, for example, whether he dyed his hair blonde, Le Pen produced a certificate from his barber to prove that he had not. In another occasion, he tied a red scarf around his face to protest the "censorship" of the Left. His controversial style attracted wide audiences and was a good "sell" for the broadcasters: His first appearance on "The Hour of Truth" attracted an audience of 7 million and his second, in 1986, an audience of 17 million. Although

comprehensive evidence for the degree of exposure of the FN on television is lacking, the analysis of data from the National Commission
for Communication and Freedoms (Commission nationale de la communication et des libertés, CNCL), which is the predecessor of the
existing media regulator, the High Council for Broadcasting (Conseil
supérieur de l'audiovisuel, CSA), shows that the FN received 462 minutes of television exposure in the last two months prior to the 1988
presidential elections. This amounted to 8.25% of the television time
allotted to political parties during the campaign. In the last phases of
the campaign the exposure granted to Le Pen exceeded considerably
that given to André Lajoinie, the candidate for the Communist party.[7]
Similarly, Le Pen received 9.9%, or ninety minutes, of all airtime on
the France-Inter radio prior to the presidential elections.[8] A systematic analysis of *Le Monde* front pages between 1980 and 1999 also
shows the enhanced visibility of the FN toward the late 1980s, which
topped that of the Communist Party during certain periods (Bizeul
2003: 295, quoted in Le Bohec 2004: 221).

    The oscillation of the governing coalition on nationality reform and
the continued visibility of the FN helped the party achieve another
electoral success in the 1988 presidential elections. An unprecedented
14.6% voted for Le Pen in the first round of the elections, forcing
Chirac to actively seek the support of FN voters for the second round
to defeat Mitterrand. To lure these voters, Pasqua stated that "the
Front has the same preoccupations and the same values as the majority. It just expresses them in a rather more brutal and noisy manner"
(Simmons 1996: 91). As in earlier elections, the typical FN voter was
predominantly male, younger, urban, and with limited education.
Moreover, the FN continued to be overrepresented among workers
(Mayer and Perrineau 1992: 127). Political commentators considered
the FN vote to be largely a protest vote, but the results of the legislative elections held a few months later showed the endurance of

---

[7] Commission nationale de la communication et des libertés, *Élection du Président de
la République. Rapport sur la campagne à la radio et à la télévision (22 Février–8
Mai 1988)*, retrieved from the archives of the National Library of France, January
2009, Paris.
[8] Commission nationale de la communication et des libertés, *Campagne Presidentielle:
Relevé du temps consacré aux candidats declares ou presumes et à leurs soutiens*,
1988 (CSA archives). The data are from February 22 to April 7; data from April 8
to April 24 are missing.

FN support, despite the return to a majoritarian system. The party received 9.7% of the vote, almost as many as it had received under proportional representation in 1986, although it won only a single seat. The electoral success of the party revived the debate about the possibility of allying with the FN in the second round of elections, despite the earlier pledge of the moderate Right not to strike any local or national deals with Le Pen. In some constituencies in Marseilles, the FN withdrew its candidates in favor of rightist candidates, with the moderate Right reciprocating in other constituencies.[9]

The Late 1980s and 1990s. After the electoral advances of the FN in the 1988 legislative elections, the moderate Right renewed its efforts to recapture the political space lost to Le Pen. In 1990, the RPR launched a petition drive against granting voting rights to immigrants. The campaign was followed by heightened rhetoric from the top leadership of the UDF and the RPR. In June 1991, Chirac stated that France suffered from an "overdose" of immigrants and claimed that the "noise and smell" from immigrants "makes the French worker crazy." Subsequently, in an interview in *Le Figaro*, former interior minister Michel Poniatowski asserted that "the immigrant population, principally North Africans and Blacks, had a high propensity to commit crimes." In September 1991, Giscard referred to immigration as an "invasion" and proposed the consideration of traditional conceptions of citizenship based on blood (quoted in Marcus 1995: 93–94; Simmons 1996: 96–97). Meanwhile, the moderate Right became less ambivalent about its dealings with the FN. It rejected national or local alliances and called for the isolation of extremism.

The return of the moderate Right to the government after the 1993 elections and the persistence of FN support reinvigorated the moderate Right's efforts to win back FN voters. Within a month after taking office, the newly appointed interior minister, Pasqua, brought a

---

[9] In the period prior to the legislative elections, the FN received about 14.7% of all television time devoted to political parties and 14.8% of all speech time. The FN also received 18% of the radio airtime devoted to the coverage of political parties by France-Inter during this period as well as 17.6% of all speech time. Commission nationale de la communication et des libertés, *Campagne pour les elections legislatives: Relevé du temps consacré aux formations politiques*, 1988 (CSA archives). The data are for the period between May 22 and June 3, 1988.

package of bills to the legislature to restrict the right to citizenship, work, and asylum. The bills were partly reinstating but also toughening his 1986 measures, which were reversed by his Socialist successor, Pierre Joxe, in 1989. The new measures passed through the National Assembly in June 1993, with a majority of 480 deputies voting for the restrictions and a small minority of Socialist and Communist deputies voting against. Pasqua insisted in an interview in November that the only way to block the FN was to demonstrate that the government was tough on law-and-order issues.

The renewed effort of the moderate Right to entice the FN electorate by toughening its stance on immigration failed to bring the expected results. In the 1989 European elections, the party received 11.8% of the vote, improving its 1984 result. Its strength was reinforced in two highly visible by-elections in Marseilles and Dreux, where the party received 33% and 42.5% of the vote in the first round, respectively. Amid the political storm and divisions caused by the "Islamic headscarf affair," Marie-France Stirbois received a spectacular 61.3% in the second round in Dreux and won a seat in the national legislature (Bréchon and Mitra 1992: 66–68). The electoral advances of the party continued during the turbulent and divisive – for the moderate Right – period of ratifying the Maastricht Treaty. The FN received 13.9% in the 1992 regional elections and 12.4% in the cantonal elections. Despite the "republican quarantine" of the moderate Right, the FN elected 33 mayors, 239 regional councillors, and 1,666 town councillors. In the 1993 legislative elections, FN support grew to 12.7%.

The organizational reach and institutional entrenchment of the party proved to be a bulwark against growing competition from a new ultra-conservative party: the Movement for France (Mouvement pour la France, MPF) launched in 1992 by a maverick UDF legislator, Philippe de Villiers. De Villiers managed to get 12.3% of the vote in the 1994 European elections, topping Le Pen's 10.6%. But the newcomer failed to pose a major threat to the FN electorate, collapsing in the subsequent presidential and legislative elections. The sustained organizational growth of the FN also helped the party spread its message at a time when the media hesitated to disseminate its views. In the run-up to the 1995 presidential elections, the FN received merely 4.2% of the total television time and 4.7% of the total speech time granted to presidential candidates. This was almost a third of its turnout in the previous legislative elections and less than the exposure granted to de Villiers.[10] In the first round of the presidential elections, Le Pen received an unprecedented 15.3% of the vote, topping the polls in seven departments. Exit polls showed the "proletarianization" of the FN vote and demonstrated the successful opening of the party toward traditional leftist constituencies: Thirty percent of workers and 25% of the unemployed voted for Le Pen (Ignazi 2003: 100–101).

The return of the moderate Right to the presidency was accompanied by a new push to stop the growth of the FN. Undeterred by previous strategic failures and by the remarkable stability of the FN electorate, Chirac launched a new attempt to court FN voters. The main targets of the newly appointed interior minister, Jean-Louis Debré, were illegal immigrants. Within a year, Debré boasted to have boarded 15,000 of them on charter flights and to have increased the expulsion rate by 25%. In August 1996, he sent armed and helmeted police to end the hunger strike of ten immigrants who protested the severity and complexity of the 1993 laws passed by his predecessor, Pasqua.[11] The renewed effort of the moderate Right to outflank the FN crystallized in a legislative bill that sought to further tighten the immigration screws by expediting the expulsion process and by granting the authorities greater discretionary powers. With an eye to the subsequent legislative elections, the conservative government of Alain Juppé pushed the bill through the legislature despite strong protest from the Left, especially from intellectuals and artists. In a 1997 ceremony marking the fiftieth anniversary of the Gaullist movement, the prime minister made no secret of his effort to recapture the "national" turf. "Let us not allow the tricolor flag and the symbols of our history to be monopolized by those who are nostalgic for the

[10] The FN received a total of 207 minutes out of a total of 4,940 minutes granted to all presidential candidates during news reports on TF1, France 2, France 3, Canal +, and M6 in the *pre-electoral* period from January 1 to April 6, 1995. Le Pen also received 105 minutes of speech time. The total speech time for all candidates was 2,255 minutes. De Villiers was granted 219 and 129 minutes, respectively. During the *electoral* period, all candidates receive, by law, two hours or an equal amount of coverage, depending on the number of candidates. Hence, television stations do not have much leverage with regard to the degree of exposure they grant to the FN. Calculated from CSA 1995 Reports; retrieved from the archives of the National Library of France, January 2009, Paris.

[11] John Follain, "Paris woos Far Right voters with show of force," *Reuters*, August 12, 1996.

people who in 1940 gave France a caricature of fascism and capitulation," he told a rally of the Gaullist RPR party. Using similar rhetoric to the one used in the 2007 presidential elections, he asserted that "the foundation stone of Gaullism is love of our homeland. Let us, as proud Gaullists, make patriotism our flag."[12]

As in 1986 and in 1993, the electoral strategy of the moderate Right failed to contain the FN. The party enjoyed considerable credibility on immigration issues, and conservative efforts to co-opt its agenda only helped to legitimize it. Moreover, the FN's exclusion from government meant that it could consistently propose policies that were tougher than everyone else's – in part because the party would never have to implement them.[13] To counter the co-optive strategy of the moderate Right, then, Le Pen renewed his calls for abolishing *jus soli*, ending immigrant family reunifications and giving a preference to French employees over foreigners. Moreover, he intensified his antisystemic rhetoric, calling for a popular insurrection in favor of an alternative system of governance: a Sixth French Republic. The extremity of these appeals allowed the FN to fend off rightist efforts to outflank it. In the 1997 legislative efforts, FN support grew to 15.2%, in part because of the continued electoral inroads of the party into worker constituencies. And in the 1998 regional elections, the FN received 15.3%, electing more regional councillors than the UDF and tempting moderate Right politicians to break their *cordon sanitaire*. Once more, the rightward shift of the moderate Right failed to deliver the desired results.

Splintering and Comeback. The FN effectively resisted attempts to outflank it, but its continuous growth gave rise to internal dissent about its future course. There were voices within the party that called for the collaboration with the moderate Right for the assumption of power. These voices became louder toward the late 1990s and led to the founding of a splinter group in 1999, the Republican National

---

[12] Helene Fontanaud, "Fly the French flag against the Far Right – Juppe," *Reuters*, April 7, 1997.

[13] As the president of the Senate rightly noted, there was no point in trying to run faster than Le Pen because "Le Pen will always be faster than us." Russell Chaddock, "How to deal with Far Right splits conservatives," *Christian Science Monitor*, September 27, 1997, p. 6.

Movement (*Mouvement National Républicain*, MNR), by the Front's number two, Bruno Mégret. The departure of nearly half its elected representatives and officials took a toll on FN support in the subsequent European elections. The FN dropped to 5.7% of the total vote, its lowest electoral result in 15 years, and the MNR polled 3.3%. In the 2001 municipal elections, the FN suffered another blow, encouraging gloomy predictions about the future of the party. But the stunning result of the first round of the 2002 presidential elections belied these predictions. Benefiting from the increased salience of law-and-order issues in the French media, Le Pen staged one of the biggest upsets in French electoral history by receiving 16.9% of the first-round vote and passing to the runoff election with Chirac. As before, efforts to outbid Le Pen on his signature issues only helped to boost his popularity. Le Pen voters were primarily concerned with immigration and with criminality: Sixty-eight percent stated that each of these were the most important issues in the first round of elections, compared to 23% and 61% of all voters, respectively (Mayer 2003: 456). In the subsequent legislative elections, FN support dropped to 11.3% but the referendum for the EU constitution in 2004 and the urban riots in 2005 gave Le Pen new opportunities for electoral mobilization.

Conclusion

This chapter probed the generalizability of the theoretical framework by testing its applicability in one of the most important Far Right cases: the French National Front. The analysis of the FN's trajectory in the early 1980s reinforces the weight placed in this study on partisan competition over national identity and on media access. The radicalization of the immigration issue by the Communist Party and its subsequent failure to sustain its position furnished the FN with an opportunity for an electoral breakthrough. The politically motivated exposure granted to Le Pen by French broadcasters helped the party capitalize on this opportunity and achieve a series of electoral advances. These early breakthroughs gave an organizational boost to the party that helped it consolidate its early support before the moderate Right could challenge its ownership of immigration issues. The temporal emphasis in the analysis has helped highlight the difficulties competitors had to reclaim the political space ceded to Le Pen after the FN entered the political system. The rightward shift of the moderate Right in the mid-1980s and in the 1990s failed to win back FN voters. Arguably, it only helped to increase the political salience of national identity issues and to legitimize the nationalist agenda of the Far Right. For almost two decades, those segments of the French populace that shared Le Pen's apprehensions over immigration followed his call to "choose the original over the copy."

Apart from showing the generalizability of this new theoretical framework, this chapter has also made room for its refinement. One aspect of the analysis that might need refinement relates to the media. The French case points perhaps to the need to qualify the emphasis placed in the Austrian chapter on the impact of the mass media in later phases of party development. Although the FN benefited enormously from the excessive visibility it got from the French media in the 1980s, the party was subsequently able to sustain or extend its electoral gains without enjoying the degree of visibility the FPÖ enjoyed. The French case hence suggests that the media is most important in earlier phases of party development, when parties need to spread their messages to the broader public. But it might be less important once parties become known. Moreover, the analysis throws more light on the effects of party organization. Although the FN is often used as a showcase of organizational effects, the sequencing of its development suggests that the organizational growth of the party was largely the effect rather than the cause of its initial breakthroughs. Party organization was more important for consolidating the early gains of the French Far Right and for resisting strategic challenges from mainstream competitors. The organizational capacity of the FN might also explain why the party sustained and extended voter support in the 1990s, when the mainstream media avoided giving it as much exposure as in the late 1980s. Finally, the French case reinforces the need to go beyond national elections to fully understand the dynamics of Far Right breakthroughs. The electoral success of the French Far Right in the legislative elections in 1986 cannot be fully appreciated without a consideration of the series of breakthroughs it achieved in secondary elections between 1983 and 1985. The French experience suggests that marginal parties can use secondary elections as entry points into the electoral market (Kitschelt with McGann 1995). Through such elections, neophytes can gain national media attention and enhance their recruitment efforts. This might be especially so in countries with strong local or regional institutions that supplement centralized decision making by national legislatures (Kitschelt 2007: 1190–1191).

The analysis of the French politics has traced the fortunes of the FN until 2002, when Le Pen shocked the world by advancing into the second round of the presidential elections. It showed the durability and growth of FN support despite repeated efforts by the moderate Right to regain the electoral ground lost to Le Pen. The 2007 elections have changed this: FN support dropped to 10.4% in the first round of the presidential elections and to a mere 4.3% in the subsequent legislative elections – its worst result in more than two decades. While it might be premature to write the FN off the French electoral map, it is worth trying to use the theoretical framework developed here to make sense of this new development.

Most analyses of the recent French elections are in line with the emphasis placed in this study on partisan competition over national identity. They note the rightward shift of Nikolas Sarkozy on national identity issues, pointing to his hardened rhetoric against immigration during the urban riots and to his controversial proposal to create an "Immigration and National Identity" ministry during the campaign. According to this view, Sarkozy managed to co-opt the agenda of the Far Right in a move that marked "a decisive break from the strategy of the party's old guard."[14] The analysis presented in this chapter shows that this interpretation is only partly true: The co-optation strategy of Sarkozy was not radically different from that of his predecessors in 1986, 1993, and 1995. Sarkozy did to the FN what Chirac had repeatedly tried to do in the past.

If the electoral slide of the FN should be attributed to the electoral strategy of the Gaullists, then the real puzzle is why this strategy worked in 2007 but not before. The answer might lie with Sarkozy's tactical maneuvering during the campaign. He was able to effectively communicate his candidacy as a clear break with Chirac's presidency and leadership. Along with his earlier stance on immigration, the break with Chirac allowed Sarkozy to regain the lost credibility of the Gaullists on national identity issues. Apart from this break from

---

[14] Martin Arnold and John Thornhill, "The will to power," *Financial Times*, May 15, 2007, p. 13.

the past, Sarkozy was also able to directly appeal to FN voters, without the inhibitions or the ambivalence the Gaullists had previously shown. Instead of oscillating between a strategy of collaboration and exclusion, Sarkozy made no secret of his effort to regain Far Right voters by stressing the themes they cared about the most. Indicative of his clear strategy toward the FN was that instead of boycotting Le Pen like his three previous predecessors had done, Sarkozy hosted consultations with the Far Right leader in the presidential palace. Another factor was arguably the credibility Sarkozy had established during the 2005 urban riots and during his tenure in the interior ministry since 2002 as being "tough on crime."

A different explanation attributes the success of the moderate Right in outflanking Le Pen to a fundamental ideological reorientation of the Union for a Popular Movement (Union pour un Mouvement Populaire, UMP). Going beyond the tactical maneuvering of Sarkozy, this explanation sees a distinctive centrifugal shift of the party on both identity and materialist politics under his leadership, which allowed it to rehabilitate some features of the Right's cognitive map. According to this explanation, Sarkozy used his dominant position within the UMP to push it to the Right on both the cultural and the socioeconomic axes of political competition – which his predecessors had not done. The 2007 elections epitomized the ideological reorientation of the UMP toward the ethnicization of the debate on immigration and crime and toward the re-actualization of anti-egalitarian rhetoric that was specifically targeted against the Left.

The ideological distance with the extreme Right was further decreased by Sarkozy's decisive and most controversial turn on national identity politics in the final stage of the presidential race. The tactical facet of this move is hardly controvertible but it nevertheless represented a significant alteration from the standard line of argumentation by the mainstream Right. Until then, the latter had been more reluctant to engage on relating immigration issues to that of national identity explicitly, most evidently because of the strong negative connotation inherited from the Vichy regime. (Ivaldi 2008: 6)

While the tactical maneuvers and the possible ideological shift of the UMP might go some way in explaining why Sarkozy was more successful than his predecessors in winning FN votes, the trespassing of the programmatic territory of the Far Right was also possible because of the FN's repositioning. In the past, the FN was able to resist

the electoral challenges posed by the rightward shifts of the moderate
Right by remaining firm on its radical views on national identity and
by moving farther to the right. After the marked failure of the FN
to escape from its electoral ghetto in the second round of the 2002
presidential elections, the party started flirting with a more moderate
programmatic platform advocated by the modernist wing of the FN
in its 2003 congress. The new strategy was evident in FN posters that
featured a young black woman instead of the seventy-nine-year-old
Le Pen and in a surprise visit Le Pen paid to an immigrant suburb of
Paris. At the same time when Sarkozy was making explicit references
to national identity, the FN sought to "de-racialize" its appeals on
immigration, placing it within a strict citizenship instead of a cultural
framework. A similar change was also noticeable in the revised program of the FN, which dropped cultural arguments against immigration and moderated its defense of French identity (Ivaldi 2008). This
"softer" approach of the FN, which contrasts with its earlier strategy
of moving rightward when challenged by the moderate Right, allowed
Sarkozy to successfully outbid it. Absent this programmatic shift of
the Far Right, it is doubtful whether Sarkozy would have been any
more successful than his predecessors in regaining Far Right votes.

Time will show whether Sarkozy will be able to sustain this rightward shift. The establishment of his new "Immigration and National
Identity" ministry shows his resolve not to cede the ground he recently
won from Le Pen. So does the introduction of a tougher immigration bill and the controversial law allowing DNA tests for would-be
immigrants, as well as the announced goal of deporting 25,000 illegal immigrants in 2007. Having recently regained much of the political space lost to Le Pen, Sarkozy seems determined to remain firm
on national identity issues and to block Le Pen's attempts to reclaim
them. Whether he eventually succeeds in eliminating the FN from the
French political map will ultimately depend on how he and his rivals
compete over French identity.

7

Conclusion

The major goal of this book was to develop and examine a novel theoretical framework for understanding the early and later development of Far Right parties in Western Europe. Using and extending the insights of the voluminous literature on this topic, this book focused on how party and media behavior affect the initial and subsequent trajectories of Far Right parties. It has shown that in earlier stages of party development, the fortunes of these parties largely depend on exogenous factors: on the availability of political opportunities and communication resources. This book has also suggested that after their initial breakthroughs, these parties increasingly rely on endogenous factors, such as their organizational capacity and their positioning in the competitive space. The study examined party and media behavior in the "most similar" cases of Austria and Germany and in the "most different" case of Greece. It showed that despite marked differences between the Greek and the other two country cases, the trajectory of the Far Right was shaped by similar processes. Moreover, this book suggested the generalizability of these findings by examining the trajectory of the French National Front. More research and further analysis would be needed to show whether the findings are valid for more country cases beyond the four considered here. While this book does not claim generalizability beyond the cases it closely analyzed, it has sought to devise useful conceptual and analytical tools for studying this phenomenon in other empirical settings. By viewing the Far Right through new angles, it has tried to provide the intellectual justification for examining (or re-examining) its trajectory in countries where it has succeeded but also in those where it is has failed. This last chapter looks in more detail at the contributions of this book as a way of summarizing its findings and of suggesting venues for future research. The chapter concludes with an overall discussion about the future of the Far Right.

National Identity and Party Competition

One of the contributions of this book stems from the qualitative analysis of party competition over national identity. Much forgotten in the postwar decades, national identity has become a potent force in party politics since the early 1980s, supplementing traditional competition over economic issues. The entry of national identity into the public domain has transformed the competitive space, inducing parties to take positions on a new axis, one that defines the boundaries of the national collective. Immigration has been the most obvious issue that came to be contested on this axis, but it is not the only one. Asylum rights, citizenship laws, and historical memory have also proved politically contentious, triggering a clash between different sociocultural views. By tracing partisan movements in this new political space, this book has shown that it deserves distinct analytical treatment: Far Right trajectories cannot be sufficiently understood without a consideration of how parties compete over national identity issues.

The main focus of this study was the competitive behavior of mainstream parties. Contrary to some strains in the literature and in line with others, this book has demonstrated that established parties politicized national identity before the Far Right did. The Christian Democrats' turn toward asylum and immigration policy, for example, pre-dated the founding of the Republikaner and the DVU. Similarly, the nationalist mobilization over Macedonia and over identity cards preceded the splintering of the conservative ND and the founding of the Political Spring and LAOS. Evidence from France and Austria also shows that the politicization of national identity was not a direct response to a perceived threat by the Far Right. The French Communists turned toward national identity at the same time Le Pen was struggling to gather the 500 signatures necessary to participate in the presidential elections. In Austria, the controversy over Reder and, later, over Waldheim erupted during a period of FPÖ slide. In all four countries, major parties ethnicized politics before they confronted credible electoral competition from the Far Right. In this sense, mainstream parties were not necessarily reacting to competitive pressures, as part of the literature suggests, but were actively seeking to expand their electoral base.

In attributing party behavior to electoral motivations, this book relied on a conventional understanding of politics that sees politicians as rational actors pursuing vote-maximizing strategies. It also underlined the limitations of these strategies. Such limitations relate to the pressures mainstream parties confront to retreat from earlier programmatic commitments. This book identified two main sources of such pressures. The first relates to the heterogeneity of partisan constituencies: By radicalizing national identity issues, catchall parties risk alienating certain segments of their electorate. In Germany, for example, the *Wende* created tensions between the conservative and the Christian-social and liberal factions of the Christian Democrats; in Austria, the Waldheim controversy caused unease in the business constituency of the conservative party; and in Greece, the nationalist turn in foreign policy in the early 1990s frustrated moderate conservatives who resigned their parliamentary seats in protest. The programmatic shift toward national identity issues is not only a problem for the Right but also for the Left. By playing the immigration card at the 1981 elections, the French Communists alienated Communist intellectuals and eventually had to retract it. The second source of pressure relates to the international context. Parties that choose to radicalize national identity issues risk being isolated by international allies. This is especially the case for parties in government. Both the Greek and the Austrian conservatives confronted the specter of international isolation over the Macedonia and the Waldheim affairs, respectively.

The wavering over national identity issues had damaging electoral consequences for mainstream parties: It legitimized the agenda of previously marginal political actors, presenting them with opportunities for entry into the electoral market. Did the parties not foresee the limitations of their electoral strategies? Or did they choose to take the electoral risk, aware of the potential costs they would have to incur should their competitors manage to capitalize on the political opportunities made available in the electoral market? The evidence presented here suggests that the choice to radicalize national identity issues was more an act of political short-sightedness than a risky political maneuver. When mainstream parties started making national identity a political issue, Far Right groupings were too marginal to pose credible electoral threats. It was hence hard for mainstream actors to foresee the political danger of being outflanked by parties that would make national identity their signature issue. The display of such political short-sightedness might also relate to the limited time horizons politicians tend to have. Their most immediate goal is to win elections; they are less concerned with the future consequences of their positioning in the competitive space. The possibility of creating policy expectations they cannot meet and the likelihood of backtracking from their programmatic positions requires the adoption of much longer time horizons than those politicians can usually afford. This is especially the case for political actors pressured by their waning electoral fortunes. Confronted with the specter of electoral defeats, political parties might be more willing to pursue short-term objectives, which might be untenable in the longer term. Two examples from the analysis presented in earlier chapters might serve to illustrate this point. The Greek Conservatives radicalized the Macedonia issue at a time when their electoral standing was constantly deteriorating because of popular dissatisfaction with their liberalization program and because of continued economic problems. Similarly, the politicization of immigration by the French Communists occurred during a period of partisan slide.

The failure of mainstream parties to fully appreciate the consequences of their strategies is not only a function of their bounded rationality and of their short time horizons but also of internal party dynamics. To analyze these dynamics, it is necessary to go beyond standard theories of political competition. The Downsian treatment of "each party as though it were a single person" (Downs 1957: 26) might be necessary for the generation of such theories, but it is seems to be less useful for understanding party positioning on new issue dimensions: those cutting across the traditional Left-Right axis. A comprehensive understanding of the political process through which parties explore new programmatic territory requires a look "inside" parties and a consideration of intraparty politics (Berman 1997).

The analysis in the empirical chapters has highlighted two different aspects of intraparty politics that might be relevant to the understanding of how new issues become politicized and evolve. The first
is the relationship between national and subnational party elites. The
analysis of party competition tends to attribute shifts in the competitive space to reactions of national party elites to their external environment. But the examination of the German case has pointed to the
influential role of subnational elites in the politicization of national
identity issues (see also Karapin 1999). The evidence presented here
suggests that the politicization of the asylum issue in the early 1980s
and the immigration issue in the early 1990s came from regional party
leaders who managed to turn this into a national political theme. The
Bavarian CSU is a case in point, as it has been the most vocal and
consistent defender of German identity, putting pressure on its sister
party to move closer to its own conservative positions. Subnational
pressures from the Bavarians might help explain why Christian
Democrats adopted a strategy that by the late 1980s seemed to be
suboptimal. It might also explain why – despite the obvious, by then,
drawbacks of this strategy – the Union parties pushed forth with their
anti-immigrant signature drive in the late 1990s.

The second aspect of intraparty politics highlighted here was the
configuration of power between various groups or factions within
parties. Representing diverse preferences within political parties,
intraparty factions usually coalesce around distinct positions on specific issues and exercise considerable pressure on their parties to adopt
these positions (e.g., Belloni and Beller 1976; Sartori 1976: chapter
4). The configuration of power among competing factions and their
respective access to institutional and organizational resources can
help account for how parties maneuver in the competitive space. The
emphasis on intraparty politics is not new, of course. Some of the
most cited accounts of Far Right performance have attributed their
electoral misfortunes to their suboptimal positioning in the competitive space (e.g., Kitschelt with McGann 1995). One of the suggestions
here is that we can learn a lot by trying to extend the intraparty focus
of these analyses to mainstream parties. For there is no reason a priori
why intraparty politics should be more relevant to the analysis of the
Far Right rather than to that of other party families. Again, Germany
serves as an example: The influence of national conservatives among

the Christian Democrats throughout most of the 1980s coincided with the politicization of national identity themes. Their weighty presence in the Union might have helped push the governing coalition in a more conservative position on national identity than the one they might have otherwise adopted. How did the national conservative faction come to prevail over the liberal and the Christian faction at that given time? What resources did it have at its disposal? How did veteran networks and other, less formal associations help the national conservatives push the CDU to a suboptimal positioning in the competitive space? More generally, what are the effects of the configuration of power within parties on their capacity to adopt optimal positions in the competitive space? By answering these questions, future research might discover interesting new ways in which intraparty politics affects interparty competition.

The Media and the Far Right

Another main goal of this book was to highlight the important and multifold role the media can play in the performance of Far Right parties. Most analyses of the Far Right implicitly assume that these parties compete in perfect electoral markets in which they have the means to publicize their views. While this assumption is valid for established parties, which have considerable institutional resources at their disposal (Katz and Mair 1995), it is problematic for marginal parties that desperately seek entry into the electoral market.

This book suggested a number of ways in which the media facilitate the rise of these parties. First, the media lower the barriers of entry into the electoral market by giving new parties the means to disseminate their message across a wider audience than their organizational or financial resources would allow. During their earlier stages of development, smaller parties can rely on media exposure to make up for their organizational weaknesses or economic difficulties. Viewed as a resource for the dissemination of political information, media access can effectively substitute organizational vigor or financial strength. Second, media exposure grants newcomers respectability and legitimacy. Far Right politicians need the media to gain recognizability among voters and to wrap their radical remarks with an aura of officialdom. Finally, the media can provide momentum to minor parties by giving the impression of a mass following that signals their political viability. Such signals can reduce the possibility that their potential voters will strategically desert them in fear of wasting their votes.

The examination of media effects would have been superfluous if the exposure granted to Far Right parties matched their electoral standing or if it followed their electoral advances – that is, if the media merely reflected political realities. The biggest challenge was to demonstrate that by granting or denying exposure to the Far Right, the media do not merely reflect but also shape politics by facilitating or blocking the entry of new players into the electoral market. The most notable effect of the media was in Austria: The mainstream press gave the FPÖ much more exposure than its electoral standing justified, turning Haider into the most visible articulator of public concerns over Austrian identity. The analysis of newspaper content showed that the conservative tabloid *NKZ* as well as the liberal press granted oversized exposure to the FPÖ. Media publicity was also important for the French National Front, which until the early 1980s was a marginal party without substantial organizational basis. The television exposure granted to the party after 1982 facilitated and amplified its secondary electoral breakthroughs and gave it a national platform to broadcast its appeals. Unlike their French and Austrian counterparts, German Far Right parties confronted serious visibility obstacles, as mainstream media purposefully avoided giving them exposure, especially after the early 1990s. Even the most telegenic Far Right leaders, such as Franz Schönhuber, rarely attracted media spotlights. The degree of exposure granted to minor or marginal parties does not only vary across countries but also across time. In Greece, the mainstream press gave enormous publicity to the Political Spring in 1993 but ignored LAOS in the 2004 elections. The markedly increased visibility of LAOS in recent years helped it stage an important breakthrough in the 2007 elections.

The willingness of some mainstream media to grant Far Right parties oversized exposure does not necessarily imply that they have sympathy for such parties. The example of the Austrian weekly news magazine *Profil* helps illustrate this point. Although *Profil* was much more willing to host Haider in its pages and to put him on its cover than the German *Spiegel*, the journalists of *Profil* were almost as critical of the Haider FPÖ as their German counterparts were of the Republikaner. By painting a Hitler-like moustache on his face or asking him whether his supporters greet him with a Nazi salute, *Profil* reporters and other liberal publications went out of their way to show their dislike for Haider and his politics. "When we put him on the cover, people bought the newspaper because they were scared of him or simply because they disliked him. The liberal media just tried to serve its own readers ... to keep up the flame of the resistance."[1] Similarly, the FPÖ made no secret of its antipathy toward the liberal media by verbally attacking journalists and by taking legal action against them. But the open confrontation of the liberal media and the FPÖ rewarded the party with even more publicity, raising questions about real effects of the critical stance some media held toward the party. Did the negative exposure Haider receive from the liberal press hinder or help the growth of the party? Does the *kind* of exposure Far Right parties get matter?

The macrolevel data presented in the empirical chapters cannot yield firm conclusions on the effects of negative exposure on the electoral performance of Far Right parties, but there are compelling reasons to think that for small or fringe parties, bad publicity is better than no publicity at all. Even when negative, the publicization of Far Right appeals makes it easier for voters to draw the critical link between the party and its program, which inadvertently helps Far Rightists draw attention for their cause. Especially when Far Rightists can speak for themselves, they get opportunities to dissociate themselves from the stigma of authoritarianism and to publicize their programmatic appeals. They are unlikely to convince large segments of the electorate about their views, but even a small fraction of the electorate is enough to boost their electoral fortunes. In Germany, for example, the media gave considerable exposure to the Republikaner in 1989 after its January breakthrough in the Berlin elections. While the publicity the party got was negative – the party leader being branded by the mainstream media as a new *Führer* – it was enough to impress 7% of the electorate, or 2 million people, to vote for the Republikaner in the June European elections. Probably shocked by the inadvertent effects of this negative publicity, the German media have since chosen

---

[1] Interview #29, Vienna, July 2004.

to avoid giving a forum to the Far Right, even after some of its most notable regional advances. Clues about the potential effects of negative publicity can also be given by rare survey data *Profil* published in response to reader and political concerns that the outsized publicity the magazine granted to Haider boosted his electoral fortunes. After nearly ten years of the magazine being highly critical of Haider, a sixth of its readership still held a "good opinion" of him.[2] The FPÖ was already a major rather than a negligible political player by that time, but the data are suggestive of the effect that negative exposure can have on small and, in many cases, previously unknown Far Right parties. It only takes a small fraction of the overall audience to be convinced for fringe parties to stage major breakthroughs and to change the political landscape. For parties that do not have alternative means to reach national audiences, the marketing truism that "bad publicity is good publicity" might be valid.

In analyzing how the media affect the electoral trajectories of Far Right parties, this book has relied on the careful examination of newspaper and, where possible, television content as well as on insights from interviews with journalists in the various cases. Preliminary evidence from other West European countries reinforces the emphasis placed in this book on media behavior. The Swedish New Democracy, for example, was a "typical media party" (Rydgren 2006: 63), receiving considerable exposure prior to its 1991 electoral breakthrough, in which it got 6.7% of the national vote. The electoral success of the party has been associated with the communication resources made available to the party before this breakthrough. Contrary to previous practice, the newly founded party was invited to participate in the televised debates broadcasted during the campaign (44). The biggest Swedish newspaper, *Dagens Nyheter*, granted the party considerable free publicity by publishing a debate article by its founders, Ian Wachtmeister and Bert Karlsson, in which they outlined their manifesto. The controversial decision of the editor to publish the article is

[2] Josef Votzi, "Sonderfall Haider?," *Profil*, September 14, 1995, pp. 30–32. Sixteen percent of *Profil* readers had a "good opinion" of Haider, and 81% held "no good opinion." The figures for the overall population were 27% and 67%, respectively. The report states, though, that the 16% was the lowest point for the FPÖ leader in ten years among *Profil* readers.

thought to have helped the party gain respectability and legitimacy and remains memorable even today, nearly two decades afterward.[3]

In Italy, the 1994 alliance with Berlusconi's Forza Italia facilitated the successful transformation of the neo-fascist Movimento Sociale Italiano to the "post-fascist" Alleanza Nazionale. Devoid of communication and financial resources but, more importantly, lacking political legitimacy, the party relied on the "unprecedented access to television" (Gallagher 2000: 74) granted to it from the Berlusconi-owned media to establish itself as a credible political actor that would make a reliable government partner. "Receiving passive support from the Berlusconi media channels, rather than being forced to compete and protect the party's image from critical news coverage like the PDS [Democratic Party of the Left] and Rifondazione Communista, has been a necessary resource for the political rehabilitation of the Alleanza Nazionale" (Statham 1996: 101). The Northern League (*Lega Nord*, LN) also benefited from its alliance with Forza Italia in the mid-1990s, but its entry into national politics occurred earlier, after a series of breakthroughs in regional elections in the late 1980s and early 1990s. These earlier breakthroughs "guaranteed the party both media attention and public funds," thereby giving it the opportunity to expand its organizational base in northern Italy (Betz 1998b: 46). The magnifying effect that local breakthroughs could have in the exposure of newer or smaller parties is evident in the publicity granted to the League by the daily *Il Corriere della Sera*, which boasts the highest circulation in Italy. While the newspaper had only 12 articles in 1987 that included the term "Lega Lombarda" in their headlines, in 1988, it had 47 articles; in 1989, headline references increased to 67, and by 1990, they grew to 217 (Biorcio 2003: 78). As in the case of the French FN's Dreux success in 1983, the local breakthroughs of the Northern League helped turn the party into a national political player.

The electoral fortunes of Dutch Far Right parties in the past few decades are also indicative of how the media can serve as a political resource for the entry of new players into the political scene. The contrasting trajectories of the failed Center Democrats (Centrum

---

[3] Discussion with political editor of the *Dagens Nyheter*, May 2007, Oxford, United Kingdom.

Democraten, CD) and Center Party (Centrumpartij'86, CP'86) in the 1990s and the (briefly) successful Pim Fortuyn List (Lijst Pim Fortuyn, LPF) in 2002 can be attributed, in part, to their varying access to the mainstream media. After a decade in the political wilderness, the CD and the CP'86 were primed for a political breakthrough in the 1994 local, European, and national elections. The mainstream People's Party for Freedom and Democracy (Volkspartij voor Vrijheid en Democratie, VVD) had already placed the immigration issue on the political agenda, and public opinion considered this to be the main national problem in the country (Mudde and Van Holsteyn 2000: 160–161). Capitalizing on the public mood, the two parties made notable gains in the March 1994 local elections, creating expectations that their electoral strength could grow from 0.9% in the previous legislative elections to over 5%. Nevertheless, these local breakthroughs did not have the amplifying effect they had for other European Far Right parties. The two parties received 2.9% in the parliamentary elections in May, and a month later, the CD received merely 1% in the European elections. In part, this failure can be attributed to the limited access the two parties had in mainstream media during the campaign. An analysis of the degree of exposure granted to the CD by the popular Dutch dailies *NRC Handelsblad* and *Algemeen Dagblad* during 1994 shows the difficulty the party has had in gaining media publicity. The CD merely got 2.9% of all references the two newspapers made to the programmatic position of Dutch parties during the campaign (Bornschier 2008: 237).[4] On account of the obstacles the CD had in attracting media spotlights, nearly a third of its voters did not know the name of the only CD MP and leader of the party: Hans Janmaal (Mudde and Van Holsteyn 2000: 157). The expansion of its parliamentary presence from one to three seats in the 1994 elections did little to boost its media presence. In the 1998 campaign, the two Dutch dailies made no references to the programmatic positions of the CD, while in 2002, coverage of party positions was limited to 0.9% of the total references to all parties (Bornschier 2008: 237).

---

[4] When media spotlights turned to the CD, it was to portray it as "a party of fascists, criminals and scum" or to expose the revelations of a local councillor that he was involved in criminal activities against foreigners (Mudde and Van Holsteyn 2000: 148).

The limited exposure of the CD and the CP'86 in the mainstream media contrasts sharply with that of the LPF. Although the List was founded only a few months before the elections, Fortuyn was "able to play an important role in the 2002 media campaign, and to present his ideas in great detail," receiving 25% of all references made in the NRC *Handelsblad* and *Algemeen Dagblad* to political parties (Bornschier 2008: 237). At a time when immigration and asylum policy were salient issues in the public discourse, Fortuyn relied on this outsized exposure to gain ownership of these issues at the expense of established parties. A columnist in the Dutch newsweekly *Elsevier* and a frequent participant on television shows, he was already a recognizable public figure when he decided in 2001 to enter politics. This granted him easy access to television studios and newspaper columns that political startups usually lack. The enormous free publicity given to the party prior to the 2002 campaign allowed Fortuyn to capitalize on his unconventional style and controversial rhetoric to become the prime articulator of widespread concerns over immigration as well as public resentment against the established parties. The newly founded LPF rode on this wave of media publicity to become the second-biggest Dutch party overnight, receiving 17% of the votes in the legislative elections, a few days after its flamboyant leader was assassinated by an animal rights' activist. While the assassination might have helped grant the party more media exposure and some sympathy votes, Fortuyn had impressed voters and surprised pollsters several months before the election and his death (Van Holsteyn and Irwin 2003). The sudden entry of the party into the political mainstream and its quick success relates to the easy access Fortuyn had to the mainstream media.

Access to communication resources can also help explain the emergence of Geert Wilders's Party of Freedom (Partij voor de Vrijheid, PVV) as the undisputed heir of the Fortuyn tradition out of the several startups that competed to attract the "anti-Islamic" vote in the 2006 national elections. A former VVD parliamentarian, Wilders was one of the most quoted politicians in the Dutch parliament prior to his defection from the VVD in 2004 and remained in media spotlights in the subsequent years, in part because of his highly controversial positions on Islam. His easy access to communication resources helped him crown himself as the true representative of the Fortuyn legacy among the LPF, the Party for the Netherlands, and the One Netherlands, which contested the 2006 elections with a similar platform. While all three failed, the PVV received a notable 5.9% and nine seats. Since then, Wilders has continued to dominate the public discourse in the Netherlands but also abroad because of reactions to his film *Fitna*, which portrays Islam as a violent religion and compares it to Nazism. After Dutch prosecutors decided to put Wilders on trial for hate speech and following a British government ban of his entry to the country, the PVV was reported in March 2009 to top Dutch polls with 18%.[5] While more groundwork needs to be done to unravel the knots linking the media with Far-Right party performance, this preliminary evidence reinforces the emphasis placed in this book on the availability of communication resources highlighting possible venues for future research.

Possible Explanations for Media Behavior. Apart from seeking to establish the link between media behavior and party performance, future work should further explore the interplay of factors explaining the way media actors operate in the political system. This book attributes media behavior to three distinct dynamics that might serve as the basis for future research. The most obvious one is commercial: Economic pressures for wider audiences push the media into a symbiotic relationship with Far Rightists. In an era of growing public distrust and political apathy, market dynamics seem to compel media outlets to continuously search for political actors that are likely to generate public interest and attract new audiences. Media spotlights reward good public performers, especially those with an unconventional rhetorical style, such as Haider or Le Pen, who can stir controversy by breaking taboos or attacking the establishment. At any given time, there are many such actors vying for political attention. But Far Rightists enjoy considerable advantages over other newcomers. In part, this is because Far Right parties profess to represent the interests of the "common people" against the political elite conspiring against them (Betz 1994; Mudde 2004; 2007). To fully understand

---

[5] Bruno Waterfield, "Geert Wilders leads Dutch polls" *The Telegraph*, March 3, 2009 (Accessed from http://www.telegraph.co.uk/news/worldnews/europe/netherlands/4933687/Geert-Wilders-leads-Dutch-polls.html on March 9, 2009).

why the media give Far Rightists exposure, though, it is also important to consider the nationalist nature of their appeals. The high public resonance and emotional appeal of the cultural frames used by
the Far Right, along with its simplified representation of the political
world, make it newsworthy, especially for those media targeting mass
audiences. As a veteran Greek reporter put it: "Fear, insecurity and
intolerance sell well! By personifying fear and by placing the blame on
particular social groups, the extremist arguments gain wide appeal.
The wide appeal of their arguments gives them a spot in the evening
news. ... The extreme left is different. It talks about fear, but it does
not personify it. And it certainly does not paint it in national hues."[6]

The symbiosis of media concerns and Far Rightists seems to cut
across ideological inclinations or media types. Regardless of whether
they are liberal or conservative or whether they seek mass or spe-
cialized audiences, mainstream media could face similar commercial
pressures to give exposure to Far Right parties. Such pressures are
likely to be strongest once competitors start giving publicity to Far
Rightists, compelling the rest of the media to follow suit. Because
of the broad resonance, controversial nature, and relative novelty of
Far Right appeals, coverage of this new phenomenon furnishes media
outlets with an opportunity to differentiate their news package from
that of competitors and to attract new audiences. To keep up with
the competition, the rest of the media need to incorporate the Far
Right into their news agendas, albeit in ways that are specific to the
ideological inclinations of the media organization. The analysis of
the exposure granted to the FPÖ by the *NKZ* and *Profil* is suggestive
of the similar push different media have, to give access and exposure
to the Far Right. While standing on opposite sides of the ideological
spectrum and targeting different audiences, both publications chose
to give outsized exposure to Haider in the mid-1980s.

Commercial dynamics are important determinants of media behavior, but even in the market-based Anglo-Saxon systems (Hallin and
Mancini 2004), the media cannot merely be thought of as economic
agents that seek to maximize profits but also as political actors trying to shape political outcomes. After all, many newspapers, magazines, and, to a lesser extent, television channels have explicit partisan

---

[6] Interview #14, Athens, February 2004.

sympathies, while some are owned by politicians. The political agendas of the media make it harder to attribute behavior to purely commercial motives. Some media might grant outsized exposure to the Far Right not only to expand their audiences but also to serve their political goals. The *NKZ*, for example, is thought to have granted considerable publicity to the Haider FPÖ because it shared its critical views of the Austrian political establishment, European Union accession, and Eastern European immigration. The programmatic appeals of the FPÖ did not only grant the newspaper novel commercial possibilities but also yielded opportunities to bring about political change. While Haider used the newspaper to publicize his controversial views, the newspaper also used these views as a means to push through its own political agenda.

While political and commercial dynamics are conceptually distinct, empirically, the dividing line is often blurry. Because the supply and demand of political views is closely intertwined, the political agenda of a news medium is also an inseparable component of its commercial strategy. A Rightist news channel seeks to tap into the pool of conservative viewers, just as a liberal newspaper seeks to attract like-minded readers. It is hence hard to distinguish what is clearly political in media behavior. The distinction between political and commercial motivations becomes even fuzzier when one considers the full range of economic interests media concerns often have. Such interests include access to lucrative public licenses or government contracts. In the 1990s, for example, the owner of the *NKZ*, Hans Dichand, fought a legal battle against the Austrian government for a commercial television channel. His efforts found support from the Haider FPÖ, "which spearheaded the fight to break up the ORF [public broadcasting] monopoly."[7] Was the free publicity the newspaper granted to Haider because of the coincidence of their political views or was the Haider FPÖ the means for the *NKZ* owner to advance his commercial interests?

The boundary between political and economic interests is even more blurry in Greece, where a row between media owners and the conservative government in the early 1990s coincided with the

---

[7] Eric Frey, "Writing on the wall for Austria TV monopoly," *Financial Times*, July 5, 1995. ORF is the Austrian public broadcaster.

outsized publicity granted to the young leader of the newly founded Political Spring. A few days before the 1993 elections, the conservative PM openly accused media owners of funding and publicizing this party to undercut his thin parliamentary majority and bring his government down. In a highly politicized media system, as the Greek one, the oversized exposure granted to the PS should not be surprising: It is almost to be expected that the media sympathizers of the political opposition try to hurt the government. This behavior is more puzzling, though, when it comes from traditional media allies of the government. Why did the most consistent supporters of the conservative party among the Greek media give such enormous exposure to the PS? The allegations of the conservative PM that the media publicized and funded the new party because the government did not grant their owners licenses or state contracts point to the complex nature of the relations the media have with the state. In a media system like the Greek one, where media owners also own big construction, shipping, or oil concerns, political considerations for media behavior can be indistinct from commercial considerations.

On account of the difficulty in distinguishing commercial from political considerations, future research on the political determinants of media behavior will benefit from a careful examination of publicly owned media. Public ownership restricts the reliance of the media on market mechanisms because part or all of their funding comes from the state. This makes it easier to observe the political rationale for media behavior, especially in those settings where public broadcasting is politicized and at the "whims" of the government of the day (Humphreys 1996).

Where political reasoning informs the behavior of the media, it can be expected that the degree of exposure granted to marginal parties will rely on political calculations about how the newcomers will affect the political landscape. Those expecting political benefits from the advent of a neophyte are likely to promote it, while those threatened by it would want to block it. The discussion of the French case illustrated this point. In the early 1980s, the Socialist government intervened, asking the three public broadcasters to grant Le Pen prime time exposure. Although Mitterrand claimed to be acting in the interest of political pluralism, his critics associated the intervention with a politically motivated attempt to split the conservative vote by helping the National Front become a visible political force in French politics. After Mitterrand's intervention, Le Pen was regularly hosted on major television shows, gaining access to national audiences.

Media behavior depends not only on commercial interests and political calculations but also on the professional norms shared by media practitioners. Such norms are more influential in media organizations or environments where editors and journalists enjoy a considerable degree of autonomy from the political and economic realm. In such circumstances, editorial decisions affecting the Far Right are likely to follow professional conventions of how to deal with extremist opinions. Some of these conventions favor granting exposure – although not necessarily excessive exposure – to the Far Right. In Britain, for example, professional norms of impartiality encourage journalists to present views that reflect the entire political spectrum. As the head of BBC's television news puts it: "We need more Taleban interviews, more British National Party interviews – of course put on air with due consideration – and the full range of moderate opinions. All those views need to be treated with the same level of sceptical inquiry and respect."[8] This view contrasts with that of many German journalists who purposefully avoid granting the Far Right any direct publicity. Interviews with German journalists and analysis of newspaper and television content suggested that there is a consensus in Germany against giving Far Rightists a forum to disseminate their views. This is not because German newspapers take extra care to avoid framing foreigners in negative terms. Just like their Austrian or English (e.g., Eatwell 2000) counterparts, some German media are often accused of feeding racism and xenophobia through their sensationalist stories on problems associated with immigration (e.g., Jäger 1993; Trebbe and Köhler 2002). German journalists differ in that they largely consider the silencing of the Far Right to be some sort of a civic duty. To some extent, this makes Germany extraordinary, as the strength and spread of this consensus seems to be unparalleled. But it is not unique: Media in other countries, such as Belgium or the Netherlands, also claim to

[8] Peter Horrocks, public lecture delivered at St. Anne's College and at the Reuters Institute of Oxford University, 28 November 2006. Downloaded from http://reutersinstitute.politics.ox.ac.uk/about/discussion/finding_tv_news_lost_audience.html (last accessed: December 24, 2007).

be following a strategy of "silencing [the Far Right] to death" (Mudde 2007: 252). Although Germany is, in many ways, an unusual case, it is not unique among European democracies in having media that are unwilling to give a forum to the Far Right. The controversies mentioned at the beginning of this book over the exposure granted to the Swedish and to the Greek Far Right are suggestive of the overall skepticism about the way the media treat the Far Right.

Each of the three dynamics explicated here can change the parameters of party competition by helping new actors enter the political market. By examining how commercial, political, and normative factors interact, we can hence gain a richer understanding of how the media affect party politics. This understanding will also benefit from a careful consideration of technological dynamics. New technologies affect the capacity of political neophytes to enter the political market, exercising similar pressures on political systems to open up. One of the most notable technological changes in the media industry is the rise of the Internet. The Web decreases the cost of disseminating information to wide audiences, giving marginal parties the capacity to overcome visibility obstacles posed by the lack of advertising funds or media access. Moreover, the Web provides the means for establishing direct contact between parties and voters through online interactive tools. West European Far Right parties are well aware of the communication potential of this medium, and they extensively use the Web to disseminate information and interact with prospective voters. At present, though, their online presence cannot substitute the importance of party visibility in the traditional media. Compared to these older media, the Internet remains a minor player, used on a weekly basis by only a third of EU citizens.[9] According to one of the most frequently cited studies on the topic, only a fraction of these users visit party Web sites (Norris 2003). Nevertheless, the dissemination of political information through the Internet can be expected to grow in the future, following the linear upward trend in Internet usage. This will mostly benefit political newcomers by decreasing their reliance on traditional means of communication. Given the higher levels

---

[9] Maria Smihily (2007). "Internet usage 2007," *Eurostat* 23: http://epp.eurostat. ec.europa.eu/cache/ITY_OFFPUB/KS-QA-07-023/EN/KS-QA-07-023-EN.PDF (last accessed: January 31, 2008).

of Internet penetration among younger users, this resource could become the means for attracting first-time voters or previous non-voters.

The Far Right Across Time

The analysis of the Far Right is largely one of political change, and the phenomenon can be best understood by examining it across time. The temporal approach in this book has marked a departure from the spatial comparisons dominant in this literature. What has this departure added to our understanding of the phenomenon? The basic claim of this book is that the relative weight of explanatory factors might vary across different phases of party development. Certain variables can best explain the initial trajectory of a party and others its subsequent development. The point of differentiation between the early and the later phase of party development is that of an initial electoral breakthrough – the time when electoral strength increases significantly from one election to the next. Prior to such breakthroughs, smaller parties are largely at the whims of bigger competitors and the mass media, but as they grow, they are better able to determine their own destinies. Electoral advances help minor parties enhance their recruitment efforts, improve their financial resources, and gain media access. After this point, their handling of these newly gained resources becomes of increased analytical relevance: The way they use them can go a long way to account for the parties' fate.

One finding of this book is that during their early stages of development, the electoral prospects of marginal or minor parties do not depend on their organizational capacity. Nearly all Far Right parties studied here had non-existent or embryonic organizational structures before achieving their initial electoral breakthroughs. Although much of the literature ascribes causal attributes to organizational factors, the careful analysis of party trajectories shows that organizational growth is largely the effect rather than the cause of electoral success. The Austrian FPÖ experienced membership decline prior to its 1986 breakthrough, and the German Republikaner had failed to set organizational roots outside Bavaria before its 1989 breakthrough in the European elections. In Greece, the Political Spring was only formed a few months before the 1993 elections, while LAOS continues to lack solid organizational structures. Even the French National Front, which is thought to be the archetype of organizational strength, seemed to be in organizational disarray prior to its series of break-throughs between 1983 and 1986. By tracing party trajectories across time, this book showed that in all these cases, organizational growth followed the parties' initial electoral success.

Another finding concerns the positioning of Far Right parties in the competitive space. While a significant body of literature consid-ers this to be an important determinant of Far Right performance, the evidence presented here suggests the need to qualify such claims. During their earlier phase of development, the specific appeals Far Right parties make seem to be inconsequential for their performance. The National Front, for example, was well-placed to benefit from public concerns over immigration, but for many years, its stance on immigration did not yield electoral gains. Other Far Right parties shifted to a more favorable position in the competitive space without alleviating their electoral misfortunes. The German NPD is a good example: Its turn to "new nationalist" themes since the late 1970s has not been rewarded in the electoral market. Two main reasons explain why the positioning of Far Right parties has a limited effect on their performance during this early phase. The first relates to the availability of political opportunities in the competitive space. Unless mainstream parties leave an opening for the Far Right, its position-ing does not matter as much. Kitschelt and McGann (1995) rightly consider the availability of such opportunities as necessary for the entry of the Far Right into the electoral market. This book adds that these opportunities are created when mainstream parties play and then retract the nationalist card. The second reason why Far Right appeals might be inconsequential during this earlier stage is because they might be unknown to national publics. This is why the media is important: It is only when they give the Far Right exposure that they enable it to capitalize on the opportunities made available in the electoral market.

This book mainly focused on the early trajectories of Far Right parties prior to their electoral breakthroughs. But it also analyzed the trajectory of these parties after their breakthroughs. In each of the four countries, Far Right parties achieved a breakthrough in a national election, increasing their electoral standing significantly. The

Austrian FPÖ nearly doubled its vote in the 1986 elections; the German Republikaner got more than 7% in its first participation in the 1989 European elections; the Greek Political Spring suddenly became the third-biggest Greek party in the 1993 legislative elections; LAOS got 3.8% of the vote and ten seats in the Greek parliament in 2007; and the National Front got approximately 10% of the vote in the 1984 European elections and the 1985 regional elections before its success in the 1986 legislative elections. In all these cases, their sudden spurt in support gave these parties access to increased funding in the form of state subventions, improving their financial resources. Moreover, it boosted their recruitment efforts and helped them widen their membership base. Finally, the breakthroughs enhanced the visibility of the parties in the mainstream media, weakening the inhibitions of some media to give them exposure. In short, the breakthroughs increased the financial, organizational, and communication resources of these parties, granting them an opportunity to permanently change the electoral map in their favor by establishing credibility on issues with relatively wide public resonance. But their subsequent trajectories varied substantially. The FPÖ and the National Front managed to sustain and improve their electoral standings after these initial breakthroughs, while support for the Republikaner and the Political Spring quickly waned. Why did some parties persist and grow after their breakthroughs but others collapse?

Given the earlier emphasis on mainstream party competition, it is tempting to attempt explaining the divergent trajectories of the Far Right by examining the behavior of their mainstream competitors. In all the cases analyzed in this book, the electoral advances of political neophytes triggered competitive efforts by mainstream parties to trespass the newcomers' programmatic territory. In Austria, the governing coalition introduced a series of tough immigration and asylum laws that sought to co-opt the anti-immigration appeals of the FPÖ. In Germany, the reunification of Germany gave the Christian Democrats the opportunity to deprive the Republikaner of a key programmatic appeal. Furthermore, the Christian Democrats got credit in the early 1990s for toughening the asylum law and in the late 1990s for rejecting the dual citizenship legislation of the social democratic government. In Greece, the conservative opposition adopted a tougher stance on Macedonia to match that of the ascendant Political Spring.

It later sought to reclaim the "national" space by its hard stance on Turkish claims in the Aegean Sea. Finally, in France, the incoming Chirac, Balladur, and Juppé governments in the 1980s and 1990s sought to win back FN defectors by introducing stricter immigration legislation and by becoming tougher on law and order issues. In each case, mainstream parties – especially the moderate Right – sought to recapture the political space lost to the Far Right by adopting more conservative positions on national identity issues. But this strategy only worked in some of the cases. In Germany and in Greece, the mainstream Right managed to quickly reclaim the political space lost to the Far Right. But in France and Austria, efforts to co-opt the Far Right miserably failed, as the FPÖ and the National Front sustained and extended their earlier electoral gains. The varying success of co-optation strategies suggests that we must go beyond mainstream party behavior to understand the reasons for the trajectories of Far Right parties after their breakthroughs.

The theoretical framework formulated in this book suggests that we can better understand the divergent fortunes of Far Right parties after their initial electoral advances if we focus on factors endogenous to their development. For while their internal characteristics have a limited effect on their early trajectory, they are important for their subsequent development. This book examined the effect of two distinct characteristics: appeals and organization. For example, it suggested that the persistence and growth of the FPÖ was partly because of the extension of its appeal beyond the issues on which it based its initial support. And it associated the sudden collapse of the Political Spring to its failure to consistently extend its ethnocentric appeals beyond the Macedonia issue. The positioning of successful Far Right parties in the competitive space might also explain the collapse of the FPÖ: Government participation and international condemnation restricted its capacity to move freely in the competitive space and compelled it to moderate its position. Similarly, the fall of the FN in the 2007 French elections might also be attributed to the perceived moderation of its anti-immigrant appeals. The divergent fortunes of Far Right parties after their breakthroughs are also related to their varying organizational capacities. The two parties that persisted after their breakthroughs already had (in the case of the FPÖ) or quickly created (in the case of the FN) effective organizational structures that helped combat efforts by their mainstream competitors to regain their voters. To the contrary, the two parties that failed to establish nationwide organizational roots – and, in the case of the Republikaner, witnessed bitter infighting – collapsed. More research and more cases would be needed to discover the exact mechanisms and processes through which internal party characteristics shape the trajectories of parties after their initial successes.

Such research will gain additional analytical traction by comparing the internal characteristics of parties belonging to other political families. So far, the literature has largely avoided such comparisons, treating the Far Right as an exceptional party family that merits a distinct analytical approach. This treatment might need more justification in the future. Is it based on the ideological distinctiveness of the Far Right? If so, how does Far Right ideology affect specific party attributes? Alternatively, is the separate treatment of the Far Right based on a distinct set of organizational attributes that make Far Right parties different from other minor or established parties? If so, how does the organization of the Far Right differ from that of Green or Christian Democrat parties? And does the effect of party organization vary across party family? Is it more important for Far Right parties than for others? Answers to these questions will illuminate our understanding of the Far Right and will provide stronger linkages between the voluminous literature on the Far Right and broader comparative work on parties and elections.

The Future of the Far Right

In the past few decades, Far Right parties have transformed the electoral landscape of Western Europe, putting more pressure on party systems than most other postwar phenomena have. Their electoral advances have raised concerns about the stability of European democracies and have evoked memories of interwar democratic disintegration. This is neither because Far Right parties are Nazi death troops nor because Far Right ballots are bullets: They are unlikely to bring about democratic collapse. The rise of the Far Right has caused so much concern because its xenophobic and exclusivist rhetoric is thought to undermine the principles of pluralist democracy. The danger the Far Right poses for basic democratic principles makes it worth speculating about its future. Is this phenomenon likely to persist in the next decades? Will West European electorates continue to vote for these parties? Or will mainstream parties eventually manage to recapture the political space lost to the Far Right and regain their lost constituencies?

The advent of the deeper economic crisis since the end of World War II makes these questions more pressing than ever. Major European economies have been hit badly by the global financial turmoil, and according to the IMF, they are expected to shrink in both 2009 and 2010, pushing unemployment rates to double-digit figures.[10] While economic conditions have not been proven to directly affect the electoral fortunes of Far Right parties, the unprecedented depth and possible length of the downturn, along with the public mistrust it has generated, is likely to exacerbate social tensions and could fuel political extremism. According to the European commissioner for social affairs, Vladimir Spidla, "if you are in a situation where lots of people are excluded from work, this will of course create social tensions." In light of the perceived increase in attacks against the Roma in countries such as Hungary and the Czech Republic, Mr. Spidla noted that "the consequences can be limited, but they can also prove dangerous: we've all seen what happened in the banlieues in France, we've seen also the rise of extremism in central Europe and elsewhere."[11] Will the Far Right, then, become the main electoral beneficiary of the crisis? Or will the economic downturn become the impetus for the abandonment of cultural politics and the return to partisan competition over materialist issues, thus benefiting mainstream parties?

Political opponents of the Far Right might hope that the economic crisis will shift the parameters of political competition away from its signature issues, turning attention to traditional materialist concerns, such as employment, redistribution, and growth. The dire economic conditions and the pressing need for government action might push European electorates away from largely untested Far Right parties, as it did during in the 1970s, which was the most "quiet" decade of the Far Right. In times of high uncertainty, voters might be more willing

[10] "World Economic Outlook: Crisis and Recovery," International Monetary Fund, April 2009.
[11] Stanley Pignal, "Europe jobs crisis poses 'threat' to social order," *Financial Times*, May 5, 2009.

to trust mainstream politicians with the delicate task of implementing sound policy solutions than to lend their support to parties with limited experience in policy making and with unproven records of political efficacy. Even to staunch government critics, the idea of having Le Pen, Wilders, Karatzaferis, or Dewinter help draft complex financial instruments for recapitalizing European banks or bailing out automakers might seem absurd.

While seemingly plausible, this scenario is unlikely to play out in the years to come. Instead of signaling the demise of identity politics, the economic crisis is likely to intensify partisan appeals to nationalist sentiments. At the most basic level, such appeals could take the form of economic nationalism. The crisis tempts European nations to start questioning the "sanctity" of the common market and introduce protectionist measures that seek to shield domestic producers from foreign competition. The suggestion by French president Sarkozy that French companies should relocate back to France in return for getting tax breaks and the launch of a "buy Spanish" campaign by the Spanish government might offer a prelude to a long period of protectionism that will reinforce the use of national origin as the basis for organizing politics. At a different level, the crisis might tempt politicians to take tougher positions against immigration or asylum at the risk of exacerbating tensions between native and foreign workers. Confronted with the prospect of cutting social expenditures or increasing taxes to make up for the budgetary shortfalls created by the fiscal stimuli and corporate bailouts, politicians on both the Left and the Right are likely to increasingly resort to identity politics in an attempt to prevent voter defections to the Far Right and in search of new electoral niches.

The findings of this book show that the strategy of pandering to nationalist sentiments is a double-edged sword for mainstream parties. Public appeals to national identity can help moderates reclaim the programmatic territory conceded to the Far Right by crowding out the political space on their Right. By playing the nationalist card, the German Christian Democrats were able to squeeze the Far Right out of the electoral market, both in the late 1980s and in the early 1990s. Similarly, Sarkozy's explicit appeals to French identity in the 2007 elections allowed the French conservatives to attract FN voters, thereby limiting Far Right support to its lowest levels in two decades.

Based on these examples, conservative strategists wishing to win back votes from the Far Right might think that taking tough positions on cultural issues is the way to do it.

Trying to outbid the Far Right, though, also has serious limitations that can potentially outweigh the gains of this strategy. As suggested in the analysis of the German case, efforts to trespass the programmatic territory of the Far Right are likely to create internal dissent and international sanction that make this strategy unsustainable in the long run. The mainstream parties examined in this book bring together heterogeneous constituencies whose simultaneous support requires the delicate balancing of party appeals. Nationalist appeals tend to disrupt fragile intraparty coalitions by alienating more liberal members of these parties. While internal dissent is more likely in parties of the Left, which usually situate themselves on the multicultural side of the identity axis, parties of the Right are not immune to internal feuds. Parties with strong Christian and liberal traditions, such as the German Christian Democrats, or those juggling the programmatic preferences of business and traditionalist constituencies pay a high price for their pandering to nationalist sentiments. As the CDU realized after its Pyrrhic 1987 victory, attempts to co-opt the agenda of the Far Right risk losing more moderate constituents. Apart from internal dissent, mainstream parties playing the nationalist card risk alienating important international allies. The international isolation of Austria in the late 1980s and Greece in the early 1990s highlight the foreign policy costs of nationalist party appeals. While seemingly an "easy" domestic issue that can help parties make catchall appeals, historical memory often has an international dimension, which complicates efforts to score domestic political points. The cost of losing allies abroad and constituents at home makes tough positions on national identity difficult to sustain over time. Playing the nationalist card can backfire, especially in settings where the Far Right has the resources to compete against its mainstream competitors.

While this book has mostly highlighted the political risks of a Sarkozy- or Kohl-like strategy, it is also worth keeping in mind the social risks. European conservatives often justify pandering to nationalist sentiments by arguing that national identity constitutes a binding force in society, giving citizens a sense of belonging and helping them confront socioeconomic challenges. Their arguments are similar to those of theorists of "liberal nationalism" who view national identity as a basic means to establish social unity and social stability or even democracy and redistribution (e.g., Tamir 1993; Kymlicka 1995; Miller 1995; Moore 2001). Despite the theoretical merits of such arguments, the experience of the past few decades has, in many cases, shown the opposite: that the politicization of national identity issues undermines social tolerance and cohesion by identifying foreigners as the source of socioeconomic malaise. Intense partisan rows over asylum, immigration, and citizenship tend to widen the gap between the native and the foreign population, making the latter feel even more isolated. In part, this is because of the irresponsible politicking of a few conservative legislators who seek to gain votes by spreading anxiety, insecurity, and intolerance. But it is also because national identity issues are difficult to address in public without legitimating extremist claims. The distinction between nationalist and more moderate positions on national identity is easy to go unnoticed among largely inattentive publics who can readily identify with the in-group and against an out-group. The series of wildcat strikes in Britain in January 2009 against the use of foreign workers by construction companies shows how difficult it is for mainstream politicians to draw a clear line between moderate appeals to national identity and racism. The protests, held under the slogan "British jobs for British workers" that Gordon Brown used in his 2007 address to the Labour Party Conference, were hijacked by members of the Far Right British National Party, who called the strikes a "great day for British nationalism."[12] Even in those cases where politicians seek to draw distinctions between moderate and extremist positions, they inadvertently provide a fertile ground for the articulation of less moderate arguments.

Given the political and social risks associated with efforts to recapture the programmatic territory of the Far Right, are there better alternatives? One possibility lies with a concerted effort to construct a new identity that takes into account the changing demographic realities of Western Europe. This identity would have to place loyalty on the

[12] "Wildcat strikes over foreign workers spread across Britain," *The Times*, January 30, 2009 (Online edition, accessed from http://www.timesonline.co.uk/tol/news/uk/article5617015.ece?token=null&offset=0&page=1 on February 5, 2009).

institutions and principles of constitutional democracy rather than on ethnic or historical constituents of identity, much like Habermas has suggested. But the construction of this civic identity is not an easy task. As critics of constitutional patriotism have noted, this concept relies on abstractions that cannot create deep attachments to the state. Moreover, the construction of a civic identity requires a broad political consensus that is difficult to achieve among political actors who are largely interested in short-term electoral gains. That major parties have failed in the past few decades to take decisive steps toward the construction of a more pluralistic identity is suggestive of this difficulty. In the absence of more effective and more realistic alternatives for dealing with public concerns over national identity, mainstream parties are likely to continue playing the nationalist card in the years to come. The growth and persistence of the Far Right is the cost they must be willing to pay.

The price to be paid for toying with cultural politics will be higher in those political settings where Far Rightists have easy access to communication resources. Far Right parties receiving outsized exposure will be able to sneak into the mainstream debate and outflank their mainstream competitors. Can the media, then, serve as a bulwark against the Far Right in the years to come? There is reason to doubt this. The commercial rationale motivating the media to give Far Rightists outsized exposure is unlikely to go away. In fact, the global economic recession will probably reinforce market-induced pressures on media outlets, granting more authority to profit-driven owners over principle-driven journalists. Even in media environments where journalistic norms keep Far Rightists off television screens and out of newspaper columns, there is likely to be a growing commercial push to give a forum to national populists in order to attract wider audiences. The dire financial conditions of quality newspapers, such as the *New York Times* or the *Boston Globe*, might not be as much of a prologue to the obituary of print journalism but might signal the beginning of an era in which media owners have increased – and perhaps unprecedented – authority over journalists. The example of the financially struggling *Le Monde*, where journalists had to choose in 2008 between firing 25% of their colleagues or ceding their controlling stake of the newspaper (that guaranteed editorial independence) to new owners might be a prelude to a period of growing proprietary meddling in newsrooms. Corporate interference will prioritize commercial profit, pushing aside journalistic qualms about granting publicity to the Far Right. In such settings, identity politics will prove costly to mainstream parties, as Far Right parties will find it easier to enter the electoral market.

To the extent that media owners are becoming the gatekeepers for the entry of Far Right parties to the electoral market, scholars and practitioners alike must try to better conceptualize and understand the input of media ownership in politics. To do so, they would need to fully consider the complex set of economic motivations that influences the way the media behave in the political sphere. The drive for bigger audiences is certainly the most important one, but in smaller media markets, such as those existing in many European countries, media conglomerates seem to have a much more intricate set of commercial preferences affecting their behavior. The most noteworthy of these interests are those that involve monetary transactions with the state. Sarkozy's €600 million rescue package for the French press announced in 2008 is one example of such transactions, showing that even in some of the biggest European markets, the media rely on state subsidies to stay afloat. State subsidies are only one of many forms of transactions between politicians and media owners. As the discussion of the Greek and the Austrian cases has shown, media conglomerates rely on the state for lucrative broadcasting licenses and public contracts. To better understand the drivers of media behavior, political scientists need to take into consideration the full range of economic transactions taking place in the increasingly narrower space separating media owners from political executives. In turn, media watchdogs must make sure that these transactions are fully disclosed. It is the job of media regulators to ensure that civil society acquires a better grasp of the dynamics driving the interplay between the media and politics; and of how these dynamics affect the quality of democracy.

Bibliography

Abedi, Amir (2002). "Challenges to established parties: The effects of party system features on the electoral fortunes of anti-political-establishment parties," *European Journal of Political Research*, 41(4): 551–583.

Art, David (2008). "The organizational origins of the contemporary Radical Right: The case of Belgium," *Comparative Politics*, 40(4): 421–440.

(2006). *The politics of the Nazi past in Germany and Austria*, Cambridge: Cambridge University Press.

Backer, Susann (2000). "Right-wing extremism in unified Germany," in Paul Hainsworth, ed., *The politics of the extreme Right: From the margins to the mainstream*, London: Pinter.

Backes, Uwe and Eckhard Jesse (1993). *Politischer extremismus in der Bundesrepublik Deutschland*, Bonn: Bundeszentrale für politische Bildung.

Baldwin, Peter (1990). *Reworking the past: Hitler, the Holocaust and the historians' debate*, Boston: Beacon.

Bartels, Larry M. (1988). *Presidential primaries and the dynamics of public choice*, Princeton, NJ: Princeton University Press.

Beiner, Ronald (1995). "Introduction," in Ronald Beiner, ed., *Theorizing citizenship*, New York: State University of New York Press.

Belloni, Frank P. and Dennis C. Beller (1976). "The study of party factions as competitive political organizations," *Political Research Quarterly*, 29: 531–549.

Bennett, Stephen Earl, Staci Rhine, Richard S. Flickinger, and Linda L.M. Bennett (1999). "'Video Malaise' revisited: Public trust in the media and government," *The International Journal of Press/Politics*, 4(4): 8–23.

Berman, Sheri (1997). "The life of the party," *Comparative Politics*, 30(1): 101–122.

Betz, Hans-Georg (2002). "Xenophobia, identity politics and exclusionary populism in Western Europe," in Leo Panitch and Colyn Leys, eds., *The Socialist Register 2003*, London: Merlin Press.

(1998a). "Introduction," in Hans-Georg Betz and Stefan Immerfall, eds., *The new politics of the Right: Neo-populist parties and movements in established democracies*, London: Palgrave Macmillan.

(1998b). "Against Rome: The Lega Nord," in Hans-Georg Betz and Stefan Immerfall, eds., *The new politics of the Right: Neo-populist parties and movements in established democracies*, London: Palgrave Macmillan.

(1994). *Radical Right-wing populism in Western Europe*, New York: St. Martin's Press.

(1990). "Politics of resentment: Right-wing radicalism in West Germany," *Comparative Politics*, 23(1): 45–60.

(1988). "*Deutschlandpolitik* on the margins: On the evolution of contemporary New Right nationalism in the Federal Republic," *New German Critique*, 44: 127–157.

Biorcio, Roberto (2003). "The *Lega Nord* and the Italian media system," in Gianpietro Mazzoleni et al., eds., *The media and neo-populism: A contemporary comparative analysis*, Westport, CT: Praeger.

Birenbaum, Guy (1992). *Le Front National en politique*, Paris: Éditions Balland.

Birenbaum, Guy and Marina Villa (2003). "The media and neo-populism in France," in Gianpietro Mazzoleni et al., eds., *The media and neo-populism: A contemporary comparative analysis*, Westport, CT: Praeger.

Bizeul, Daniel (2003). *Avec ceux du FN. Un sociologue au Front National*, Paris: La Découverte.

Bluhm, William T. (1973). *Building an Austrian nation: The political integration of a western state*, New Haven, CT: Yale University Press.

Bornschier, Simon (2008). *The transformation of historical cleavages and the rise of Right-wing populist parties in Western Europe*, Doctoral Dissertation: University of Zurich.

Bréchon, Pierre and Subrata Kumar Mitra (1992). "The National Front in France: The emergence of an Extreme Right protest movement," *Comparative Politics*, 25(1): 63–82.

Brubaker, Rogers (1992). *Citizenship and nationhood in France and Germany*, Cambridge, MA: Harvard University Press.

Bruckmüller, Ernst (2003). *The Austrian nation: Cultural consciousness and sociopolitical processes*, Riverside, CA: Ariadne.

Budge, Ian and Dennis Farlie (1983). "Party competition – Selective emphasis or direct confrontation? An alternative view with data," in Hans Daadler and Peter Mair, eds., *Western European party systems: Continuity and change*, London: Sage.

Budge, Ian, Hans-Dieter Klingemann, Andrea Volkens, Judith Bara, and Eric Tanenbaum (2001). *Mapping policy preferences: Estimates for parties, electors, and governments 1945–1998*, Oxford: Oxford University Press.

Bundeswahlleiter (2005). "Wahl zum 16. Deutschen Bundestag am 18. September 2005," Wiesbaden: Statistisches Bundesamt.

Camus, Jean-Yves (1996). "Origine et formation du Front National (1972–1981)," in Nonna Mayer and Pascal Perrineau, eds., *Le Front National à découvert*, Paris: Presses de la Fondation Nationale des Sciences Politiques.

Caramani, Daniele (2000). *Elections in Western Europe since 1815: Electoral results by constituencies*, London: Macmillan.

Carmines, Edward G. and James A. Stimson (1989). *Issue evolution: Race and the transformation of American politics*, Princeton, NJ: Princeton University Press.

Carter, Elizabeth L. (2005). *The Extreme Right in Western Europe: Success or failure?* Manchester: Manchester University Press.

(2002). "Proportional representation and the fortunes of Right-wing extremist parties," *West European Politics*, 25(3): 125–146.

Castles, Stephen (1985). "The guests who stayed – The debate on 'Foreigners Policy' in the German Federal Republic," *International Migration Review*, 19(3): 517–534.

Cooper, Alice Holmes (2002). "Party-sponsored protest and the movement society: The CDU/CSU mobilizes against citizenship law reform," *German Politics*, 11(2): 88–104.

Dalton, Russel J., Scott C. Flanagan, and Paul Allen Beck, eds. (1984). *Electoral change in advanced industrial democracies: Realignment or dealignment?* Princeton, NJ: Princeton University Press.

Danforth, Loring M. (1995). *The Macedonian conflict: Ethnic nationalism in a transnational world*, Princeton, NJ: Princeton University Press.

Davies, Peter (1999). *The National Front in France: Ideology, discourse and power*, London: Routledge.

DeClair, Edward G. (1999). *Politics on the fringe: The people, policies and organization of the French National Front*, Durham: Duke University Press.

Demertzis, Nicolas, Stylianos Papathanassopoulos, and Antonis Armenakis (1999). "Media and nationalism: The Macedonian question," *Harvard International Journal of Press/Politics*, 4(3): 26–50.

Dimitras, Panayote E. (1992). "Greece: The virtual absence of an extreme right," in Paul Hainsworth, ed., *The Extreme Right in Europe and the USA*, Pinter: London.

Downs, Anthony (1957). *An economic theory of democracy*, New York: Addison Wesley.

Downs, William M. (2002). "How effective is the Cordon Sanitaire? Lessons from efforts to contain the Far Right in Belgium, France, Denmark and Norway," *Journal für Konflikt- und Gewaltforschung*, 4(1): 32–51.

Durand, Géraud (1996). *Enquête au coeur du Front National,* Paris: Jacques Grancher.

Eatwell, Roger (2005). "Charisma and the revival of the European extreme right," in Jens Rydgren, ed., *Movements of exclusion: Radical right-wing populism in the Western world,* Hauppage: Nova Science.

(2002). "The rebirth of Right-wing charisma? The cases of Jean-Marie Le Pen and Vladimir Zhirinovsky," *Totalitarian Movements and Political Religions,* 3(3): 1–23.

(2000). "The rebirth of the 'Extreme Right' in Western Europe," *Parliamentary Affairs,* 53(3): 407–425.

Eley, Geoff (2000). "Historical accountability and the contest of memory: Nazism and business history," *The Public Historian,* 22(3): 139–145.

Ellinas, Antonis (2007). "Phased out: The Far Right in Western Europe," *Comparative Politics,* 39(3): 353–372.

Esser, Hartmut and Hermann Korte (1985). "Federal Republic of Germany," in Thomas Hammar, ed., *European immigration policy: A comparative study,* Cambridge: Cambridge University Press.

Faist, Thomas (1994). "How to define a foreigner? The symbolic politics of immigration in German partisan discourse, 1978–1992," in Martin Baldwin-Edwards and Martin A. Schain, eds., *The politics of immigration in Western Europe,* London: Frank Cass.

Faux, Emmanuel, Thomas Legrand, and Gilles Perez (1994). *La main droite de Dieu: Enquête sur François Mitterand et l'extrême droite,* Paris: Éditions du Seuil.

Feldblum, Miriam (1999). *Reconstructing citizenship: The politics of nationality reform and immigration in contemporary France,* New York: State University of New York.

Flanagan, Scott G. and Russell J. Dalton (1984). "Parties under stress: Realignment and dealignment in advanced industrial societies," *West European Politics,* 7(1): 7–23.

Freiheitliche Partei Österreichs (1997). *Program of the Freedom Party of Austria,* Vienna: FPÖ.

Friedrichsen, Mike, Wolfram Schulz, and Jens Wolling (1995). "Die Republikaner als Medienereignis," *Publizistik,* 40(2): 129–151.

Fysh, Peter (1987). "Government policy and the challenge of the Front National. The first twelve months," *Modern and Contemporary France,* 31: 9–20.

Fysh, Peter and Jim Wolfreys (1992). "Le Pen, the National Front and the Extreme Right in France," *Parliamentary Affairs,* 45(3): 309–326.

Gallagher, Tom (2000). "Exit from the ghetto: The Italian far right in the 1990s," in Paul Hainsworth, ed., *The politics of the Extreme Right: From the margins to the mainstream,* London: Pinter.

Gamson, William A. (1992). *Talking politics,* Cambridge: Cambridge University Press.

Gamson, William A. and Gadi Wolfsfeld (1993). "Movements and media as interacting systems," *Annals of the American Academy of Political and Social Science: Citizens, Protest and Democracy*, 528: 114–125.

Gärtner, Reinhold (2002). "The FPÖ, foreigners and racism in the Haider era," in Ruth Wodak and Anton Pelinka, eds., *The Haider phenomenon in Austria*, New Brunswick, NJ: Transaction.

Gaspard, Françoise (1995). *A small city in France*, Cambridge, MA: Harvard University Press.

Geddes, Andrew (2003). *The politics of migration and immigration in Europe*, London: Sage.

Gehmacher, Ernst, Frank Birk, and Guenther Ogris (1989). "1986 – The year of election surprises: From the perspective of the Electoral Behavior Theory," in Anton Pelinka and Fritz Plasser, eds., *The Austrian party system*, Boulder, CO: Westview Press.

Gellner, Ernest (1983). *Nations and nationalism*, Ithaca, NY: Cornell University Press.

Gerring, John (2001). *Social Science methodology: A criterial framework*, Cambridge: Cambridge University Press.

Givens, Terri E. (2005). *Voting Radical Right in Western Europe*, Cambridge: Cambridge University Press.

(2004). "The Radical Right gender gap," *Comparative Political Studies*, 37(1): 30–54.

Golder, Matt (2003). "Explaining variation in the success of Extreme Right parties in Western Europe," *Comparative Political Studies*, 36(4): 432–466.

Green, Simon (2004). *The politics of exclusion: Institutions and immigration policy in contemporary Germany*, Manchester: Manchester University Press.

(2001). "Immigration, asylum and citizenship in Germany: The impact of unification and the Berlin Republic," *West European Politics*, 24(4): 82–104.

Gunther, Richard and Anthony Mughan, eds. (2000). *Democracy and the media: A comparative perspective*, Cambridge: Cambridge University Press.

Hainsworth, Paul (2000). "Introduction: The Extreme Right," in Paul Hainsworth, ed., *The politics of the Extreme Right: From the margins to the mainstream*, London: Pinter.

Hallin, Daniel C. and Paolo Mancini (2004). *Comparing media systems: Three models of media and politics*, Cambridge: Cambridge University Press.

Hargreaves, Alec G. (2007). *Multi-ethnic France: Immigration, politics, culture and society*, second edition, London: Routledge.

Harmel, Robert and Lars Svåsand (1993). "Party leadership and party institutionalisation: Three phases of development," *West European Politics*, 16(2): 66–87.

Heilbrunn, Jacob (1996). "Germany's New Right," *Foreign Affairs*, 75(6): 80–98.

Herf, Jeffrey (1997). *Divided memory: The Nazi past in the two Germanys*, Cambridge, MA: Harvard University Press.

Hillgruber, Andreas (1986). *Zweierlei Untergang: Die Zerschlagung des Deutschen Reiches und das Ende des europäischen Judentums*, Berlin: Siedler.

Höbelt, Lothar (2003). *Defiant populist: Jörg Haider and the politics of Austria*, Indiana: Purdue University Press.

Humphreys, Peter (1996). *Mass media and media policy in Western Europe*, Manchester: Manchester University Press.

Husbands, Christopher (1991). "The Mainstream Right and the politics of immigration in France: Major developments in the 1980s," *Ethnic and Racial Studies*, 14(2): 170–198.

Ignazi, Piero (2006). *Extreme Right parties in Western Europe*, paperback edition, Oxford: Oxford University Press.

(2003). *Extreme Right parties in Western Europe*, Oxford: Oxford University Press.

(1992). "The silent counter-revolution: Hypotheses on the emergence of Extreme Right-wing parties in Europe," *European Journal of Political Research*, 22(1): 3–34.

Ignazi, Piero and Colette Ysmal (1992). "New and old Extreme Right parties. The French Front National and the Italian Movimento Sociale," *European Journal of Political Research*, 22(1): 101–121.

Immerfall, Stefan (1998). "The Neo-populist agenda," in Hans-Georg Betz and Immerfall, eds., *The new politics of the Right: Neo-populist parties and movements in established democracies*, London: Palgrave Macmillan.

Inglehart, Ronald (1997). *Modernization and postmodernization: Cultural, economic, and political change in 43 societies*, Princeton, NJ: Princeton University Press.

(1990). "From class-based to value-based politics," in Peter Mair, ed., *The West European party system*, Oxford: Oxford University Press.

(1977). *The silent revolution: Changing values and political styles among Western publics*, Princeton, NJ: Princeton University Press.

(1971). "The silent revolution in Europe: Intergenerational change in post-industrial societies," *American Political Science Review*, 65(4): 991–1017.

Inglehart, Ronald and Christian Welzel (2005). *Modernization, cultural change and democracy: The human development sequence*, Cambridge: Cambridge University Press.

Ivaldi, Gilles (2008). "Inequality, identity and the people: New patterns of right-wing competition and Sarkozy's 'Winning Formula' in the 2007 French Presidential election," Paper presented at the Annual American Political Science Association Meeting, Boston.

(1998). "The Front National: The making of an authoritarian party," in Piero Ignazi and Colette Ysmal, eds., *The organization of political parties in Southern Europe*, Westport, CT: Praeger.

Ivarsflaten, Elisabeth (2005). *Immigration policy and party organization: Explaining the rise of the Populist Right in Western Europe*, Doctoral Dissertation: University of Oxford.

Iyengar, Shanto (1991). *Is anyone responsible? How television frames political issues*, Chicago, IL: University of Chicago Press.

Iyengar, Shanto and Donald R. Kinder (1987). *News that matters: Television and American opinion*, Chicago, IL: University Chicago Press.

Jackman, Robert W. and Karin Volpert (1996). "Conditions favouring parties of the Extreme Right in Western Europe," *British Journal of Political Science*, 26(4): 501–521.

Jäger, Margret (1993). "BrandSätze und SchlagZeilen. Rassismus in den Medien," in *Entstehung von Fremdenfeindlichkeit: die Verantwortung von Politik und Medien*, Bonn: Friedrich-Ebert-Stiftung.

Joppke, Christian (2001). "The legal-domestic sources of immigrant rights: The United States, Germany and the European Union," *Comparative Political Studies*, 34(4): 339–366.

Joskowicz, Alexander (2002). "Austria," in Jesika ter Wal, ed., *Racism and cultural diversity in the mass media*, Vienna: European Monitoring Center for Racism and Xenophobia.

Kapetanyannis, Vassilis (1995). "Neo-fascism in modern Greece," in Luciano Cheles et al., eds., *The Far Right in Western and Eastern Europe*, London: Longman.

Karapin, Roger (2002). "Far-right parties and the construction of immigration issues in Germany," in Martin Schain et al., eds., *Shadows over Europe: The development and impact of the Extreme Right in Western Europe*, New York: Palgrave Macmillan.

(1999). "The politics of immigration control in Britain and Germany: Subnational politicians and social movements," *Comparative Politics*, 31(4): 423–444.

Katz, Richard S. and Peter Mair (1995). "Changing models of party organization and party democracy," *Party Politics*, 1(1): 5–28.

Katzenstein, Peter J. (1976). *Disjoined partners: Austria and Germany since 1815*, Berkeley, CA: University of California Press.

Kazamias, Alexander (1997). "The quest for modernization in Greek foreign policy and its limitations," *Mediterranean Politics*, 2(2): 71–94.

Keridis, Dimitris (1998). *The foreign policy of nationalism: The case of Serbia (1986–1995) and Greece (1991–1995)*, Doctoral Dissertation: Fletcher School of Law and Diplomacy.

Kinder, Donald R. (1998). "Communication and opinion," *Annual Review of Political Science*, 1: 167–197.

Kitschelt, Herbert (2007). "Growth and persistence of the radical right in postindustrial democracies: Advances and challenges in comparative research," *West European Politics*, 30(5): 1176–1206.

Kitschelt, Herbert with Anthony McGann (1995). *The Radical Right in Western Europe: A comparative analysis*, Ann Arbor, MI: The University of Michigan Press.

    (1994). *The transformation of European social democracy*, New York: Cambridge University Press.

Klapper, Joseph T. (1960). *The effects of mass communication*, Glencoe: Free Press.

Klingemann, Hans-Dieter, Andrea Volkens, Judith Bara, Ian Budge, and Michael McDonald (2006). *Mapping policy preference II: Estimates for parties, electors and governments in Eastern Europe, the European Union and the OECD, 1990–2003*, Oxford: Oxford University Press.

Klingemann, Hans-Dieter and Jürgen Lass (1996). "The dynamics of the campaign," in Dalton Russel, ed., *Germans divided: The 1994 Bundestag elections and the evolution of the German party system*, Oxford: Berg.

Knigge, Pia (1998). "The ecological correlates of Right-wing extremism in Western Europe," *European Journal of Political Research*, 34(2): 249–279.

Kolovos, Yiannis (2005). *Far Right and Radical Right in Greece and in Western Europe, 1974–2004*, Athens: Pelasgos [Κολοβός, Γιάννης (2005) Άκρα Δεξιά και Ριζοσπαστική Δεξιά στην Ελλάδα και στην Δυτική Ευρώπη, 1974–2004, Αθήνα: Εκδόσεις Πελασγός].

Kriesi, Hanspenter, Edgar Grande, Romain Lachat, Martin Dolezal, Simon Bornschier, and Timotheos Frey (2008). *West European politics in the age of globalization*, New York: Cambridge University Press.

Krosnick, Jon A. and Donald R. Kinder (1990). "Altering the foundations of popular support for the president through priming: Reagan and the Iran-Contra affair," *American Political Science Review*, 84(2): 497–512.

Krüger, Udo Michael, Karl H. Müller-Sachse, and Thomas Zapf-Schramm (2005). "Thematisierung der Bundestagswahl 2005 im öffentlich-rechtlichen und privaten Fernsehen," *Media Perspektiven*, 12: 598–612.

Krüger, Udo Michael and Thomas Zapf-Schramm (2002). "Wahlberichterstattung im öffentlich-rechtlichen und privaten Fernsehen," *Media Perspektiven*, 12: 610–622.

    (1999). "Fernsehwahlkampf 1998 in Nachrichten und politischen Informationssendungen," *Media Perspektiven*, 5: 222–236.

Kuhn, Raymond (1994). *The media in France*, London: Routledge.

Kymlicka, Will (1995). *Multicultural citizenship*, Oxford: Clarendon Press.

Langenbacher, Eric (2002). *Memory regimes in contemporary Germany*, Doctoral Dissertation: Georgetown University.

Lawson, Kay and Peter H. Merkl, eds. (1988). *When parties fail: Emerging alternative organizations*, Princeton, NJ: Princeton University Press.

Le Bohec, Jacques (2004). *L'implication des journalistes dans le phénomène Le Pen*, Paris: L'Harmattan.

Lewis-Beck, Michael S. and Glenn E. Mitschell (1993). "French electoral theory: The National Front test," *Electoral Studies*, 12(2): 112–127.

Linz, Juan (1980). "Political space and Fascism as a late-comer: Conditions conducive to the success or failure of Fascism as a mass movement in inter war Europe," in Stein Ugelvik Larsen et al., eds., *Who were the Fascists?: Social roots of European Fascism*, Bergen: Universitetsförlaget.

Lipset, Seymour Martin and Stein Rokkan (1990). "Cleavage structures, party systems and voter alignments," in Peter Mair, ed., *The West European party system*, Oxford: Oxford University Press.

Lipset, Seymour Martin and Earl Raab (1978). *The politics of unreason: Right-wing extremism in America, 1790–1977*, Chicago, IL: University of Chicago Press.

Loizides, Neophytos (2005). *Majority group crisis behaviour: Restraint vs. confrontation*, Doctoral Dissertation: University of Toronto.

Lubbers, Marcel, Mérove Gijsberts, and Peer Scheepers (2002). "Extreme Right-wing voting in Western Europe," *European Journal of Political Research*, 41(3): 345–378.

Luther, Kurt R. (2006). "Die Freiheitliche Partei Österreichs und die Bündnis Zukunft Österreich," in Herbert Dachs et al., eds., *Politik in Österreich: Das Handbuch*, Vienna: Manz.

(2000). "Austria: A democracy under threat from the Freedom Party?," *Parliamentary Affairs*, 53: 426–442.

(1988). "The Freiheitliche Partei Österreichs: protest party or governing party?," in Emil J. Kirchner, ed., *Liberal parties in Western Europe*, Cambridge: Cambridge University Press.

(1987). "Austria's future and Waldheim's past: the significance of the 1986 elections," *West European Politics*, 10(3): 376–399.

Luther, Kurt R. and Wolfgang C. Müller, eds. (1992). *Politics in Austria: Still a case of consociationalism?* London: Routledge.

Mackie, Tom and Richard Rose (1997). *A decade of election results: Updating the international almanac*, Glasgow: Centre for the Study of Public Policy, University of Strathclyde.

Maier, Charles S. (1988). *The unmasterable past: History, holocaust, and German national identity*, Cambridge, MA: Harvard University Press.

Manoschek, Walter (2002). "FPÖ, ÖVP, and Austria's Nazi Past," in Ruth Wodak and Anton Pelinka, eds., *The Haider phenomenon in Austria*, New Brunswick, NJ: Transaction.

Marcus, Jonathan (1995). *The National Front in French Politics: The resistible rise of Jean-Marie Le Pen*, London: Macmillan.

Mavrogordatos, George Th. (2003). "Orthodoxy and nationalism in the Greek case," *West European Politics*, 26(1): 117–136.

Mayer, Nonna (2003). "Le Pen's comeback: The 2002 presidential election," *International Journal of Urban and Regional Research*, 27(2): 455–459.

(1998). "The French National Front," in Hans-Georg Betz and Stefan Immerfall, eds., *The New politics of the Right: Neo-populist parties and movements in established democracies*, London: Palgrave Macmillan.

Mayer, Nonna and Pascal Perrineau (1992). "Why do they vote for Le Pen?," *Journal of European Political Research*, 22(1): 123–141.

Mazzoleni, Gianpietro (2003). "The media and the growth of neo-populism in contemporary democracies," in Gianpietro Mazzoleni et al., eds., *The media and neo-populism: A contemporary comparative analysis*, Westport, CT: Praeger.

Mazzoleni, Gianpietro, Julianne Stewart, and Bruce Horsfield, eds. (2003) *The media and neo-populism: A contemporary comparative analysis*, Westport, CT: Praeger.

McGuire, William J. (1968). "Personality and susceptibility to social influence," in Edgar F. Borgatta and William W. Lambert, eds., *Handbook of personality theory and research*, Chicago: Rand McNally.

Meckstroth, Theodore W. (1975). "'Most different systems' and 'most similar systems': A study in the logic of comparative social inquiry," *Comparative Political Studies*, 8(2): 132–157.

Meguid, Bonnie M. (2005). "Competition between unequals: The role of mainstream party strategy in niche party success," *American Political Science Review*, 99(3): 347–359.

Mendelberg, Tali (2001). *The race card: Campaign strategy, implicit messages, and the norm of equality*, Princeton, NJ: Princeton University Press.

Mihas, D.E.M. (1998). "New political formations in Greece: A challenge to its party system?," *Journal of Modern Greek Studies*, 16(1): 49–72.

Miller, David (1995). *On nationality*, Oxford: Oxford University Press.

Minkenberg, Michael (2003). "The politics of citizenship in the new republic," *West European Politics*, 26(4): 219–240.

(2001). "The Radical Right in public office: Agenda-setting and policy effects," *West European Politics*, 24(4): 1–21.

(1997). "The new Right in France and Germany: *Nouvelle Droite, neue Rechte*, and the new Right radical parties," in Peter H. Merkl and Leonard Weinberg, eds., *The revival of Right-wing extremism in the nineties*, London: Frank Cass.

(1995). "What's left of the Right? The new Right and the Superwahljahr 1994 in perspective," in David P. Conradt et al., eds., *Germany's new politics: Parties and issues in the 1990s*, Oxford: Berghahn.

(1992). "The new Right in Germany: The transformation of conservatism and the Extreme Right," *European Journal of Political Science*, 22(1): 55–81.

Minkenberg, Michael and Martin Schain (2003). "The Front National in context: French and European dimension," in Peter H. Merkl and Weinberg, eds., *The revival of Right-wing extremism in the twenty-first century*, London: Frank Cass.

Minkenberg, Michael and Ronald Inglehart (1989). "Neoconservatism and value change in the USA: Tendencies in the mass public of a postindustrial society," in John R. Gibbins, ed., *Contemporary political culture: Politics in a postmodern age*, London: Sage.

Mitra, Subrata (1988). "The National Front in France: A single-issue movement?," *West European Politics*, 11(2): 47–64.

Mitten, Richard (1994). "Jörg Haider, the anti-immigrant petition and immigration policy in Austria," *Patterns of Prejudice*, 28(2): 27–47.

(1992). *The politics of antisemitic prejudice: The Waldheim phenomenon in Austria*, Boulder, CO: Westview.

Money, Jeannette (1999). *Fences and neighbors: The political geography of immigration control*, Ithaca, NY: Cornell University Press.

Moore, Margaret (2001). "Normative justifications for liberal nationalism: Justice, democracy and national identity," *Nations and Nationalism*, 7(1): 1–20.

Mudde, Cas (2007). *The populist radical right in Europe*, Cambridge: Cambridge University Press.

(2004). "The populist Zeitgeist," *Government and Opposition*, 39(4): 542–563.

(2000). *The ideology of the Extreme Right*, Manchester: Manchester University Press.

(1996). "The war of words defining the extreme right party family," *West European Politics*, 19(2): 225–248.

Mudde, Cas and Joop van Holsteyn (2000). "The Netherlands: Explaining the limited success of the extreme right," in Hainsworth, ed., *The politics of the Extreme Right: From margins to the mainstream*, London: Pinter.

Müller, Jan-Werner (2000). *Another country: German Intellectuals, unification and national identity*, New Haven, CT: Yale University Press.

Müller, Sybille (1996). "Rechtsradikale im Bild: Die Darstellung rechtsextremer Politiker im deutschen und französischen Fernsehen," in Sabine Jungk, ed., *Zwischen Skandal und Routine? Rechtsextremismus in Film und Fernsehen*, Marburg: Schüren.

Müller, Wolfgang (2002). "Evil or 'Engine of democracy?' Populism and party competition in Austria," in Yves Mény and Yves Surel, eds., *Populism in Western democracies*, Houndmills: Palgrave-Macmillan.

(1993). "After the 'Golden Age': Research into Austrian political parties since the 1980s," *European Journal of Political Research*, 23(4): 439–463.

(1992). "Austria (1945–1990)," in Richard S. Katz and Peter Mair, eds. *Party organizations*, London: Sage.

Müller, Wolfgang, Fritz Plasser, and Peter A. Ulram (2004). "Party responses to the erosion of voter loyalties in Austria: Weakness as an advantage and strength as a handicap," in Peter Mair et al., eds., *Political parties and electoral change: Party responses to electoral markets*, London: Sage.

Murray, Laura M. (1994). "Einwanderungsland Bundesrepublik Deutschland? Explaining the evolving positions of German political parties on citizenship policy," *German Politics and Society*, 33: 23–56.

Nagle, John David (1970). *The National Democratic Party: Right radicalism in the Federal Republic of Germany*, Berkeley, CA: University of California Press.

Newton, Kenneth (1999). "Mass media effects: Mobilization or media malaise?," *British Journal of Political Science*, 29: 577–599.

Nicolacopoulos, Elias (2001). *The cachectic democracy: Parties and elections, 1946–1967*, Athens: Pataki Publications [Νικολακόπουλος, Ηλίας (2001) Η καχεκτική δημοκρατία: Κόμματα και εκλογές, 1946–1967, Αθήνα: Εκδόσεις Πατάκη].

Norris, Pippa (2005). *Radical Right: Voters and parties in the electoral market*, Cambridge: Cambridge University Press.

   (2003). "Preaching to the converted? Pluralism, participation and party websites," *Party Politics*, 9(1): 21–45.

   (2000). *A virtuous circle: Political communication in postindustrial democracies*, Cambridge: Cambridge University Press.

Papathanassopoulos, Stylianos (2000). "Election campaigning in the television age: The case of contemporary Greece," *Political Communication*, 17: 47–60.

Papathemelis, Stelios (1992). *Counterattack: Proposals for our national issues*, Paratiritis: Salonica [Παπαθεμελής, Στέλιος (1992) Αντεπίθεση: Προτάσεις για τα εθνικά μας θέματα, Παρατηρητής: Θεσσαλονίκη].

Patterson, Thomas E. (1993). *Out of order*, New York: Knopf.

Patterson, Thomas E. and Robert D. McClure (1976). *The unseeing eye: The myth of television power in national elections*, New York: Putnam.

Pedersen, Mogens N. (1990). "Electoral volatility in Western Europe, 1948–1977," in Peter Mair, ed., *The West European party system*, Oxford: Oxford University Press.

   (1982). "Towards a new typology of party lifespans and minor parties," *Scandinavian Political Studies*, 5(1): 1–16.

Pelinka, Anton (1998). *Austria: Out of the shadow of the past*, Boulder, CO: Westview Press.

Pelinka, Anton and Fritz Plasser, eds. (1989). *The Austrian party system*, Boulder, CO: Westview Press.

Perlmutter, Ted (2002). "The politics of Restriction: The effect of xenophobic parties on Italian immigration policy and German asylum policy," in

Martin Schain et al., eds., *Shadows over Europe: The development and impact of the Extreme Right in Western Europe*, New York: Palgrave Macmillan.

Perrineau, Pascal (2000). "The conditions for the re-emergence of an Extreme Right wing in France: The National Front, 1984–98," in Edward J. Arnold, ed., *The development of the Radical Right in France: From Boulanger to Le Pen*, New York: St. Martin's Press.

(1997). *Le symptôme Le Pen: Radiographie des électeurs du Front National*, Paris: Fayard.

(1996). "Les étapes d'une implantation électorale (1972–1988)," in Nonna Mayer and Pascal Perrineau, eds., *Le Front National à découvert*, Paris: Presses de la Fondation Nationale des Sciences Politiques.

Pick, Hella (2000). *Guilty victim: Austria from the Holocaust to Waldheim*, London: I.B.Tauris.

Plasser, Fritz (1989). "The Austrian party system between erosion and innovation: An empirical long-term analysis," in Anton Pelinka and Fritz Plasser, eds., *The Austrian party system*, Boulder, CO: Westview Press.

(1987). "Die populistische Arena: Massenmedien als Verstärker," in Anton Pelinka, ed., *Populismus in Osterreich*, Wien: Junius.

Plasser, Fritz and Peter A. Ulram (2003). "Striking a responsive chord: Mass media and Right-wing populism in Austria," in Gianpietro Mazzoleni et al., eds. *The Media and Neo-Populism: A contemporary comparative analysis*, Westport, CT: Praeger.

(1989). "Major parties on the defensive: The Austrian party- and electoral landscape after the 1986 National Council Election," in Anton Pelinka and Fritz Plasser, eds., *The Austrian party system*, Boulder, CO: Westview Press.

Pontusson, Jonas (1995). "Explaining the decline of Social Democracy: The role of structural economic change," *World Politics*, 47(4): 495–533.

Prodromou, Elizabeth (2004). "Christianity and democracy: The ambivalent orthodox," *Journal of Democracy*, 15(2): 62–75.

Przeworski, Adam and John Sprague (1986). *Paper stones: A history of electoral socialism*, Chicago, IL: University of Chicago Press.

Przeworski, Adam and Henry Teune (1970). *The logic of comparative social inquiry*, New York: Wiley-Interscience.

Putnam, Robert (1995). "Bowling alone: America's declining social capital," *Journal of Democracy*, 6(1): 65–78.

Rallis, George (1995). *To ears of non-listeners*, Ellinoekdotiki: Athens [Ράλλης, Γεώργιος (1995) Εις ώτα μη ακουόντων, Ελληνοεκδοτική: Αθήνα].

Reisigl, Martin and Ruth Wodak (2001). *Discourse and discrimination: Rhetorics of racism and anti-Semitism*, London: Routledge.

Riedlsperger, Max E. (1996). "The FPÖ and the Right," in Günter Bischof and Anton Pelinka, eds., *Austro-corporatism: Past, present, future*, New Brunswick, NJ: Transaction.

(1978). *The lingering shadow of Nazism: The Austrian independent party movement since 1945*, Boulder, CO: East European Quarterly.

Robinson, Michael J. (1976). "Public affairs television and the growth of political malaise: The case of the 'selling of the Pentagon'," *American Political Science Review*, 70(2): 409–432.

Rose, Richard and Derek W. Urwin (1970). "Persistence and change in Western party systems since 1945," *Political Studies*, 18(3): 287–319.

Roth, Dieter (1990). "Die Republikaner: Schneller Aufstieg and tiefer Fall einer Protestpartei am rechten Rand," *Aus Politik und Zeitgeschichte*, 37–38: 27–39.

Roudometof, Victor (2002). *Collective memory, national identity and ethnic conflict: Greece, Bulgaria and the Macedonian question*, Westport, CT: Praeger.

Ruzza, Carlo E. and Oliver Schmidtke (1993). "Roots of success of the Lega Lombarda: Mobilisation Dynamics and the Media," *West European Politics*, 16(1): 1–23.

Rydgren, Jens (2006). *From tax populism to ethnic nationalism: radical right-wing populism in Sweden*, Oxford: Berghahn Books.

Sainteny, G. (1995). "Le cens médiatique. L'accès des petites forces politiques à l'audiovisuel," *Médiaspouvoirs*, 38: 91–102.

Sartori, Giovanni (1976). *Parties and party systems: A framework for analysis*, Cambridge: Cambridge University Press.

Schäuble, Wolfgang (2000). *Mitten im Leben*, Munich: Bertelsmann.

Schain, Martin A. (1988). "Immigration and changes in the French party system," *European Journal of Political Research*, 16(6): 597–621.

(1987). "The National Front in France and the construction of political legitimacy," *West European Politics*, 10(2): 229–252.

Schain, Martin, Aristide Zolberg, and Patrick Hossay, eds. (2002). *Shadows over Europe: The development and impact of the Extreme Right in Western Europe*, New York: Palgrave Macmillan.

Schellenberg, Britta (2005). "Rechtsextremismus und Medien," *Aus Politik und Zeitgeschichte*, 42: 39–45.

Semetko, Holli A. (2000). "Great Britain: The end of *News at Ten* and the changing news environment," in Richard Gunther and Anthony Mughan, eds., *Democracy and the media: A comparative perspective*, Cambridge: Cambridge University Press.

(1989). "Television news and 'The Third Force' in British Politics: A case study of election communication," *European Journal of Communication*, 4(4): 453–481.

Shepherd, Gordon (1957). *The Austrian odyssey*, London: Macmillan.

Shields, James G. (2007). *The extreme right in France: From Pétain to Le Pen*, London: Routledge.

Simitis, Costas (1992). *Nationalist populism or national strategy?* Gnosis: Athens [Σημίτης, Κώστας (1992). *Εθνικιστικός λαϊκισμός ή εθνική στρατηγική;* Γνώση: Αθήνα].

Simmons, Harvey G. (1996). *The French National Front: The extremist challenge to democracy*, Boulder, CO: Westview Press.

Skylakakis, Thodoros (1995). *In the name of Macedonia*, Athens: Hellenic Europublishing [Σκυλακάκης Θόδωρος (1995). *Στο όνομα της Μακεδονίας*, Αθήνα: Ελληνική Ευρωεκδοτική].

Smith, Anthony D. (1999). *Myths and Memories of the Nation*, Oxford: Oxford University Press.

——— (1991). *National identity*, Reno: University of Nevada Press.

Stadler, Karl R. (1981). "The Kreisky phenomenon," *West European Politics*, 4(1): 5–18.

Statham, Paul (1996). "Berlusconi, the media, and the New Right in Italy," *Harvard International Journal of Press/Politics*, 1(1) 87–105.

Steiner, Niklaus (2000). *Arguing about asylum: The complexity of refugee debates in Europe*, New York: St. Martin's.

Stöss, Richard (1991). *Politics against democracy: Right-wing extremism in West Germany*, New York: Berg.

——— (1990). *Republikaner: Woher sie kommen, was sie wollen, wer sie wählt, was zu tun ist*, Köln: Bund-Verlag.

——— (1988). "The problem of Right-wing extremism in West Germany," *West European Politics*, 11(2): 34–46.

Sully, Melanie A. (1997). *The Haider phenomenon*, New York: East European Monographs.

——— (1981). *Political parties and elections in Austria*, London: C. Hurst & Company.

Swyngedouw, Marc (1998). "The Extreme Right in Belgium: Of a non-existent Front National and an omnipresent Vlaams Blok," in Hans-Georg Betz and Stefan Immerfall, eds., *The new politics of the Right: Neo-populist parties and movements in established democracies*, London: Palgrave Macmillan.

Taggart, Paul (1996). *The new populism and the new politics: New protest parties in Sweden in comparative perspective*, New York: St. Martin's.

Tamir, Yael (1993). *Liberal nationalism*, Princeton, NJ: Princeton University Press.

Tarrow, Sidney (1998). *Power in movement: Social movements, collective action and politics*, 2nd edition, Cambridge: Cambridge University Press.

Thaler, Peter (2001). *The Ambivalence of identity: The Austrian experience of nation-building in a modern society*, Indiana: Purdue University Press.

Thränhardt, Dietrich (1995). "The political uses of xenophobia in England, France and Germany," *Party Politics*, 1(3): 323–345.

Toumbas, Rosemary Casey (2001). *Impact and impasse: The role of the media in the formation of Greek national consciousness with a special emphasis on the Macedonian conflict 1992–1995*, Doctoral Dissertation: Boston University.

Trebbe, Joachim and Tobias Köhler (2002). "Germany," in Jesika ter Wal, ed., *Racism and cultural diversity in the mass media*, Vienna: European Monitoring Center for Racism and Xenophobia.

Tziampiris, Aristotle (2000). *Greece, European political cooperation and the Macedonian question*, Aldershot: Ashgate Press.

Uhl, Haidemarie (1997). "The politics of memory: Austria's perception of the Second World War and the National Socialist period," in Günter Bischof and Anton Pelinka, eds., *Austrian historical memory and national identity*, New Brunswick, NJ: Transaction.

Van der Brug, Wouter and Anthony Mughan (2007). "Charisma, leader effects and support for Right-wing populist parties," *Party Politics*, 31(1): 29–51.

Van der Brug, Wouter, Meindert Fennema, and Jean Tillie (2005). "Why some anti-immigrant parties fail and others succeed: A two-step model of aggregate electoral support," *Comparative Political Studies*, 38(5): 537–573.

Van der Brug, Wouter and Joost van Spanje (2004). "Consequences of the strategy of 'Cordon Sanitaire' against anti-immigrant parties," Paper prepared for Workshop 17 of the ECPR joint sessions of workshops, 13–18 April in Uppsala, Sweden.

Van Holsteyn, Joop J.M. and Galen A. Irwin (2003). "Never a dull moment: Pim Fortuyn and the Dutch parliamentary election of 2002," *West European Politics*, 26(2): 41–66.

Veugelers, John (1997). "Social cleavage and the revival of far right parties: The case of the National Front," *Acta Sociologica*, 40(1): 31–49.

Von Beyme, Klaus (1988). "Right-wing extremism in post-war Europe," *West European Politics*, 11(2): 1–18.

Von Weizsäcker, Richard (1986). *A voice from Germany: Speeches*, London: Weidenfeld & Nicolson.

VPRC (2000). *Greek Public Opinion 1999–2000*, Athens: VPRC Institute [VPRC (2000) *Η κοινή γνώμη στην Ελλάδα 1999–2000:* Αθήνα: Ινστιτούτο VPRC].

Walgrave, Stefaan and Knut De Swert (2004). "The making of the (issues of the) Vlaams Blok," *Political Communication*, 21(4): 479–500.

Warnecke, Steven (1970). "The future of Rightist extremism in West Germany," *Comparative Politics*, 2(4): 629–652.

Westle, Bettina and Oskar Niedermayer (1992). "Contemporary Right-wing extremism in West Germany," *European Journal of Political Research*, 22: 83–100.

Wodak, Ruth and Anton Pelinka, eds. (2002). *The Haider phenomenon in Austria*, New Brunswick, NJ: Transaction.

Young, Brigitte (1995). "The German political party system and the contagion from the Right," *German Politics and Society*, 13(1): 62–78.

Ysmal, Colette (1984). "Le RPR et l'UDF face au Front National: concurrence et connivances," *Revue Politique et Parlementaire*, 86: 6–20.

Zaller, John R. (1992). *The nature and origin of mass opinion*, Cambridge: Cambridge University Press.

Index